Sex Testing

SPORT AND SOCIETY

Series Editors
Randy Roberts
Aram Goudsouzian

Founding Editors
Benjamin G. Rader
Randy Roberts

*A list of books in the series appears
at the end of this book.*

Sex Testing

Gender Policing in Women's Sports

LINDSAY PARKS PIEPER

UNIVERSITY OF ILLINOIS PRESS

Urbana, Chicago, and Springfield

Contents

Acknowledgments

AS WITH ALL BOOK PROJECTS, this was not a single-person venture. I am grateful for the assistance I received from a variety of individuals. First, I would like to thank Willis G. Regier, director of the University of Illinois Press. Without him this book would not be a reality. Bill assisted me throughout the entire venture, even taking the time to provide feedback on my dissertation. I am thankful for his guidance, support, and kindness. Sarah K. Fields introduced me to Bill, and for that I am indebted to her. Not only did her reputation open the door for me, but Sarah was also involved with this project from the beginning, when it started as a seminar paper in a graduate class. She offered endless advice and, perhaps most importantly, kept me on track in the writing process. Judy Wu also provided invaluable guidance from the start, offering important suggestions regarding historical context.

Leading Olympic scholars Ian Ritchie and Alison M. Wrynn reviewed the manuscript and provided substantial feedback. Ian helped the work flow and asked me to expand my thoughts on the significance of gender testing. Alison read the manuscript, twice. She not only contributed to the depth of the work's analysis but also went through it with a fine-tooth comb. Ian's and Alison's comments greatly enhanced this project and I am grateful for their time and insights. The members of the Beth Emory Virtual Writer's Workshop also read several drafts. I am thankful for the energy, efforts, and advice offered by Andrew D. Linden, Susan J. Bandy, Melissa C. Wiser, and Dain TePoel. Friends who voluntarily agree to edit chapters are hard to find.

Several archivists and librarians also helped me locate documents and other materials. I appreciate the help I received from Nuria Puig of the

Olympic Studies Centre; Emma Yan, Sam Maddra, and Claire Daniel of the University of Glasgow; Ann K. Sindelar of the Western Historical Society; Andre Gailani of *Punch* magazine; Lauren Leeman of the State Historical Society of Missouri; Renata Balewska of the Narodowe Archiwum Cyfrowe; and the staff of the University of Illinois Archives. Sharon Kinney Hanson also offered both assistance and encouragement. Furthermore, research for this project was funded in part by the Postgraduate Research Grant Programme, 2013, of the IOC Olympic Studies Centre.

I am also appreciative of the historical actors who took time out of their busy schedules to speak with me. Kirsten Wengler Burton and Nancy Hogshead-Makar shared their experiences of actually undergoing sex testing, while María José Martínez Patiño shared her thoughts and photographs. Albert de la Chapelle recalled his efforts in the protest and shared insights into the current sex/gender protocol. Richard Budgett discussed the IOC's perspective. This project was greatly enhanced as a result of their insights.

Melvin L. Adelman brought me into the world of sport history. Although the Olympics may not be his favorite sporting forum, he nevertheless engaged in the project and offered ceaseless support. Kristen Worley kept me in the loop regarding recent occurrences and illuminated the athletes' view, a perspective often ignored. Katie Krisko and Alan D. Rogol helped me understand the scientific complexities of the human body. Danny Hedrick surpassed his duties as a colleague and showed encouragement throughout the entire process. Kelsey Pieper used her statistical expertise to format several tables. I need to also thank her for our writing days. Kyle Krisko, my best friend, embodied encouragement; he offered the necessary reassurances in the (numerous) moments of stress. Additionally, Kyle's graphic design prowess came in handy more than once. I would not have finished this project without his support, patience, and help.

Finally, I owe a lot to George and Lucy Pieper. George was my first coach and helped me develop a passion for sport. Importantly, his positive interpretation of girl's and women's sports fostered my beliefs about gender equality in athletics. Lucy read the entire manuscript. Twice. I am grateful for her editing assistance, but also for a number of other reasons. She signed me up for my first team and ensured that I never viewed my participation in sport as inferior because of my gender. I owe them more than words can describe.

Introduction

IN THE 1960 SUMMER OLYMPICS, Irina and Tamara Press gained international notoriety. Each sister won a gold medal in the Rome Games: Irina in the 80-meter hurdles and Tamara in the shot put. The Ukrainian-born duo dominated women's track and field, collectively acquiring a total of five Olympic medals and establishing twenty-six world records, all under the Soviet flag. While the Soviet Union applauded the Press sisters' astounding achievements, many ridiculed the Olympians, citing their strength and stature as suspiciously abnormal. The reports disparaged the "Russian muscle molls" for being too big, too "burly," and "heftier" than their Western counterparts.[1] For example, New York Times reporter Arthur Daley complained that Tamara was "big enough to play tackle for the Chicago Bears," and Irina, he wrote, was "about the size of a running guard."[2] Journalist Sid Ziff similarly mocked that when contrasted against the stature of Rocky Marciano, the former world heavyweight boxing champion, Tamara made him "look like a midget."[3] These repeated comparisons to male athletes were not accidental. Such accounts belittled women's success in sport and simultaneously constructed feats of speed and strength as antithetical to femininity. Accordingly, because Irina and Tamara did not embrace Western notions of gender, neither in appearance nor choice of vocation, the two sisters could not be real women.

Based on this assumption that sporting prowess contradicted womanhood, the International Association of Athletics Federation (IAAF) and the International Olympic Committee (IOC) instituted sex testing from the 1920s through the 1990s. In the interwar era, sport organizations first used a physical exam for this purpose. Whenever there was "a definite question as to sex," the IAAF and IOC required women to undergo an examination.[4] Observing numerous examples of masculine women, the IAAF mandated an on-site anatomical investigation for all female participants in 1966. One year later the track and field federation implemented a chromosomal check, with the IOC following suit in 1968. Editor of *Track & Field News* Dick Bank explained that the verification measures were intended "to drive out types who really had no business in women's track." In other words, the sex tests sought to preclude women, like the Press sisters, who "had more male characteristics than female."[5] Upon introducing the check, the IAAF and IOC consequently controlled womanhood in sport for much of the twentieth century.

To assess the significance of sex testing, this book explores its history from the 1930s to the early 2000s. The IOC used different tests to both guarantee the authenticity of female athletes and identify male masqueraders in Olympic sport. Although the IOC Medical Commission never discovered a single male imposter—and the various iterations of the exam actually illustrated the impossibility of neatly delineating sex—the IOC nevertheless continued to implement the control. Olympic officials thus authorized a policy of sex/gender conformity, as sex testing/gender verification required that female athletes demonstrate conventional notions of white Western heterofemininity. Through these regulations, the IOC, a powerful and influential authority, continuously reaffirmed a binary notion of sex, privileged white gender norms, and hampered female athleticism.

The Significance of Language

Scholars have increasingly recognized the significance of language in the construction of the social world.[6] Following a generally accepted paradigm, this book uses the term "sex" to denote biological and anatomical distinction and "gender" to reflect socially and culturally constructed differences, roles, and attributes deemed appropriate for the sexes.[7] Furthermore, the IOC regularly conflated sex and gender in its policies; therefore, this work incorporates "sex/gender" to acknowledge the often inseparable nature of the two ideologies. Some scholars have also criticized the existing sex testing/gender verification literature for using the two labels interchangeably.[8] To best illustrate the mind-sets of those responsible for the scrutiny, this project employs the various English terms used by the IOC Medical Commission at different moments, as demarcated in the Olympic *Official Reports*. Accordingly, the commission referred to the required examination as shown in the accompanying table. However, sex/gender testing serves as an umbrella term to denote the entirety of the practice, from 1968 to 2000.

The discursive shift from sex control to femininity test to gender verification—and *contrôle de sexe* to *contrôle de féminité*—is telling. Although always deeply concerned with muscular female Olympians, the IOC Medical Commission initially expressed fears of male masqueraders in women's competitions. Hence, the test's original purpose was to detect sex imposters. With both the impossibility of discovering a clear sex divide and the increased presence of female dopers, however, the IOC adjusted its semantic framework to encapsulate gender normativity. The conspicuous adjustment from sex to femininity to gender underscored the medical commission's changing anxieties. Rather than to catch men disguised as women, the test evolved into a measure to prohibit female Olympians with biological advantages. In other words, the commission eventually viewed gender verification as a tool to eliminate competitors whom it deemed too strong, too fast, too successful, or too unfeminine for women's competition.

Furthermore, the medical commission, medical literature, and medical practitioners regularly distinguished "abnormal" from "normal." Such diagnoses were medical constructions shaped by social expectations.[9] As historian Elizabeth Reis explains, doctors proved unable to escape the ideologies and anxieties of the larger society, "which render any medical management a cultural, rather than simply a scientific, endeavor."[10] An objective, value-free delineation of sex was impossible to denote. This book therefore uses "nor-

Table 1. Sex/Gender Control Labels, 1968–1998

Year	Host City	Terms in English	Terms in French
1968	Grenoble	*Sex Verification*	*Contrôle du Sexe chez la Femme*
1968	Mexico City	*Women's Medical Examination*	*Examens Médicaux pour Femmes*
1972	Sapporo	*Sex Check*	*Contrôle de Sexe*
1972	Munich	*Sex Control*	*Contrôle de Sexe*
1976	Innsbruck	*Sex Check*	*Contrôle du Sexe*
1976	Montreal	*Femininity Testing*	*Contrôle de Féminité*
1980	Lake Placid	*Femininity Test*	*Contrôle de Sexe*
1980	Moscow	*Femininity Test*	*Contrôle de Féminité*
1984	Sarajevo	*Femininity Test*	*Contrôle de Féminité*
1984	Los Angeles	*Gender Verification*	*Contrôle de Féminité*
1988	Calgary	*Gender Verification*	*Contrôle de Féminité*
1988	Seoul	*Gender Verification*	*Contrôle de Féminité*
1992	Albertville	*Gender Control*	*Tests de Féminité*
1992	Barcelona	*Gender Test*	*Contrôles de Féminité*
1994	Lillehammer	*Gender Testing*	*Contrôle de Féminité*
1996	Atlanta	*Gender Verification*	*Contrôle de Féminité*
1998	Nagano	*Gender Verification*	*Contrôle de Féminité*
2000	Sydney	*Gender Verification*	*Contrôles de Féminité*

mal" and "abnormal" to indicate popular ideology, not to reify problematic binaries. When the terminology is used, it reflects the sentiments shared by medical practitioners, scientists, the IOC, and athletes alike.

Biological Constructions of Sex

Along with shifting terminology, the IOC Medical Commission's views of biology also fluctuated. To first prevent male imposters, and later to curtail competitive advantages, the group relied on several different techniques to distinguish women from men. Unfortunately, as sports writer David Epstein explains, "Human biology does not break down into male and female as politely as sport governing bodies wish it would."[11] Sex is not a binary system established by a singular qualification. Rather, most people in the medical profession recognize a collection of markers, including chromosomes, external genitalia, gonads, hormones, internal genitalia, and secondary sex characteristics. Despite these recognized complexities, the medical commission used anatomy, chromosomes, and genetics—in isolation—to determine sex.

External anatomy served as the first indicator approved by the international governors of sport. In the 1930s women whose gender came under suspicion by athletic officials had to prove their womanhood through physical examinations. By 1966 the IAAF made the check mandatory in track and field. Not only did women find this procedure humiliating, but the investigations failed to unequivocally establish competitors' sex. Ambiguous genitalia in genetic females can stem from an enlarged clitoris, fused labia, undescended testicles, or an abnormal location of the urethral opening. Consequently, the female athletes' disdain of physical examinations, combined with the inaccuracies of the method, eventually convinced the officials to turn to chromosome tests.

In the middle of the twentieth century, scientists prioritized chromosomes as the signifier of sex. Chromosomes exist in the nucleus of human cells and are comprised of DNA tightly coiled around proteins. Men and women usually possess forty-six chromosomes, arranged in twenty-three pairs. Of these forty-six, two are identified as sex chromosomes, which control the development of sex characteristics. Women are typically believed to possess forty-six somatic chromosomes, including two XX sex chromosomes (46,XX); men are typically believed to possess forty-six somatic chromosomes, including one X and one Y sex chromosome (46,XY). Sport authorities focused on this dichotomy. In 1967 the IAAF implemented a chromosomal analysis in competition, barring all women who did not possess XX chromosomes. Believing the method successful, the IOC embraced the method in 1968.

Various chromosomal constitutions regularly undermined the test. For example, individuals with androgen insensitivity syndrome (AIS), chromosomal mosaicism, Klinefelter's syndrome, and Turner syndrome all challenged the notion that men and women could be separated neatly into XY and XX. Perhaps most notably in sports, AIS occurs when a person who is considered chromosomally male (46,XY) is resistant to male hormones and therefore demonstrates the physical characteristics of a female. Chromosomal mosaicism exists when an individual possesses cell populations with different chromosomal makeups. For example, a person with 46,XX/XY mosaicism has both XX and XY chromosomes. Klinefelter's syndrome occurs when men inherit extra X chromosomes (46,XXY or 46,XXXY) and, as a result, produce less than average amounts of testosterone. Finally, Turner syndrome is present when women inherit only one X chromosome (46,X0) and consequently do not develop ovaries.[12] The IAAF and IOC did not consider the reality of such chromosomal differences.

When protests surrounding the use of chromosomes surfaced, the IOC again changed tactics. In the 1990s its medical commission implemented DNA testing to establish competitors' sex. Olympic officials copied specific DNA sequences through polymerase chain reaction (PCR) to determine the presence of the SRY (sex-determining region Y) gene. PCR is the technology that amplifies specific DNA sequences. Found on the Y chromosome, the SRY gene initiates the production of testosterone. Put simply, the presence of the SRY gene typically corresponds with maleness and the development of male genitalia. However, sexual development is a multistep process influenced by an assortment of genetic factors. For example, individuals with Swyer syndrome appear outwardly feminine, with a uterus and Fallopian tubes, but may have a mutated SRY gene. Despite the multifaceted nature of biological sex, at different moments the IOC embraced anatomical inspections, chromosomal checks, and PCR testing as the gateways to enter women-only events.

Constructing "Western" Womanhood

Geopolitical and racial concerns also shaped the history of sex testing/gender verification. Influentially, Euro-centered medical science promoted both sex and racial difference. Social concerns about race consequently seeped into physicians' opinions. For example, US medical journals historically depicted more black than white bodies when discussing sexual abnormalities, and European medical texts similarly suggested that malformed or ambiguous genitalia were common among women of African descent.[13] As Reis notes, physicians fixated on such malformations "as if to suggest that monstrosity . . . and blackness went hand in hand."[14] Perhaps as the most illustrative historical example, in 1810 French imperialists Henri de Blainville and Georges Cuvier placed the body of South African Saartjie Baartman, known as the

"Hottentot Venus," on display in both Paris and London exhibits. Baartman's breasts, genitals, and buttocks served as a visual anomaly against which white Western European onlookers could contrast.[15] Doctors and scientists alike inscribed cultural notions of sex/gender and race onto female patients—and later onto female athletes—in the name of medical advancement.

The creation of dichotomous categories also separated the East from the West and promoted the supposed superiority of Western culture. However, the notion of the "East" and "West" encapsulated various meanings and locations in different historical moments. During the Cold War, "East" and "West" referred to the group of countries that aligned culturally, ideologically, and politically upon the conclusion of World War II. Comprised mainly of North American and Western European nations, the West promoted capitalism and democracy. This proved oppositional to the communist East, constituted primarily by the Soviet Union and countries in Eastern Europe. Importantly, the two embraced divergent opinions about the use and presentation of female athletes in international competition. For the Western-dominated IOC, many women from the East did not resemble femininity as prescribed by the West. Whereas the Western bloc demanded petite, graceful athletes, the Eastern bloc encouraged strength and muscularity. Consequently, in the West, Eastern European women, particularly track and field athletes, were ridiculed and derided. As historian Susan K. Cahn argues, "Descriptions of 'ponderous, peasant-type Russian athletes' and 'Amazons from the Russian steppes' created a contrasting 'other' whose very presence lent some legitimacy to the less talented US team."[16] Thus, although more talented in many aspects, the Eastern bloc women were constructed as different and non-feminine along Western standards.

Moreover, Western doctors, journalists, and sport organizations treated white women and women of color contrastingly. While women in general have historically experienced ridicule for their involvement in sport, black women in particular have faced contempt for not displaying white femininity. As sociologist Patricia Hill Collins notes, "Within a Western sex role ideology . . . the seeming role reversal among African Americans has been used to stigmatize Black people."[17] In the midst of the Cold War, US reports held up white women as icons of appropriate femininity and contrasted them against both black Americans and Eastern Europeans.

Finally, with the collapse of the Soviet Union in 1991, the divisions between the East and West somewhat dissipated.[18] After the Cold War the terms "East" and "West" referred to the group of countries that affiliated culturally, geographically, and politically. In particular, the People's Republic of China emerged as a new global enterprise that challenged countries in the West. China's increased economic authority and improved international influence created new political and geographical tensions between the East and the West. This threat extended into sport as Chinese teams achieved unprecedented success and dominated international competition. The Chinese female athletes emerged in the 1990s as sport's new "other" against which practitioners constructed Western femininity. Although arising in different time periods and locations, Western norms of femininity and race underlined sex/gender anxieties throughout the Olympic movement.

The Fair Play Discourse

Finally, to justify sex/gender testing, the IOC Medical Commission repeatedly espoused rhetoric that cited equality and fair play. For example, according to Eduardo Hay, the Mexican gynecologist responsible for overseeing the control in the 1968 Mexico City Olympics, in cases of anatomical difference, "The athlete in question must be withdrawn, in order to allow the others to compete on '*equal terms*.'" He further restated this position, noting that "the sole purpose of the Medical Commission in this investigation of femininity is to ensure that the *physical equality* of the women athletes competing against each other."[19] This sentiment underlined the medical commission's objective for the duration of sex/gender testing. Two decades later, in the 1988 *Official Report* of the Seoul Olympics, the organizers similarly noted that "female competitors participating in events for women only were required to undergo gender verification in order to ensure *fair competition*."[20]

This discourse is problematic for two reasons. First, as both sport philosophers and scientists recognize, genetic and physiological equality simply does not exist in sport.[21] Certain biological differences, such as cardiovascular ability, height, and lung capacity, foster athletic excellence.[22] For example, US swimmer Michael Phelps, who earned a record-number eight medals in the 2012 London Olympics, was almost literally "built to swim." His longer than average arm span, elongated torso, short legs, size-fourteen feet, and double-jointed ankles, which allowed Phelps to bend fifteen degrees farther at the ankle than most swimmers, provided him with certain physiological advantages.[23] Similarly, athletes who have been diagnosed and treated for Marfan syndrome, a genetic variance that produces tallness, long limbs, and slender fingers, could be perceived as having a positive predisposition for sporting success.[24] Despite the awareness and acceptance of such naturally produced abnormalities, only sex/gender differences resulted in disqualification. As sport scholar Jaime Schultz questions: "Why are genetic variations that affect autosomal chromosomes an advantageous endowment while those that affect sex chromosomes amount to a curse that can effectively drum one out of competitive sport?"[25] One can assume that fears of powerful, non-feminine female athletes forged such a position. Accordingly, only stronger than average women aggrieved the IOC's sensibilities.

Second, the presumed need to protect women athletes degraded female athleticism and reaffirmed a belief in male physical superiority. Jacques Thiebault, the French doctor responsible for sex testing at the 1968 Grenoble Winter Olympics, explained that some type of control was necessary, for "it is inevitable that sooner or later, the representatives of the weaker sex should feel persecuted and ask that the feminine records be awarded to them."[26] Such rhetoric established athleticism and femininity as oxymoronic and criminalized powerful female Olympians. Accordingly, sport authorities found it inconceivable that strong, muscular women could be authentic or natural. With this line of reasoning, "real" women were those who preserved Western notions of white femininity. Moreover, the fear of male imposters bolstered the conviction in masculine advantage. The belief that any man could don a wig or a skirt and defeat all women in athletic competition both promoted sport as a male domain and diminished women's skills and talents. The IOC Medical Commission thus deployed the rhetoric of equality and fair play to preserve its vision of appropriate female athleticism.[27]

Chapter Outline

Some scholars have analyzed sex/gender testing as a creation of the Cold War, while others have explored the influence of the IOC on the reaffirmation of gender norms, but a complete historical evaluation of the policy remains unwritten.[28] This study interrogates the long history of sex/gender testing in sport, which started before the Cold War. Rather than international finger-pointing, deeply rooted anxieties about the appropriateness of women in sport convinced officials to verify participants' womanhood. Moreover, the IAAF and IOC targeted specific women for investigations; those who did not exhibit white Western notions of femininity frequently came under scrutiny. This book therefore intends to more fully interrogate sex/gender testing in sport and to extend the conversation both chronologically and topically.

To move the discussion beyond the Cold War, this book examines the sexed, gendered, racial, and geopolitical concerns sport authorities maintained when implementing testing. Chapter 1 illustrates the sex-segregated framework of sport and highlights the historical threats to the sex/gender status quo. When the IOC reluctantly added women's track and field—a sport originally deemed too masculine for female competitors—to the Olympic program, suspicions of male imposters immediately ensued. The supposed threat of masqueraders encouraged officials to require physical examinations of some participants. Chapter 2 examines how Cold War tensions heightened the fear of fraudulent competitors. In particular, sport leaders disliked the sudden successes of the Eastern European track and field athletes. Consequently, as noted in chapter 3, the international tensions that surfaced during the Cold War played a large role in the initial institution of sex verification at the 1968 Olympics.

The IOC created its medical commission to deter athletes from consuming performance-enhancing substances and to bar sex/gender-transgressive women from competition. Not surprisingly, the purposes of doping controls and sex tests became conflated in the 1970s, as discussed in chapter 4. The victories of the German Democratic Republic at the 1976 Olympics allowed the IOC to envision all muscular women as unethical, substance-enhanced cheaters. Moreover, the IOC's belief in categorical divisions proliferated throughout the West. Although the subject was never mentioned explicitly, white Western women served as the foils to the supposed transgressors of femininity, reinscribing certain stereotypes about women of color.

While the US-USSR rivalry dissipated somewhat in the 1970s, the two countries experienced an escalation of hostilities in the 1980s. Chapter 5 evaluates the impact of the heightened animosities on sport and examines the IOC's response. In line with the increased international resentments between the two global powers, the IAAF started to disagree with the IOC regarding the ethics of gender verification. The different opinions would eventually help dismantle sex/gender testing.

Although the IOC sought to differentiate women from men, the methods employed repeatedly illustrated the difficulty in determining the exact composition of womanhood. Chapter 6 argues that rather than showing a clear-cut biological divide, the policy highlighted a range of chromosomal varieties and DNA diversity. The IOC disregarded these well-documented variations and continued testing. Officials never discovered a man posing as a woman; however, several female athletes with biological differences were barred from competition. Eventually, protests by medical authorities and athletes in the 1980s encouraged the IOC to abandon all gender verification practices.

However, as chapter 7 demonstrates, alternative requirements merely rendered gender verification moot. The spandex apparel preferred by competitors, for example, decreased the possibility for anatomical male masqueraders, and doping controls required visual examinations during urination. Furthermore, the Stockholm Consensus, penned for the 2004 Athens Olympics, dictated specific norms for transgender athletes. Sport leaders thereby maintained their authority over sex/gender without the aid of scientific verification for more than ten years. Yet concerns never actually abated and the IOC resumed control in 2012, this time through hormonal controls.

This book explores the history of sex/gender testing in order to demonstrate society's deeply rooted concerns about female athletes' appropriate place in physical contests. As both a historically male purview and a powerful social institution, sport's sex/gender policies extended far beyond the courts, fields, and stadiums, and the testing impacted women's inclusion, reception, rejection, and ability at all levels of competition. Sex/gender testing therefore not only reflected the larger cultural perception of womanhood throughout the twentieth century but also continues to shape our interpretation of acceptable gender and sex in sport.

1 "A Careful Inquiry to Establish Her Sex beyond a Doubt"

Sex/Gender Anxieties in Track and Field

IN THE 1936 BERLIN SUMMER OLYMPICS, nineteen-year-old Missouri runner Helen Stephens finished first in the 100-meter finals. Her speed proved both unprecedented and unbelievable. As reporter Bill Henry recounted, she "literally [ran] away from the fastest field of girl flyers ever assembled on an athletic field."[1] With an unparalleled time of 11.5 seconds—actually a tenth of a second slower than her first qualifying time—the "Fulton Flash" earned the gold. The "Missouri farm girl" also eclipsed the world record held by runner-up Stanisława Walasiewicz, who was known in the West by her anglicized name, Stella Walsh.[2] Although the IAAF refused to ratify Stephens's result due to the presence of an advantageous tailwind, no woman officially surpassed her time for nineteen years.[3]

While Stephens's hometown, Fulton, Missouri, burst into celebration upon receiving news of her victory, others remained unmoved.[4] Few people believed a woman could run at such a fast pace; therefore, many questioned Stephens's sex. Notably, a special correspondent to the Polish newspaper *Kurier Poranny* alleged that the United States had allowed a man to compete in the women's event.[5] The reporter reasoned that silver medalist "Miss Walasiewicz would have gained first place if she had competed only against women." He further suggested that Stephens "should have been running with [Jesse] Owens and the other American male stars."[6] Public condemnations of the US victor ensued.

Stephens's mother, Bertie May Stephens, attempted to dispel the attacks by citing her daughter's courtship practices. "Helen is absolutely a girl," she explained. "Helen leads a normal girl's social life. She enjoys dating and attends dances regularly at college." Bertie May's underlying assumption—one

Helen Stephens's American Olympic Committee portrait, date unknown. Courtesy of the State Historical Society of Missouri, Helen Stephens Papers. (WUNP6118)

she shared with the larger public—was that participation in heterosexual rituals ensured femininity, which proved womanhood. Nevertheless, the innuendos surrounding the Olympic victor failed to dissipate. To quiet the suspicions, sport authorities quickly disclosed that Stephens had undergone a physical exam prior to competition. According to the *Los Angeles Times*, German officials, suspicious of Stephens's tremendous athletic talent, conducted "a careful inquiry to establish her sex beyond a doubt" when she arrived in Berlin.[7] This inquiry marked the first widely publicized sex test of the modern Olympic movement.

Strong, successful women in track and field, like Stephens, challenged the deeply rooted Olympic sex/gender divide. Throughout the history of the

Olympic Games, sport officials mandated sex categorization and attempted to uphold a dichotomous gender divide. In ancient Greece men and women competed separately and in different events. Men participated in a variety of activities, including boxing, discus, equestrian, javelin, running, and wrestling. Women participated in only a short footrace. This setup helped establish sex segregation in sport and fostered hierarchal gender assumptions. When Pierre de Coubertin founded the modern games centuries later, he maintained this sex/gender paradigm. He required sex classification and entrenched conventional gender beliefs in the Olympic movement. Coubertin notably barred women from the 1896 Athens Games and later limited their participation to events deemed socially acceptable. Although women's involvement in archery, golf, and tennis received tempered support, track and field remained strictly proscribed.

Track and field was the most popular and prestigious Olympic pastime in the early twentieth century. The United States, for example, celebrated athletics as the epitome of international sporting excellence. It was also an activity explicitly reserved for men. Thus when female activists successfully fought for women's inclusion in international competition, many people balked. The IAAF and IOC, in particular, begrudged the presence of female track and field athletes and painted the victors as mannish oddities. It was in track and field, then, where questions of sex/gender first surfaced and continued throughout the twentieth century.

The Origin of Olympic Sex Segregation and Gendered Ideals

Although the IOC eventually introduced sex/gender testing, sex segregation in sport has much deeper historical roots. Contests in ancient Greece tellingly excluded women. To celebrate the masculine body and pay tribute to the gods, male athletes competed naked, a practice that helped deter female infiltration.[8] This requisite of nudity therefore served as the first method to ensure separation in sport; paradoxically, a similar type of test later would be required of female participants to bar men from women's competitions. In addition, not only did the ancient games forbid female involvement, but women were also disallowed from spectating. The penalty for female intrusion was death by being thrown from the top of Mount Typaion, a peak near Olympia. With such severe punishments, only one such incident is known to have occurred. Greek traveler Pausanias testified that the widow Kallipateira, or Pherenike, from the famed athletic family of Diagoras of Rhodes, disguised herself as a male trainer in order to bring her son, Peisirodos, to compete.

Unable to contain her excitement when he triumphed, Kallipateira exposed herself. Pausanias relayed that she was released unpunished out of respect for her family.[9]

While Kallipateira's artifice provided a singular (recorded) example of female infiltration in the ancient Olympic Games, some scholars speculate that women, specifically unmarried virgins, participated in a separate forum. In advance of the male festival, women held female-only competitions to honor the Greek goddess Hera. Known as the Heraean Games, the contests occurred in Olympia's stadium and consisted of "stade" races, footraces that were five-sixths of the length males were required to run.[10] The shorter distance—coupled with the privileging of men's achievements and the prioritization of the male festival—indicates a belief in women's lesser status. A similar attitude was later exhibited by Coubertin, the "father" of the modern Olympic movement.

Coubertin reformulated the ancient competitions and birthed the modern games at the end of the nineteenth century. Born into an aristocratic French family, and a child during the Franco-Prussian War, he wanted to avenge the humiliating military defeat that included France's loss of the Alsace and Lorraine provinces. As a nationalist the baron initially considered a military career but instead followed an educational track that gradually prompted his enamor of sports.[11] Coubertin's intentions for Olympic revival therefore aimed primarily at revitalizing French masculinity; however, he also desired European camaraderie to eliminate the possibility of further warfare—and French defeat.[12] For example, in 1894 he proclaimed that an international sports forum held every four years would "give the youth of all the world a chance of a happy and brotherly encounter which will gradually efface the peoples' ignorance." Coubertin further explained that left unaddressed, such ignorance "feeds hatred, accumulates misunderstandings, and hurdles events along a barbarous path toward a merciless conflict."[13] Although he revived the Olympic Games to promote athletic reform and encourage international goodwill, Coubertin nevertheless established several incongruities. As sport scholar Alan Tomlinson notes, his "declared egalitarianism concerning the politics of the body was bounded by principles of privilege, patronage, and misogyny."[14] In alignment with the beliefs of the time, the French baron opposed female inclusion.

Coubertin's sex/gender beliefs both paralleled contemporary society and dominated the Olympic policies of his tenure. Shaped by the nineteenth century's social acceptance of "separate spheres," which encouraged strength, physicality, and sociability for men while mandating passivity, fragility, and domesticity for white, middle-class women, he repeatedly espoused such gendered ideals in his formulation of the Olympic movement. Coubertin suggested that "the Olympic Games must be reserved for men" and justified this assertion by infamously declaring female competition "impractical, uninteresting, ungainly, and . . . improper."[15] The founder of the modern games further rationalized the denial of women by pointing out complications with female inclusion; he noted that permitting women Olympians would require the construction of separate facilities and argued that social norms eschewed viewing females in athletic costumes.[16]

Although he succeeded in barring women from officially partaking in the first modern Olympics, Coubertin's prohibitions eventually dwindled and female athletes competed from the Paris Games onward. Significantly, the addition of 22 women in the 1900 Olympics occurred against the behest of Coubertin and the IOC. With the success of the 1896 Games, the IOC was forced to delegate organizational responsibilities to various committees. Women first entered Olympic competition under these more localized authorities.[17] However, Coubertin did not completely acquiesce, as female Olympians remained limited to separate, often modified competitions and participated only in those deemed appropriately feminine—such as archery, golf, swimming, tennis, and yachting—throughout his reign. As a result, the 22 women who competed in 1900 (compared to the 975 men) overtly adhered to Western notions of appropriate femininity.

Furthermore, Coubertin established the consummate Olympic authority as an elite male domain. His classed and gendered beliefs led to the naming of fifteen affluent men in the creation of the IOC in 1894.[18] Because Coubertin desired an independent, nonpolitical organization, he selected individuals who could both afford the necessary travel and contribute to the burgeoning IOC. In the words of historian Allen Guttmann, "The members, who were much more likely to be enthusiasts for turf than track, were selected for their wealth and for their social status."[19] Of the original members, IOC president Demetrios Vikelas (Greece), officer Viktor Balck (Sweden), Alexei General de Boutowsky (Russia), Coubertin, Jiří Guth-Jarkovský (Bohemia), Ferenc Kemény (Hungary), and classics professor William Milligan Sloane (United States) were the most active. Other members included Lord Ampthill (Britain), Count Maxime de Bousies (Belgium), Ernest F. Callot (France), Duke of Andria Carafa (Italy), Leonard A. Cuff (New Zealand), Charles Herbert (Britain), Count Mario Lucchesi Palli (Italy), and Dr. José Benjamín Zubiaur (Argentina).[20] Coubertin assumed the presidency in 1896 and held the office for almost three decades. Although he retired in 1925, his principles remained rooted in the IOC's policies. As historians Kay Schiller and Christopher Young explain, throughout the twentieth century the IOC "behaved on occasion with the random unaccountability of a self-electing gentleman's club."[21] With regard to sex and gender, perhaps the greatest influence of this "gentlemen's club" was its decision to implement sex testing.

Sex/Gender Anxieties in Track and Field

Due to the historical association of physicality and maleness, whispers of ambiguously sexed female athletes and men posing as women for athletic achievement surfaced almost from the onset of women's inclusion in sport. The interwar period proved notably rife with such accusations as female competitors advanced in track and field, the era's most popular international pastime for men. Athletics had masculine connotations—thereby deterring women's participation—for a variety of reasons. Foremost, female track and field competitors experienced resistance from the medical community. According to sport historian Jennifer Hargreaves, "Because of the intrinsically vigorous nature of running, jumping and throwing events, female athletes were particularly vulnerable to reactionary medical arguments."[22] Doctors not only suggested that the sport harmed women's health and damaged the female physique but also specifically described its detrimental effects on reproduction.

Heeding these precautionary warnings, female physical educators sought to limit women's involvement in the sport, a restraint appreciated by many in the West. The larger public found the muscularity required for track and field unsettling, and the power and speed necessary for success, unmediated by an apparatus or teamwork, only exacerbated such concerns. Finally, race and class dynamics underlined all of these anxieties. That women of color and working-class women more frequently competed in athletics kept middle- and upper-class white women off the track. As a result, argues Susan Cahn, "Where sports in general connoted masculinity, track and field had a particularly masculine image."[23] Consequently, as women organized and participated in events deemed socially unacceptable—such as discus, distance running, and javelin—they stepped into an arena previously reserved for men and subsequently faced hostility, resentment, and suspicion.

The Amsterdam Olympics and Women's World Games

In the wake of World War I, Coubertin attempted to reclaim the authority he had previously delegated to national committees. The IOC proved unable to eliminate the already-added female events, which included diving, figure skating, swimming, and tennis, and therefore opted to reject any proposal that suggested expanding the women's program.[24] Because the IOC repeatedly denied the addition of women's track and field in the Summer Games, female sports organizations created new, alternative forums for athletics.

As the most notable example, French feminist Alice Milliat formed the Fédération Sportive Féminine Internationale (FSFI). She founded the FSFI in 1921 after several failed lobbying attempts to secure women's track and field in the 1920 Games. Denied by the IOC, the FSFI hosted the Jeux Olympiques Féminins (Women's Olympic Games) in 1922, during which sixty-five competitors from five countries participated in eleven events—the 60-meter race, 100-yard race, 100-yard hurdles, 300-meter race, 1,000-meter race, 4 x 110-yard relay, high jump, javelin, long jump, standing long jump, and shot put.[25] The Women's Olympics continued to grow and were repeated in 1926, 1930, and 1934. Despite its short tenure, this initiative accomplished three significant goals: it maintained affiliation with the same number of countries as other male international federations; it expanded the role of women in sport; and it simultaneously challenged the gender order.[26]

Not everyone viewed women's inclusion in track and field quite so positively. In the United States, for example, white female physical educators disdained the competitive and masculine nature of athletics. In the early twentieth century, female instructors had gained control over women's sport by highlighting biological dissimilarities between the sexes. They reasoned that the peculiarities of women's bodies and the shortfalls in their physical capabilities required female leadership over separate activities. In other words, the women "staked their programs and authority on female-appropriate exercise."[27] By focusing on their differences, the physical educators cast female athletes as ill-equipped to handle the most commonly practiced (male) versions of sport and instead offered moderated approaches that upheld white, middle-class feminine norms.[28] Thus when the Amateur Athletic Union (AAU) opened track and field to women in 1924, the physical educators quickly protested. On the surface, many of them questioned the motives of the men in promoting women's athletics. The sudden interest "struck women instructors as opportunistic and simply wrong."[29] Yet underlying such concerns were the gendered, raced, and classed realities of the sport. Because African American and working-class women largely populated track and field, several instructors denounced the sport as inappropriate and the participants as mannish. Such indictments led to increased associations of track and field as both masculine and masculinizing and encouraged white, middle-class women to further abandon the sport.

Despite the disproval of women's track and field, Milliat's efforts finally convinced the IAAF to incorporate women in international competitions. Although seemingly altruistic, IAAF president Sigfried Edström never intended equality but instead sought to envelop women's sport under his domain.[30] Therefore, only when the IAAF requested Coubertin's assistance did the IOC acquiesce and permit track and field for both men and women in 1928, although in only half as many events as previously promised. In a compromise, Milliat agreed to remove "Olympics" from the title of her international event, renaming the forum the Women's World Games. Eventually, male dominion over all of track and field, combined with a worldwide economic depression and the rise of fascism, extinguished both the Women's World Games and female control over women's athletics.[31]

With the IAAF and IOC in control of women's track and field, the two organizations dictated and determined appropriate womanhood for female participants. The 1928 Amsterdam Olympics thereby shaped the sport authorities' viewpoints and proved disastrous for women's advancement in international athletics. In particular, the 800-meter final vindicated the IOC's previous stance on women's supposed fragility. The 800-meter event was the longest footrace permitted for women in 1928 and was therefore touted as the debut of female potential in track and field. After the elimination of sixteen competitors in the semifinals, nine athletes raced the following day.[32] Lina Radke (Germany) earned gold, followed by Hitomi Kinue (Japan) and Inga Gentzel (Sweden); all three women finished in world record time. However, rather than celebrate the astonishing efforts of these competitors, the *New York Times* reported hysterically that "at the finish six runners were completely exhausted and fell headlong to the ground."[33] Although similar dramatics occurred in men's races, public outcry quickly emerged.[34] A panicked IOC subsequently voted in 1929 to drop all future female athletic events, using the "collapse" as proof that women were unfit for such physical endeavors. However, US AAU president Gustavus Kirby threatened a boycott of men's track and field if the IOC did not alter its decision. Again backpedaling, the IOC reintroduced women's track and field for the 1932 Los Angeles Games but barred participation in mid- and long-distance races.[35] This "elimination of the 800 meter race meets with approval," noted a *Boston Transcript* reporter. "The revamped program promises to leave a more pleasant taste."[36] As a result, races longer than 200-meters remained closed to women until the 1954 European Athletics Championships and the 1960 Rome Olympics.

Furthermore, skepticism regarding the sex/gender of one runner materialized in the wake of the tumultuous 1928 race. Second-place finisher Hitomi was the first Japanese woman to participate in the Olympics and the first female from the country to win an Olympic medal—an accomplishment that was not replicated until the 1992 Barcelona Olympics. Despite earning international recognition at a young age, she faced constant scrutiny about her apparent disregard of conventional gender norms.[37] Born in 1907 in Okayama, a farming village in western Japan, Hitomi broke her first national record at the age of sixteen in the long jump and unofficially eclipsed the world record for the triple jump one year later. Her excellence in track and field, which included thirty national records and eight medals in the Women's World Games, allowed many to portray her as an *otenba* or *bassai,* a tomboy.[38] Although lauded as a pioneer, Hitomi did not escape gender-based criticisms. Tellingly, the Japanese media frequently compared and contrasted her physicality with leading male athletes. According to historian Dennis Frost, "Such comparisons, perhaps intended as praise, also served to highlight the fact that in terms of her appearance, Hitomi seemed more like a man (and an impressive man, at that) than a woman."[39] In the same vein, historian Robin Kietlinski argues that many in the popular press actually believed Hitomi was a man, a rumor that was only exacerbated when she earned silver in the 1928 Games.[40] For example, male social critic Murobuse Kōshin penned a piece for *Fujn gabō,* a Japanese women's magazine, that questioned Hitomi's sex/gender. Based largely upon Hitomi's athletic successes and her unmarried status, the reporter deduced that she was "40 or 50 percent male and 50 or 60 percent female." He further explained that "Hitomi's 'prestigious records' were not those of a woman, but a man."[41] In the midst of the ceaseless speculations, Hitomi died from pleurisy at age twenty-four, three years after her international debut in Amsterdam.

Although the rumors surrounding Hitomi crystallized in the wake of the 1928 Olympics, some insinuated that the sex/gender anxieties sparked by the Japanese runner also circulated prior to the start of the 800-meter race. According to US sports reporter Grantland Rice, in Amsterdam the IOC required verification of her sex. In a 1936 *New York Times* article Rice divulged that a 1928 "case concerned a Japanese girl in Amsterdam, where the investigating committee was out two hours before it decided predominant sex."[42] He did not mention Hitomi by name; however, one can reasonably deduce the article referenced her, as she served as the lone female representative of Japan. Furthermore, while one journalist's vague account does not guarantee that a sex test occurred in the 1928 Summer Games, it is believable that Hitomi's embodiment of strength and muscularity worried the IAAF and IOC. Even if an examination was not used in Amsterdam, it is plausible that Hitomi motivated the groups to consider requiring proof of womanhood prior to participation in track and field.

While sport authorities pondered the possibility of sex control, powerful female Olympians continued to excel in athletics. In the 1932 Los Angeles Summer Olympics, US athlete Babe Didrikson "was the undisputed star of

Japanese runner Hitomi Kinue (second from left) competes in the 1928
Amsterdam Olympic 800-meter race. Photo by the Asahi Shimbun.
Courtesy of Getty Images.

the women's games." The "Texas Tomboy" set world records in the 80-meter
hurdles and javelin and received a controversial silver medal in the high
jump.[43] In spite of the accolades Didrikson added to the US team's honors,
she was regularly criticized for her appearance, capabilities, and conceit. Her
flagrant disregard of conventional gender norms worried those who feared
that athletics produced mannish women. As noted by sport historian Jennifer
H. Lansbury, successful track athletes like Didrikson, Stephens, and Walsh,
"who initially spurred interest in the sport, eventually did more harm than
good for its image."[44] Many lambasted their muscular physiques, unfeminine
appearances, working-class backgrounds, and (only partially concealed)
rejection of amateurism. Such sentiments proliferated throughout the 1930s,
derived from both the fear of mannish female athletes and the threat they
posed to the gendered status quo. Critics warned that track and field masculinized competitors and applauded overt displays of hetero-femininity.[45]
As sportswriter Paul Gallico jokingly recalled, in 1932 "the accepted method
of determining that a lady was indeed a girl—less clinical and more de-
lightful—was to date her and take her out."[46] The assumption that hetero-
femininity was the appropriate incarnation of womanhood underlined the
calls to implement testing.

Whereas some people sought to verify the sex/gender of female track and field participants, others desired to simply eliminate women's athletics from the Olympic program. After the 1932 Los Angeles Summer Games, calls for the sport's termination increased. Female physical educators again led the charge in the United States. When the IOC first announced the addition of the events for 1928, the Committee on Women's Athletics, the National Association of Physical Education for College Women, and the Women's Division of the National Amateur Athletic Federation all renounced women's involvement.[47] Following the Los Angeles Games, many others shared similar sentiments. For example, *Washington Post* journalist Betty Hardesty asked whether or not "sports, overdone often by the too-zealous, sports-minded woman, rob her of the femininity which has been her birthright and upon which she has always traded."[48] Similarly, A. F. Carylon-Hendry of the *Times of India* implored, "Are we going to breed a race of Amazons, a race of strong brawny women of masculine habits?"[49] Carylon-Hendry further dreaded the encroachment of women into the arts, education, and workforce.

Such public discord permitted sport authorities to consider abandoning all female track and field events. In 1933, for example, *Los Angeles Times* columnist Bill Henry assured his readers that they would not again be forced to witness women's athletics. "There 'ain't gonna be no' ladies events in the 1936 Olympic Games," he explained, "at least not in track and field." Henry supported his postulation by noting, "There is a lot of quiet conversation . . . that may result in the ladies' events being dropped." According to Henry, IOC president Henri de Baillet-Latour publicly disapproved of women's athletics and wanted its deletion.[50] Despite this backlash against women's track and field, the events remained a staple in Olympic competition. Sex and gender anxieties, though, did not abate. Concerns continued to surface in track and field throughout the 1930s and increased the desires to implement sex controls for women.

Milliat's Women's World Games also did not escape such alarms. According to Canadian sports leader Alexandrine Gibb, several overtly masculine athletes competed in the 1934 Women's World Games in London, as well as in the British Empire Games that same year. In her *Toronto Daily Star* sports column titled "No Man's Land of Sport," Gibb publicly lamented the inclusion of muscular victors, disdaining the successes of the "six-foot mannish" Stephens and the "huge and husky, deep voiced" Walsh. Contrastingly, she applauded the triumphs of the "dainty" Canadian runners, the "most feminine team that ever stepped out on cinder paths in Old England." Following the two international events, Gibb recounted that several Canadian athletes wept, for "they had to toe the mark against girls who shaved and spoke in mannish tones!"[51]

As a leader of female athletics, Gibb outlined two recommendations for track and field, one glib and one serious. Sarcastically she suggested an additional category of competitors for the 100-meter race at the Olympic Games. "In it I would put Stella Walsh, Helen Stephens, a couple of special German contestants, at least two English girls, and one or two other Europeans," Gibb explained.[52] On a more serious note, in 1934 she called for the "proper physical examination" of any athlete who wished to compete as a woman.[53] After the Berlin Olympics, many others echoed her demand.

The 1936 Berlin Olympics

With Stephens and Walsh both vying for gold in the Berlin Olympics, the 1936 Games proved rife with accusations of male masqueraders. Several Olympic historians have detailed the increased drive for grandeur instigated by Nazi Germany.[54] Adolf Hitler and the Nazi Party not only demanded victories but also sought to create a memorable international festival to showcase both the authority of the new government system and the superiority of the Aryan race to the world. Perhaps not surprisingly, then, the 1936 Games sparked nascent concerns of nations using sex/gender-transgressive competitors for medals.

As previously mentioned, Stephens finished first in the 100-meter race and, as a result of her speed, was forced to prove her sex. Such suspicions

Helen Stephens (United States) defeats Stanisława Walasiewicz (Poland) in the 1936 Berlin Olympic 100-meter final. Courtesy of the State Historical Society of Missouri, Helen Onson Papers. (C4043, folder 2.)

were not atypical for the "Fulton Flash." Stephens's assistance with the daily operations of her family's farm both developed her strength and allowed her to disregard contemporary gender mores. As biographer Sharon Kinney Hanson explains, "Helen's father, badly needing her help, treated his strong, strapping daughter much as he would have treated a stepson."[55] A childhood accident that wounded her throat and rendered her voice low and raspy, combined with her exceptional height—Stephens reached almost six feet by the age of fifteen—further enhanced her image as a masculine female.[56] It is not surprising, then, that her record-setting performance in 1936 surprised and flummoxed fans and officials.

Immediately after the race, Polish reports disparaged Stephens's victory and claimed she was a man. Some credit Walsh's coach and the Polish Olympic

Helen Stephens and Stanisława Walasiewicz shake hands, August 6, 1936. Courtesy of the Polish National Digital Archive.

Committee for starting the rumor; others suggest Walsh was the culprit. Nevertheless, the Associated Press printed the story and the news traveled around the world.[57] When asked her thoughts on the accusations, Stephens told the media to confer with the physician who sex tested all track and field athletes before competition.[58] This suggestion that female athletes were checked before participating in the Olympics raises an important question: was Stephens singled out, or were other women also required to undergo a physical exam? An account in the *Los Angeles Times* insinuates that Berlin organizers selected the "Missouri Express" for control. The article explained that German Olympic officials, wary of Stephens's physique and speed, "had ascertained her true sex before admitting her to participate in the 1936 games."[59] Contrastingly, according to Gallico, it was the AAU that "had La Stephens frisked for sex" before boarding the Olympic-bound boat and "checked her in as one hundred percent female."[60] In addition, the minutes of the 35th Session of the IOC support the latter claim that US authorities were responsible for Stephens's examination. On July 31, 1936, days before the start of the Berlin sex test saga, IOC members discussed "*athlétes femmes anormales*" (abnormal women athletes). According to the meeting minutes, the IOC forwarded a letter from the American Olympic Committee (AOC) to all international federations on the topic. The excerpt suggests that the AOC was cognizant of the concerns and handled the situation in advance of the competition.[61]

Nevertheless, if Stephens alone was examined, whether by the German officials, AAU, or AOC, one could argue that the decision to test her stemmed solely from her physical appearance and observable success. However, if the AAU or AOC checked all US women prior to participation, it insinuates that US sport organizations questioned the sex/gender of anyone who competed in track and field, a sport considered masculine in the United States. Both scenarios reveal the anxieties sparked by women's participation in interwar athletics.

Furthermore, Walsh—the second-place finisher who some suggest was responsible for sparking the accusations against Stephens—also regularly defended herself against sex/gender criticisms. Born in Poland, she immigrated to the United States and grew up in Cleveland. As an adolescent, Walsh excelled in many sports; however, her triumphs were more often met with misgivings than with cheers. For example, because of her European roots and supposed lack of femininity, classmates criticized Walsh's appearance and pejoratively nicknamed her "Bull Montana," a reference to professional wrestler Lewis Montagna. In addition, some acquaintances retrospectively suggested that Clevelanders were aware of Walsh's unique biological composition from the onset of her career. Casimir Bielen, a childhood friend, Polish community leader, and one of the runner's biggest advocates, later acknowledged that "other boys and girls knew she had these physical deformities. . . . It was common knowledge that she had this accident of nature. She wasn't 100% female."[62] Similarly, Beverly Perret Conyers, one of Walsh's track pupils, admitted to seeing her coach undress in the locker room when she was ten years old and later claimed that she viewed both male and female genitalia.[63]

Despite experiencing cruel treatment, Walsh shined in athletics. Notably, she set twenty-two world records and was the first woman to run the 100-meter race in less than twelve seconds. Importantly, as recounted by Bielen,

Stanisława Walasiewicz training, 1932. Courtesy of the Polish National Digital Archive.

Stanisława Walasiewicz at the 1938 European Athletics Championships, Vienna, Austria. Courtesy of the Polish National Digital Archive.

medical doctors inspected Walsh prior to several events, and she "passed qualifying medical examinations" as a requisite to compete. Such an account is telling for two reasons. First, Bielen's description that Walsh "was medically examined by hundreds of doctors" implies that US and international sport authorities were suspicious of the runner—likely because of her appearance and athleticism—and repeatedly forced her to undergo a visual check to verify her womanhood.[64] Second, if Walsh was regularly inspected, she was not a male imposter, but an example of biological ambiguity.

Therefore, she presumably passed all the necessary tests, competed in the 1932 Summer Games, and set a world record in the 100-meter race. As she secured the gold medal in Los Angeles, Walsh intended for Berlin to serve as the forum for her back-to-back titles. After Stephens deflated such plans, the "Cleveland Flyer" retired and continued to serve as a role model to the Polish community in Ohio. Her murder in 1980 not only shocked the Cleveland populous but also would help the IOC rationalize the continuation of its sex testing policy throughout the 1980s and 1990s.

Along with the Stephens-Walsh feud in the 1936 Games, it was also reported that a man posed as a woman in Berlin. German high jumper Dora Ratjen, who finished fourth in the women's event and set a world record

Dora Ratjen at the 1937 German Athletics Championships.
Courtesy of the German Federal Archives, German
News Service.

in the 1938 European Athletics Championships, later identified as a man, Heinrich Ratjen. Some initially speculated that the Nazi Party forced the faux participation due to its anti-Semitic desire to replace Gretel Bergmann, a world-class Jewish high jumper, with Ratjen.[65] However, police records and medical reports show the incorrectness of this explanation.

Two years after placing fourth in the Olympics, and mere days after setting the women's world record in the high jump, Ratjen was arrested for "cross-dressing" while wearing feminine clothing aboard a German train. Not only does the corresponding police file refer to the Nazi Party's ignorance on the matter, but the documents also highlight the medical uncertainties surround-

Dora Ratjen (left) and Elfriede Kaun take a break during the German Athletics Championships. Courtesy of the German Federal Archives, German News Service.

Dora Ratjen wins the high jump in the 1937 German Athletics Championships. Courtesy of the German Federal Archives, German News Service.

ing the case.[66] According to the report, the midwife present at Ratjen's birth first declared the baby a boy before quickly asserting that the actual sex of the child was female. After deliberation the midwife informed the parents it was best to raise Ratjen as a girl, which they did. Only after the 1938 legal proceedings and medical examinations did the civil registry officially change Ratjen's sex from female to male. Thus, as the public prosecutor explained, "Fraud cannot be deemed to have taken place because there was no intention to reap financial reward. . . . After all, Dora had never been told he was a man."[67] Ratjen was exonerated of all charges but forced to return his medals. Although his position on the 1936 German Olympic team stemmed from "a mundane and human case of gender uncertainty, medical error, fear and embarrassment," Ratjen's case was used by the IAAF and IOC as an infallible example of a male imposter in women's sport.[68]

Transgender Athletes in International Competition

The 1936 Berlin Olympics thereby cemented sex and gender concerns in international track and field. Future IOC president Avery Brundage served as the chaperone of the US athletes in Berlin. While in Germany, he grew anxious about the participation of ambiguously sexed/gendered women. "I am fed up to the ears with women as track and field competitors," he explained after the games. Their "charms sink to less than zero. . . . [And] they are ineffective and unpleasing on the track."[69] Brundage's unease only increased when newspaper accounts surfaced that described the sex-reassignment surgeries of several successful female athletes.[70] Transgender individuals sparked anxieties by blurring boundaries and demonstrating the fluidity of sex and gender, clear challenges to the sex-segregated nature of sport.[71] Brundage particularly disdained the fact that two former European champions, Zdeňka Koubková and Mary Edith Louise Weston, underwent sex-reassignment surgery, becoming Zdenek Koubek and Mark Edward Louis Weston, respectively. Both had excelled in European track and field events as women.[72]

In 1934 Koubková set the Czechoslovakian women's records in the broad jump, high jump, and several short and mid-distance races. As a woman, Koubková also broke the world record in the 800-meter run and was labeled the "fastest woman on legs." However, appearance-based suspicions led to an investigation in 1935, and the inconclusive results convinced the Fédération Sportive Féminine Internationale to strip the Czechoslovakian athlete of the victories.[73] Having combated feelings of masculinity as a child and adolescent, Koubková opted to undergo surgery in Podil, Ukraine.[74] "I always thought I was a girl in the first part of my life," he later recounted through a translator.

"And then . . . I began to realize that I wasn't a girl. . . . I went to a doctor and he told me that I was right—that I was a man."[75] The story gained traction in the United States when the former women's champion traveled to New York City in 1936 to perform in a Broadway club, where he ran on a treadmill chasing a woman.[76]

In a similar manner, Mary Weston competed for Great Britain as a woman and won several events throughout a six-year career. As Mary, Weston earned the British Women's Amateur Athletic Association (WAAA) shot-put title in 1925 and in 1928 and represented the United Kingdom in the 1926 Women's World Games. Three years later Weston placed first in the 1929 WAAA Championships in the discus, javelin, and shot put. Despite the national recognition devoted to athletics, questions surfaced about the validity of the achievements. Studies in anatomy led Weston, who was vying for a career in medicine, to question his biological sex and gender expression. "I found that I had to shave regularly, and that I was not very feminine," he explained in a later interview. "I began withdrawing from athletics, feeling it unfair to women competitors, who undoubtedly were 100 percent feminine."[77] Accordingly, feeling more male than female, Weston underwent surgery in 1934. While *Time* magazine characterized the procedure as sex-reassignment surgery, the overseeing surgeon, L. R. Broster, described it as a corrective measure, one that reformed a biological abnormality.[78] Broster explained that "Mark Weston, who has always been brought up as female, is a male and should continue to live as such."[79] Weston followed the recommendation and lived as a man, eventually marrying his longtime friend Alberta Bray in 1938. The widely disseminated story allowed many to use Weston's case as proof that athletics masculinized women.

Both Koubek and Weston received international recognition. Their celebrity status showcased the new technologies that rendered sex-reassignment surgery a possibility and also highlighted additional occurrences of other athletes changing sex. For example, twenty-three-year-old Polish javelin thrower Sophia Smetkowna announced plans to transition to a man in 1937. More importantly, Koubek's and Weston's notoriety increased the demands for a control method in women's events. "I was laughed at when I suggested medical examinations at these international games," recounted Gibb. "Since then two so-called girls have become men legally. . . . Some day [*sic*] those in charge of women's international competitions will waken and realize their responsibilities to the 100 percent girls."[80] Voicing similar concerns, Brundage wrote a letter to IOC president Baillet-Latour describing women with "apparent characteristics of the opposite sex" and asked if a sex check policy had been enacted. "If not," Brundage reasoned, "it might be well to insist on a medical examination before participation in the Olympic Games."[81] Additionally, in his first meeting as an IOC member, he advocated for increased visual scrutiny of women, "to make sure they were really 100% female."[82] After listening to Brundage's concerns, the IOC voted on the matter and agreed to defer to individual sport federations.[83] The IAAF hence emerged as the forerunner in sex testing, with the IOC eventually following suit later, during Brundage's presidency.

Despite the pleas, both the IOC and IAAF avoided the implementation of sex control with the onset of World War II. Due to the war, the 1940 and 1944 Olympic Games, 1942 European Athletics Championships, and 1942 and 1946 Commonwealth Games were canceled. Talks of ambiguous female athletes therefore quieted. However, when international competitions resumed, speculations and suspicions again abounded. In the 1946 European Championships in Oslo, Norway, French runner Léa Caurla earned bronze in the 200-meter race and participated on the French 4 x 100-meter relay team that finished second. Yet when asked to undergo a compulsory examination, Caurla refused. Consequently barred from the French Athletics Federation in 1948, Caurla transitioned from Léa to Leon and underwent surgery two years later.[84] Similarly, Caurla's 4 x 100-meter relay teammate Claire Bressolles also transitioned to a man, Pierre, following the 1946 European Championships.[85] Finally, Helga Cordes, a 1952 Olympic hopeful, also transitioned. Unlike the previously recorded cases, Cordes "had apparently changed sex over a period of years. . . . [The] conversion apparently was a slow and natural development." Nevertheless, a medical examination proved the athlete unable to compete in the Helsinki Games.[86] The widely discussed examples of female-to-male transgender competitors concerned sport authorities, seemingly provided evidence of the masculinizing effects of track and field, and increased the demands for sex control in international sport.

Early Control Measures and "Failures"

Armed with such speculations, in 1946 the IAAF incorporated one of the first compulsory sex/gender regulations in international competition. In order to participate in women's events, female competitors had to obtain a physician's letter verifying their sex.[87] The British Women's Amateur Athletic Association similarly requested written confirmation from medical personnel for all female participants.[88] Finally, also convinced that threats to the sex/gender binary existed in track and field, the IOC instituted a check for the 1948 London Summer Olympics. Officials required female Olympians to submit an affidavit, signed by a doctor, certifying that they were women.[89]

For almost two decades, sport authorities determined womanhood based upon physicians' interpretations of sex/gender.

Female athletes experienced difficulties with the controls from their inception. In 1949 Dutch track athlete Foekje Dillema defeated national rival Fanny Blankers-Koen. Blankers-Koen, Holland's "Flying Housewife," had previously won four gold medals in the 1948 London Summer Olympics and was an international star, celebrated for her athleticism, femininity, and motherhood. Dillema, on the other hand, was a relatively unknown runner who gained attention for both defeating the famous mother of two and concurrently establishing a new Dutch record in the 200-meter race. However, her victory proved short-lived, as Dillema was barred from competition in 1950.

Reasons regarding her expulsion vary. Some accounts note that the Royal Dutch Athletics Federation sidelined Dillema after she refused to undergo a sex test at the 1950 European Championships.[90] Other reports suggest she was expelled due to the results of a mandated gynecological examination. Despite the rationale, the Dutch athlete was banned from athletics for life and her records erased. Depressed, Dillema returned to Friesland, a small village in the Netherlands, and did not leave her house for an entire year; she also refused to discuss her case with reporters or physicians.[91] After her death in 2007, scientists posthumously discovered that Dillema had 46,XX/46,XY chromosomal mosaicism and should have been allowed to compete as a woman.[92] Although Dillema's story illustrates the inaccuracies of sex testing, the IAAF and the IOC interpreted her plight as justification for continued control.

Problems with sex testing continued. In the 1960 Rome Olympics, for example, a protest emerged regarding the sex and gender of one of the British Olympians. Two European nations reported that a member of the women's athletics team had developed masculine characteristics and was likely a man. In defense, K. S. "Sandy" Duncan, the head of the British Olympic team, referred to the allegations as a "slur" and noted that all entrants possessed a "certificate signed by a doctor certifying their sex."[93] Jack Crump, secretary of the British Amateur Athletic Board, similarly assured the press that all female track and field members possessed proper forms signed by a physician. "It would be unthinkable for us and for anybody else to challenge the integrity and capability of a registered practitioner," he explained. "In that respect we have completely complied with the rule."[94] Nevertheless, concerns that unscrupulous individuals might utilize fraudulent documents eventually pushed the IAAF and IOC to reconsider their control measures.

* * *

It was within track and field where anxieties surfaced and tests resulted. Sex and gender beliefs permeated the ancient Olympics, and Coubertin later imposed similar norms into the modern games. The founder not only continued sex segregation but also instilled gender ideals. Bolstered by the prevailing sex/gender mores, Coubertin completely denied female inclusion in the 1896 Athens Games. The expansion of the Olympics eventually forced him to begrudgingly accept women, albeit only in a handful of socially acceptable events. Furthermore, for much of his tenure, track and field, the most prestigious and masculine of Olympic sports, remained off-limits to women. Consequently, when women fought for inclusion, they repeatedly faced denials from both male and female sport authorities. Only the activism of Milliat and the foresight of Edström finally convinced the reluctant IOC to include women in 1928.

Neither the IAAF nor the IOC amiably embraced female track and field athletes. Rather, as women excelled in the sport, officials fueled the fears of masculinized women and male masqueraders. When muscular victors like Hitomi, Stephens, Walsh, and Didrikson dominated athletics, many decried the loss of femininity and suggested they could not be "real" women. Accordingly, only men could run as quickly, jump as high, or throw as far as these Olympians. The initial physical examination thus targeted female athletes who succeeded in international athletics events and who did not display Western standards of femininity. In addition, the presence of transgender athletes in track and field exacerbated the growing sex/gender anxieties in the sport. Recognition of sex/gender-transgressive track and field participants compelled the IAAF and IOC to eventually outline rules dedicated to the certification of women. The prestige of track and field, combined with its masculine undertones, allowed the sport to serve as the first in which questions of sex/gender appeared.

However, when the Soviet Union returned to the international sport scene, an even greater emphasis on sex testing emerged. The immediate triumphs of the Soviet women in a variety of events convinced the IAAF and IOC that compulsory examinations for all female athletes was a necessity. Therefore, although sex/gender fears first arose in track and field, the continued successes of powerful female athletes resulted in the eventual implementation of compulsory sex tests for all women in all sports.

2 "Because They Have Muscles, Big Ones"

Cold War Gender Norms and International Sport, 1952–1967

THREE DAYS AFTER THE OPENING ceremonies of the 1960 Rome Olympics, *New York Times* reporter William Barry Furlong bemoaned the tendency for female Olympians to destroy "The Image." According to the author, The Image referred to the innate beauty possessed by petite, aesthetically pleasing, non-muscular women. In a three-page article titled "Venus Wasn't a Shot-Putter," Furlong complained that certain sports destroyed this natural feminine appeal, specifically admonishing discus, field hockey, shot put, and snooker pool, because in these activities the athletes' "force of intellect—if any—was subordinated to harsher disciplines." However, he noted that a "girl" athlete could maintain The Image if she selected a socially sanctified pastime. "Those that frolic athletically in swim suits or brief tennis skirts find it easy to preserve, not to say enhance, that Image," Furlong explained.[1] His disdain for women's sports that required strength and power, such as shot put, and appreciation for those that mandated grace and skirts, such as tennis, mirrored the predominant gender ideology of the West during the onset of the Cold War.

In the wake of World War II, the Soviet Union and the United States emerged as ideologically polarized superpowers. The two nations disagreed on numerous fronts throughout the Cold War, from governmental practices to social dynamics. Sport became an influential medium through which each country sought to showcase its supremacy. While the Soviet Union and the United States both propagated athletic victories as signifiers of national prowess, they diverged on the acceptability of women's involvement in physical contests. Female athletes in the United States remained bounded by Western notions of femininity, but women in the Soviet Union were encouraged to succeed in a variety of sports. This rare promotion of female athleticism extended from the Soviet Union's egalitarian beliefs in physical labor. Soviet women thus dominated international sport, excelling in the activities that destroyed what Furlong labeled The Image. Notably, Soviet female athletes competed unhindered—and successfully—in track and field. As male sports columnist Shirley Povich noted before the 1956 Melbourne Olympics, "The Russian women indeed are favored again over the American women, mostly because they have muscles, big ones, in the places United States gals don't want 'em."[2] The USSR women earned first-place finishes in the European Championships, gold medals in the Olympic Games, and condemnation from abroad.

Consequently, the gender anxieties that had previously plagued interwar track and field were amplified during the early phases of the Cold War. After witnessing the Soviet women's remarkable achievements in athletics, the IAAF decided that all female competitors should verify their womanhood prior to competition. In 1966 the federation introduced a "nude parade," the first compulsory sex test of modern sport. Although the desire to police womanhood was not entirely sparked by the Soviet Union's triumphs in international sport—as illustrated by the sporadic interwar-era examinations—the rise of the Cold War allowed many to point to the USSR athletes as the sole reason for the policy's implementation. "Let's take a hard look at some facts," suggested Frank True of the *Sarasota Herald Tribune*. "If the Commies hadn't been guilty of substituting men for women in the first place, the new rule of the IAAF wouldn't have been necessary."[3] Similar to the gender-transgressive women of the interwar period, the strong, successful female athletes of the Soviet Union became targets for not embodying conventional femininity as prescribed by the West. The heightening of the Cold War merely exacerbated the earlier sex/gender concerns and resulted in a mandatory examination for all female track and field competitors. Encouraged but not caused by the Soviet's victories, sport authorities grew increasingly worried that powerful female athletes in the 1950s and 1960s were either unnaturally inauthentic women, men posing as women, or dopers. Using the USSR women as scapegoats, the IAAF established tests to eliminate all three categories and delineate "true" womanhood.

The Cold War and International Relations

The IAAF and IOC grew more concerned about sex/gender transgressions as Cold War tensions developed internationally. At the close of World War II the United States and the Soviet Union emerged as uneasy allies. Under the leadership of President Harry S. Truman, US policy makers sought to maintain the country's power by rebuilding the world system to align with the democratic and capitalistic ambitions of the United States. Concurrently, headed by General Secretary Joseph Stalin, Soviet authorities underscored the virtues of communism and demanded territorial extension into Eastern Europe. Relations between the two superpowers thus declined precipitously and divided the world ideologically into East versus West. As Cold War historian John Lewis Gaddis explains, World War II was "won by a coalition whose principal members were already at war—ideologically and geopolitically if not militarily—with one another."[4] Although direct military conflict between the United States and the Soviet Union never materialized, the two nations did clash on several cultural fronts, which included gender and sport.

Less than one year after the end of World War II, Stalin orated a 1946 election speech (in a one-candidate election) at Moscow's Bolshoi Theatre in which he proposed a solution for any future international turmoil. In his view, monopoly capitalism fostered uneven economic development and was the culprit of the recent multi-country conflict. "The capitalist world is split into two hostile camps," Stalin declared, "and war breaks out between them." Furthermore, he argued that the results of World War II demonstrated the success of the Soviet social system and its stability as a viable form of government. Most alarmingly, from the US perspective, Stalin explained that "as regards long-term plans, our Party intends to organize another powerful upswing of our national economy."[5] Stalin's Bolshoi Theatre speech detailed the USSR's expansionist intentions and illustrated the new postwar entanglements. The division of Europe into spheres of influence—which moved the Soviet Union's borders several hundred miles to the west and permitted the implementation of subservient Eastern bloc regimes—the joint occupation of Germany, and the development of the atomic bomb collectively fostered novel international anxieties.[6]

In response to Stalin's election oration, US diplomat George F. Kennan assessed the dictator's intent and proposed a proactive foreign policy in a hastily drafted, eight-thousand-word telegram to Secretary of State James Byrnes. Kennan, who at the time worked in the American embassy in Moscow, identified three main issues in his cable, which was later dubbed the "Long Telegram." First, he argued that USSR leaders viewed the world as divided into a capitalist and socialist binary in which the Soviet Union felt circumscribed by antagonistic capitalist regimes. Such a conviction appeared rooted more in popular lore than reality, yet it nevertheless nurtured insecurity and generated neurotic foreign policies.[7] As a second point, the US diplomat noted that not all USSR citizens agreed with the Soviet authorities on the necessity of destruction; many posited that peaceful coexistence was possible. Finally, Kennan foreshadowed an image of the Soviet Union as a devastating force and suggested that the United States confront the country directly; he reasoned that attempts at cooperation would be futile. In his view the Soviet Union was a political entity "committed fanatically to the belief that with the U.S. there can be no permanent *modus vivendi*," peaceful agreement.[8] Although Kennan concluded that the United States should avoid acting with hysteria, his later suggestion that "vigilant containment of Russian expansive tendencies" was necessary cemented the United States' foreign policy.[9]

Cold War apprehensions were further aggravated three years later when US informants discovered Soviet atomic weaponry. With the confirmation of the USSR's nuclear capabilities, the United States responded by accelerating its own production of atomic bombs. Both countries consequently engaged in a nuclear arms race; each was convinced that the only way to deter its perceived enemy from deploying catastrophic technology was to possess more of such armaments. Therefore, taking the reins from Truman in 1953, successor Dwight D. Eisenhower rejected limited notions of war and instead prepared the country for total nuclear engagement. USSR leader Nikita Khrushchev, who presided after Stalin's death in 1953, similarly attempted to conceal vulnerability through atomic buildup.[10] However, unlike Eisenhower, Khrushchev initially voiced overt threats toward the West, occasionally pinpointing specific targets.[11] He foreshadowed that any missile confrontations would be "fought on the American continent."[12] This arms-race mentality dominated foreign policy throughout the Cold War. When President John F. Kennedy entered office in 1961, he was "shocked to discover that the only war plan Eisenhower had left behind would have required the *simultaneous* use of well over 3,000 nuclear weapons against *all* communist countries."[13]

Cold War Gender Norms

Although the possibility of mutual catastrophic destruction actually limited overt warfare, the conflict increased the depth and distribution of propaganda. This, in turn, led to a variety of cultural confrontations between the United States and Soviet Union. One of the most notable examples occurred when US vice president Richard Nixon and Soviet premier Khrushchev extemporaneously discussed the plight and purpose of women in what was later dubbed the "Kitchen Debate." During the 1959 opening of the American National Exhibition at Sokolniki Park in Moscow, the leaders contrasted the gender ideologies of the two nations, illustrating the centrality of such constructs in the Cold War. While touring the kitchen of a model American home—which exhibitors claimed anyone in the United States could afford—Nixon pointed to a dishwasher and explained, "What we want to do, is make life more easy [*sic*] for our housewives." Khrushchev quickly rebuffed the sentiment and noted, "Your capitalistic attitude toward women does not occur under Communism."[14] The at times terse conversations between Nixon and Khrushchev highlighted the different gender norms that existed in the United States and Soviet Union during the onset of the Cold War. As each nation frequently measured progress and superiority by the status of its women, the dialogue often devolved into an "our-women-are-better-off-than-your-women-no-they-aren't-yes-they-are kind of masculine debate."[15]

The perceived role of women, and thus of female athletes, differed significantly between the two superpowers. In the United States, conventional white gender norms and heterosexuality—exhibited primarily through marriage, domestic work, and child rearing for women—was exalted to counteract the supposed threats from abroad. The Soviet Union highlighted the egalitarian nature of the Soviet state, paying particular attention to gender equality under the law and in the workplace. Both superpowers used their women to demonstrate international superiority; their dissimilar ideology would eventually extend into sport.

Gender and Sexuality in the Cold War United States

After the momentary dismantling of gender and sexuality norms during World War II, US citizens sought a return to the previously established social order of the interwar era. The necessities of war had briefly opened the door for women and disrupted gender roles; notably, white, middle-class women entered the workforce and discarded the limitations of domesticity. However, after the Allied victory, many feared the war-induced changes and urged these white female workers back into domestic positions. According to women's historian Nancy Cott, "Men and women alike were expected to relinquish their emergency roles and settle into domestic life—men as breadwinners, women as homemakers."[16] Hence the "June Cleaver" ideal—women as white, heterosexual housewives—proliferated. The nuclear family, domestic femininity, and heterosexuality consequently gained importance during the Cold War.

Americans turned to nuclear families for protection. As historian Elaine Tyler May demonstrates, "domestic containment"—the idea that the dangerous social forces of the atomic age could be combated within the home—served to prioritize specific gender roles and privilege heterosexuality.[17] A public belief in "reproductive morality" also demanded that prospective parents consider their offspring's impact on the strength and "progress" of the United States before conception. In other words, parents were asked to contemplate their future children's race, class, gender, and sexuality before reproducing.[18] When contrasted against the Soviet Union's supposedly perverse familial framework, the nuclear family in the United States evolved into an icon of stability that many believed was necessary to survive the Cold War.

Also connected to this familial endorsement, sexuality mores in the postwar era grew to embrace heterosexual interaction and denounce all other forms of sexual relationships. Earlier, during World War II, wartime needs had softened sexuality norms. As historian Allan Bérubé explains, "The massive mobilization for World War II relaxed the social constraints of peacetime that had kept gay men and women unaware of themselves and each other."[19] Thus, gay Americans found community and experienced momentary—albeit still very limited—toleration. However, because the Cold War context mandated social control, which included the management of sexuality, US authorities started to construct deviancy from heterosexuality as treasonous. In particular, lesbianism came under increased scrutiny and was deemed "a social problem." As a result, gay men and women experienced a reduction of rights during the Cold War stemming from the hardening of the sexual binary and the criminalization of same-sex relationships. Heterosexuality became the embodiment of US sexual citizenship during this era.[20]

Not all people experienced such a dramatic shift in opportunities. Likewise, the social control of gender and sexuality was not always omnipresent in the postwar era. As women's historian Joanne Meyerowitz illustrates, women of color and poor working-class white women labored both before and after World War II.[21] In addition, anxieties and uncertainties about domestic femininity appeared in various forms, from popular music to best-selling cookbooks, suggesting that postwar gender norms were not ubiquitous nor always authoritative.[22] Nevertheless, the US public largely disregarded such accounts and prized the white, middle-class, heterosexual, domestic experience. Thus, the hegemonic womanhood that eventually prevailed in the West during the Cold War encompassed white, middle-class femininity and heterosexuality.

Gender and Sexuality in the Cold War Soviet Union

Gender norms in the Soviet Union differed. Not only did female leaders prove highly visible in the Russian Revolution of 1917, but also the Bolshevik Party transformed traditional gender patterns to help consolidate its rule. For example, the Bolsheviks garnered female support by contrasting the *"baba,"* a pejorative Russian term that depicted an illiterate, superstitious, and backward woman, against the "comrade," a progressive, educated, communist woman who worked for the creation of a better Soviet state.[23] Furthermore, under the new provisional government, laws largely promoted women's sameness to men—politically, legally, and economically. Russian women earned the right to vote in 1917, and the 1918 Code of Laws further diminished their inferior status by permitting marital divorce. The government also encouraged female workers to labor in the same capacity as their male counterparts. According to labor scholar Sarah Ashwin, this disruption of the gender order "was both a potent symbol of the triumph of the new regime and a means of undermining the social foundations of the old order."[24] The Bolsheviks may have declared the complete abolishment of gender inequality; however, attempts for a truly egalitarian society proved unrealistic, as several traditional stereotypes remained intact. Perhaps most notably, women became "worker-mothers" and had the dual responsibilities of public labor and domestic chores.[25]

As the Bolsheviks sought to promote gender equality in the 1920s, they also eased restrictions on sexuality. The desire to abolish tsarist cannons and customs—such as religious marriages and female inferiority—led to the legalization of abortion, the dissemination of contraceptive information, and the tempered acceptance of same-sex sexuality. Significantly, the Bolsheviks removed anti-sodomy statutes from the 1922 Criminal Code, becoming the first European country to decriminalize the act.[26] While the Russian Revolution helped legalize same-sex sexuality, the movement's leaders maintained inconsistent ideas about the appropriateness and purpose of intimate sexual encounters. As Russian philosopher Igor Kon explains, "Bolshevism abolished, on the one hand, God, ecclesiastical marriage, and absolute moral values, and, on the other, the individual's right to personal self-determination and love that might stand higher than all social duties."[27] In other words, socialist authorities hoped to dismantle the social order of tsarist Russia yet simultaneously viewed individual pleasure as a diversion from the greater good of the state. They thereby conveyed contradictory acceptance of both unbridled sexuality and sexual restraint. Furthermore, as Russian scholar Dan Healey notes, "Bolshevik attitudes toward male same-sex love beyond the revolutionary heartland were very different."[28] As Soviet power expanded geographically, leaders on "civilizing" missions outlawed sodomy in "primitive" societies. For example, the Bolsheviks criminalized sodomy in Azerbaijan in 1923, Uzbekistan in 1926, and Turkmenistan in 1927. Nevertheless, although the Bolsheviks embraced conflicting views on same-sex sexuality, according to Healey, the evidence suggests that "many individuals with same-sex inclinations experienced tolerance and even acceptance" during the 1920s, particularly when contrasted against other European countries.[29]

During Stalin's reign, gender and sexuality norms dramatically changed. The double burden of "worker-mothers," first expected of women during the Bolshevik construction of the Soviet state, extended under Stalin. Women continued to internalize the regime's prescriptions regarding the centrality of labor in everyday affairs. According to sociologist Marina Kiblitskaya, "to work in the Soviet Union was to work for the state—and to work for the state was seen to be the highest purpose in life."[30] Labor and social issues therefore took priority over personal concerns. Reproduction was also an important obligation; the government was both interested and involved in the process. As sociologist Olga Issoupova explains, the Soviet Union viewed motherhood as a state function. Leaders envisioned childbirth as the natural destiny of women—not a private venture, but a social one—for which mothers should be rewarded. Hence the regime supported women and highlighted their role as the creators of future workers. As this ideology gained traction, Stalin adjusted the laws to strengthen the traditional family and increase the Soviet birth rate; he subsequently decreased the opportunities for divorce and deemed abortion illegal. Finally, the Soviet Union depicted child rearing as a matter of public concern, for children needed to be raised properly as communists.[31]

Along with prioritizing reproduction for women and strengthening the family, Stalin also attempted to repress sexuality and eliminate the sexual culture that the Bolsheviks had unintentionally allowed to flourish. Most influentially, he added an anti-sodomy order to the Soviet Union Criminal Code in 1933. Under Article 121, voluntary sodomy was punishable by up to three years of hard labor.[32] Healey argued that this "homophobic turn" in the Soviet Union stemmed largely from the enactment of Stalin's First Five-Year Plan, an outline of the nation's economic goals. As part of his proposal, Stalin identified alcoholics, beggars, homeless adults, and female prostitutes as "social anomalies," those who threatened economic productivity. When campaigns against these "social anomalies" combined with efforts to remove all "socially dangerous elements" from urban areas, the gay subculture came under attack. "Socially dangerous elements" was a fluid category Stalin used to persecute socially marginalized groups, such as anticommunists, gay men and women, political enemies, spies, and tsarist supporters. In addition, Stalin had other motivations for the inclusion of Article 121, including his hopes to mend the relationship with the Eastern Orthodox Church and his fear of an influx of gay Nazi spies into the country.[33]

After World War II, these gender and sexuality norms remained entrenched, yet the pervasive power of the ideologies somewhat waned. The state still expected women to labor but did not require them to devote their entire lives to work. As Ashwin explains, the paradox of the Soviet era can be surmised as "strong, independent women who nevertheless ended up doing all the housework."[34] Moreover, a gradual expansion of sexual freedoms occurred when Khrushchev took control of the nation. Despite their occasionally shared expectations of domesticity and comparable intolerance of same-sex sexuality, the Soviet Union and United States each believed that the gender and sexuality norms of the other nation were unnatural and harmful.

Gender and Sexuality Stereotypes in the Cold War

With their differing enactments of gender and sexuality, the United States and Soviet Union used the status of their women to demonstrate superiority. US citizens disparagingly depicted women of the USSR as "graceless, shapeless and sexless." Degrading the Soviet's physiques as masculine and unsexed served to discredit the nation's government, suggesting that the "ills of communism were inscribed on the bodies of women."[35] In addition, Americans claimed that the Soviet Union inverted the natural gender order by forcing women into labor. The hard, physical work—similar to athletic training—transformed the muscularity of the Russian women, which contradicted the United States' dominant understandings of the female form. This stereotype allowed US women to contrast themselves against the Soviets and reassert the boundaries of appropriate womanhood in the West.

The Soviet Union, on the other hand, viewed capitalism as harmful to women. The Kremlin juxtaposed the United States' unwillingness to promote equal pay and inability to pass the Equal Rights Amendment with the Soviet's successes in supporting economic, legal, and political equality. Tellingly, the Soviet Union also painted female domesticity as an all-consuming hardship. USSR propaganda suggested American women were unhappily anchored to the kitchen. As historian Helen Laville notes, "The Kremlin argued that if the status of women was indeed a barometer of the progress of a nation, then this status should be understood by her place in politics, economics, and society, not her place in the home."[36] The divergent norms would come to shape women's acceptance into sport at a time when international victories gained significant cultural capital.

Cold War Sport

Sport emerged as a contested arena during the Cold War, one in which the two superpowers not only sought to demonstrate nationalistic superiority but also faced each other directly. As the Cold War intensified, international competitions evolved into significant measures of national vitality. When contrasted against the athleticism of the Soviet Union, perceived reductions in US physical vigor encouraged Eisenhower to create the President's Council on Youth Fitness (PCYF) in 1956. Appalled by the results of the Kraus-Weber Minimal Fitness Test—which found that 57.9 percent of US schoolchildren failed to meet minimum fitness standards compared to only 8.7 percent of European children—the president conceived the cabinet-level council through an executive order. The PCYF intended to serve as a "catalytic agent" that focused primarily on public awareness. Despite the PCYF's ambivalent results, the president's actions nevertheless likened the United States' supposed "muscle gap" to the "missile gap," consequently molding sport into a critical component of foreign relations. Akin to the contemporaneous arms race, Eisenhower instigated a Cold War "body race."[37]

Continuing Eisenhower's fitness crusade, Kennedy extended the PCYF and further articulated the importance of national vitality in international affairs. He declared, "In a very real and immediate sense, our growing softness, our increasing lack of physical fitness, is a menace to our security."[38] Kennedy thereby extended the power of the PCYF and changed the organization's name to the President's Council on Physical Fitness (PCPF), ensuring the incorporation of all age groups. To preempt any accusations of softness, Kennedy hired famed University of Oklahoma football coach Charles "Bud" Wilkinson to head the PCPF and launched a public service advertising campaign to inform citizens of the importance of national vigor.

At first, fears of a muscle gap in the United States primarily focused on the physical ineptitude of young white men. However, when the Soviet female athletes helped push their country to the top of international contests, anxieties extended into US women's sport as well. Questions arose regarding the role girls and women should play in the efforts to outscore the Soviet Union. As sport scholar Jaime Schultz explains, "The 1950s marked a time of intense debate about whether and how to invigorate American women's sport."[39] Consequently, white female physical educators mobilized. On the collegiate level the instructors attempted to enhance competition while simultaneously preserving their "sport for all" ideals. Such adjustments went hand in hand with the increased victories earned by the Soviet female athletes. Hence, when the United States Olympic Committee (USOC) sought to improve women's performances at the games, physical educators arranged to oversee the progress as the Women's Advisory Board of the US Olympic Development Committee. Through this committee the instructors hoped to improve women's sport while upholding a democratic vision of participation.[40] As historian Martha H. Verbrugge argues, this seemingly contradictory promotion of elite and modified contests rendered female athletes both "admirable and deficient." Within this framework, girls and women proved capable of some activities but were still viewed as not equipped to excel in other competitive endeavors. In other words, the physical educators "accepted feminine skill but not unfettered athleticism."[41] Western femininity continued to limit US women's inclusion in and enactment of sport.

The Soviet Union also viewed elite competition as a tool to demonstrate governmental excellence during the Cold War. However, in the early twentieth century the country had essentially sidelined formal sport. Immediately following the Russian Revolution of 1917, no coordinated policy existed, as many groups rejected sport as a pastime of the bourgeois. For example, the *Proletkultists*, an influential group at the time, condemned organized contests and instead promoted mass activities such as excursions, "labour gymnastics," and pageants.[42] While individuals did engage in worker-sports associations, and tsarist Russia participated in the 1912 Stockholm Olympics, no Soviet team competed in the interwar Olympics due to the reluctance of the government to support international contests against Western teams.[43]

Eventually Soviet leaders changed tactics and started to use sport as a tool to advance the nation's political ambitions. In 1921 the Soviet Union sponsored the Red Sport International to rival the capitalistic IOC. All events supported the Soviet agenda and appealed to socialist workers.[44] Moreover, in 1934 Stalin consolidated power and concentrated on formal sport to further the country's foreign objectives. According to sport scholar Rob Beamish, "After 1934, the Soviets focused on the bourgeois, competitive, high-performance forms of sports, with the goal of outperforming the capitalist world in this arena."[45] The government terminated its practice of athletic isolation and viewed participation in international contests as an important feature of the state. Sporting opportunities thereby dramatically expanded. For example, in 1946 the Soviet Union participated in only two international athletic events; between 1946 and 1955 the country competed in an additional twenty-five, including the Olympics.[46] Perhaps more importantly, the Soviet Union fostered a nationalistic drive for victory, offering its athletes financial compensation for world records and Olympic medals.[47]

During the Cold War the Soviet Union envisioned sport as fulfilling five broad objectives. First, victorious participation in international competition helped nurture relationships with pro-Soviet nations abroad. In the same vein, the Soviet Union also sought to promote friendly relations with its border states, using sport as an influential diplomatic and nationalistic medium. Third, the country hoped to garner support for its policies, particularly from the developing nations in Africa, Asia, and Latin America. Fourth, Soviet leaders viewed sport as a tool to reinforce the global socialist community. Finally, underscoring the first four aims, the Soviet Union desired victories, particularly at the Olympics, to demonstrate its national power.[48]

Because both the United States and the Soviet Union heralded sport as a universal standard of achievement, the two nations increasingly saw the Olympics and other international competitions as important measures of authority. Yet the IAAF and IOC, led by individuals from the West, remained rooted in antisocialist beliefs and resistant to Eastern European prowess.[49] The IOC slowly allowed Eastern European nations to compete in the Olympics; however, it refused to elect communist representatives into the organizational body. Moreover, when the IOC finally recognized the USSR National Olympic Committee (NOC) in 1951, differences between oppositional ideologies led to recurrent friction. Despite efforts to promote sport as apolitical, the Cold War politicized sport, the IAAF, and the IOC.[50]

Cold War Sex/Gender Concerns in Sport

As Cold War fears aggrandized the importance of sport and nationalistic ideals underlined international competitions, the IAAF and the IOC grew increasingly concerned with the potential for inauthentic human achievement. With the Soviet Union's 1946 debut in the European athletics circuit, along with its return to the Olympic movement six years later, sport victories gained unprecedented significance. Furthermore, unlike most countries in the West, the Soviet Union's accolades stemmed almost evenly from its male and female competitors, an unheard-of breakdown for the time. Many people worried that the communist countries used inauthentic women, male imposters, and female dopers.[51] The Soviet Union's embrace of muscular women, particularly in track and field, eventually encouraged the IAAF to implement a compulsory sex test for all women in track and field.

The successful performances of the muscular Eastern European women challenged Western gender norms. Upon the USSR's first appearance in the European Athletics Championships, the nation finished second overall with seventeen medals. Not only was this achievement exceptional for an inaugural entry, but the USSR's gender breakdown also proved notable: women earned a majority of the country's medals. Sweden and Finland, first and third in the medal count, respectively, had no female victors. The tremendous success of the Soviet Union, bolstered by its female performances, continued throughout the 1950s.

Rumors of gender-transgressive competitors consequently heightened during the Cold War. This amplification of sex/gender anxieties occurred

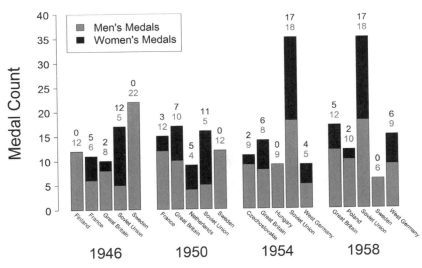

European Athletics Championships medal breakdown by sex, 1946–1958. (GBR Athletics, "European Championships," *GBR Athletics*, 2005, http://www.gbrathletics.com/ic/ecw.htm.)

despite a history of random testing and a lack of confirmed male masquer-aders in sport. When images of unapologetically powerful Soviet women flooded the West, many decried the loss of femininity, invasion of men into women's competition, and end of fairness in sport. As sport scholar Stefan Wiederkehr explains, "Western media displayed a clear tendency to juxtapose attractive females from the West with ugly and virilized sportswomen from the Soviet bloc."[52] Western norms of femininity mandated slender stature, passivity, and grace; muscular builds, aggression, and power, on the other hand, raised concerns and threatened Western dominance in sport.

As a result, speculations again marred track and field, exacerbated by both politics and the addition of new events. The IAAF incorporated the women's 800-meter and 400-meter races into the 1954 and 1958 European Athletics Championships, respectively; the IOC added the 800-meter race in 1960 and the 400-meter race in 1964. Shortly thereafter the IAAF permitted the recording of women's world records in the two events. Not surprisingly, innuendos about inauthentic female competitors increased.[53] The historical anxieties associated with longer track distances, compounded by the Soviet Union's immediate successes in the races, fostered fears in the West and seemingly provided justification to those who called for the introduction of sex/gender examinations.

The runners who set the world records in the 400-meter race experienced the most disdain. Unlike the winners of the 800-meter race, the victors of the 400-meter race were largely from the East during the Cold War. Although four athletes from the Soviet Union dominated the 800-meters for much of the 1950s, by the time the IAAF recognized the world record, runners from Australia and Great Britain had regained control of the title. Hence, the shorter race accrued greater contempt from the West. Australia's Marlene Mathews first claimed the 400-meter world record in 1957, only to be outperformed by teammate Nancy Boyle within one month. Boyle's time of 56.3 seconds was also short-lived as weeks later Soviet star Polina Lazareva crossed the finish line in 55.2 seconds. The scramble for the world record momentarily halted when "Red Speedster" Mariya Itkina—previous 220-yard title holder—eclipsed the 55.0-second mark and held the honor for five years. Despite her racing prowess, Itkina's legacy proved controversial. Because she retired almost contemporaneously to the IAAF's introduction of sex testing, many in the West claimed that Itkina stopped competing because she feared failing the exam.[54]

North Korean runner Shin Keum-dan, commonly referred to as Sin Kimdan in English, was similarly criticized by the Western press. Born in 1938 in Korea, she was separated from her father in 1950 due to the outbreak of civil war. As the country divided, Shin was in the north while her father remained in the south. It was in a Pyongyang factory where the nineteen-year-old lathe operator was discovered by a track and field coach in 1959. After one year of rigorous and scientific training, Shin quickly excelled in athletics. She eclipsed Itkina's record in 1960 and again in 1962; however, the IAAF refused to ratify her results because North Korea was not an official member of the international federation.[55] Along with the IAAF's dismissal of Shin's times, many in the West disproved of her muscularity and impressive feats. For example, according to the London *Times*, Shin's 800-meter finish "was enough to make mere male hopefuls blush," implying that she was fast enough to defeat men.[56]

Her anomalous success continued in the 1963 Games of the New Emerging Forces (GANEFO). Indonesia organized GANEFO after the IOC banned the country from the Tokyo Olympics. In 1962 Jakarta had hosted the Asian Games and prohibited Taiwanese and Israeli athletes from the competition; this refusal struck the IOC as contrary to the Olympic Charter and resulted in Indonesia's sanction. This interdict galvanized the country and fostered its desire to host an anti-imperialist forum that promoted the unity of Africa, Asia, Latin America, and various socialist nations.[57] The IOC eventually rescinded Indonesia's 1964 Olympic ban; however, the IAAF denied participation to any track and field athlete who had competed in GANEFO. In addition, the federation refused to ratify any records from the forum, including Shin's world marks set in the 400-meter and 800-meter races.

Because Shin ran in GANEFO, the IAAF banned her from the 1964 Olympics. Upon learning of the disbarment, many female runners expressed relief, citing Shin's abnormal speed and physique. Furthermore, North Korean track and field athletes traveled to Japan in an attempt to convince the IOC to overturn the IAAF's decision.[58] The IOC's refusal led the entire North Korean Olympic team to boycott. While returning home, Shin reunited with her father for five minutes in a Japanese airport; she was granted this rare opportunity because the meeting occurred outside of both North and South Korea. According to reports, the reunion was emotional and brief.[59] The five-minute meeting also helped cast doubt on Shin's legacy. Two years after the reunion, *Time* magazine published a report that declared "an overjoyed elderly gentleman in South Korea recognized Sin as the son he had lost in the war."[60] Although the account was likely erroneous—later reports noted that Shin had passed all examinations and conceived a child—the insinuation nevertheless bolstered claims of sex/gender fraudulence in track and field.

Such threats of sex/gender transgression proved worrisome from the US standpoint. Female athleticism in the United States remained bounded by ideals of grace and appeal, consequently pushing women's sport into a secondary position. This greatly diminished the possibility for Olympic success. For example, in the 1952 Helsinki Olympics, the Soviet Union earned eleven of the possible twenty-seven medals in women's athletics; the United States earned one. In women's gymnastics—which in the 1950s and 1960s produced larger, more muscular competitors than it did from the 1970s onward—the Soviet Union earned eleven of the possible twenty-one medals; the United States earned zero. Furthermore, of the Soviet Union's seventy-one total medals accumulated in 1952, USSR women earned twenty-two; of the United States' seventy-six medals, eight were earned by women, seven of these in swimming and diving.[61] This trend continued for decades.

The difference in the medal breakdown did not go unnoticed in the United States. As Povich reflected in the *Washington Post*, "These 1952 Games wouldn't even have been close between Russia and the United States save for the almost complete dominance of the Russian women in the heftier field events and the gymnastics. . . . In the non-bicep division, though, in the more graceful swimming and diving events where feminine form counts more than feminine muscle, the American girls were all-conquering. Each to her liking, perhaps."[62] While this passage highlights significant Cold War gender themes, Povich's comment also proves telling in terms of race. Sig-

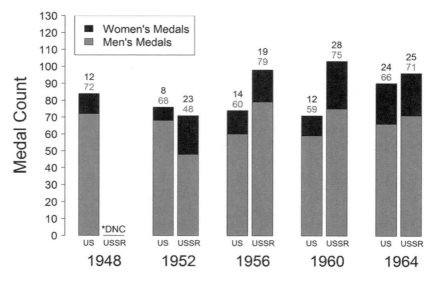

Summer Olympics medal breakdown by sex, 1948–1964. (Information derived from "Olympic.org," *Official Website of the Olympic Movement*, http://www .olympic.org, and cross-referenced with information from "Olympic Statistics and History Database Online," http://www.databaseolympics.com.)

nificantly, he failed to consider the efforts, successes, and composition of the US track and field team.

Due to femininity prescriptions in the United States, few white women opted to compete in track and field in the first half of the twentieth century. White, middle-class female physical educators largely discouraged female participation in the sport, deeming it too competitive, too strenuous, and too unfeminine.[63] Postwar gender norms also helped society further imagine the sport as a masculine pastime. Therefore, any woman who opted to participate in track and field frequently faced stigmatization as an "amazon" or a "muscle moll." Spurred by this racial and classed castigation—along with a belief in a more active ideal of femininity—black female athletes excelled in athletics. As Cahn explains, "Black women stepped into an arena largely abandoned by middle-class white women . . . and began to blaze a remarkable trail of national and international excellence."[64] For example, in the 1956 Melbourne Olympics, the United States earned three medals in track and field (the Soviet Union earned eight), all from the efforts of black athletes. Millie McDaniel finished first in the high jump; Willye White placed second in the long jump; and Isabelle Daniels, Wilma Rudolph, Mae Faggs Starr, and

Margaret Matthews Wilburn earned bronze in the 4 x 100-meter relay. Even more impressively, in the 1960 Rome Olympics, Rudolph earned three gold medals, the first US woman to accomplish such a feat. Such successes laid a foundation for the future achievements of other black women in athletics.

Even though these athletes helped dismantle certain racial prejudices, their triumphs simultaneously reinforced stereotypes of black women as being less feminine than white women. Black women were excluded from dominant understandings of womanhood in the United States, and their victories in sport "could be interpreted not as an unnatural deviation but, rather, as the natural result of their reputed closeness to nature, animals, and masculinity."[65] The victorious figure of the black female runner consequently fused together gender and racial stereotypes.

Additionally, the interpretation of track and field as a masculine enterprise—one that was considered inappropriate for feminine white women—allowed many in the West to question the sex/gender of those who excelled in the sport. As noted by sport scholar Ian Ritchie, "It was in track and field in particular that female Soviet athletes had been most successful, most visible, and most derided."[66] Not surprisingly, the victories of the USSR female Olympians allowed the West to construct Eastern bloc women as "others." Although they were white, Eastern European women were also viewed differently due to their overt disregard of Western norms of femininity during the Cold War.

The Introduction of Compulsory Testing in Track and Field

Lingering anxieties about female track and field competitors, compounded by the Soviet Union's victories in Cold War sport, encouraged athletic authorities to push for increased sex/gender control. As a result, in 1966 the IAAF instituted compulsory examinations for women athletes in area games and championships.[67] "Sport had no other means of asserting the gender of participants other than having them parade naked in front of a panel of doctors," explains Arne Ljungqvist, an IAAF member in the 1970s. "After this 'examination,' the panel decided whether the case presented to them was a woman or a man."[68] The supposed success of the IAAF in delineating womanhood in track and field eventually convinced other organizations to outline similar stipulations for all women, not just for those who competed in athletics.

The IAAF first mandated sex testing in the 1966 British Empire and Commonwealth Games in Kingston, Jamaica.[69] British athlete Mary Peters, who later won a gold medal in the 1972 Summer Olympics, vividly remembered the ordeal. She recalled being ordered to lie on a couch, pull up her knees, and remain still while doctors checked her anatomy. Peters likened the examination to a "grope." The test was "the most crude and degrading experience I have ever known in my life," she explained.[70] Canadian runner Abby Hoffman similarly described a manual component to the compulsory control. "You were undressed (and) they examined your breasts," she recalled. "They may have laid a hand on the genital area to make sure there were no hidden genitals."[71] The IAAF eventually eliminated the manual aspect for the 1966 European Athletics Championships in Budapest, which occurred two weeks after the games held in Jamaica. During the European Athletics Championships, three female doctors visually inspected the 243 women participants.[72]

The inspections continued in the 1966 Asian Games. Philippine star sprinter Mona Sulaiman—who had, in record-setting-times, won the 100-meter and 200-meter races in the previous Asian Games—refused to undergo the examination. She later explained that a severe case of the flu had led her to forgo the procedure.[73] Officials and the public alike dismissed her illness and expressed doubt. For example, when solicited for a comment regarding Sulaiman's refusal, the Philippine team physician, Antonio Vergara, responded, "Of course, I have my doubts," inferring that athletic successes stemmed from non-feminine characteristics. A teammate similarly voiced skepticism, noting, "She acts like a girl, but she talks like a man." More overtly, *Sports Illustrated* writer Marvin Zim chided that "still left unanswered is the question of whether Mona is a Filipino or Filipina."[74] This comment also demonstrates the racial undertones of sex/gender testing. Sulaiman returned home under a cloud of suspicion, her athletic career desecrated. She fended off the ensuing local incertitude by boldly daring those who challenged her identity to allow their husbands to join her for an overnight visit.[75] This line of reasoning insinuated that femininity could be verified through an intimate act of heterosexuality.

A parallel belief that overt displays of femininity rendered the sex test moot underlined most athletic competitions. Many female athletes thought that by highlighting a feminine appearance, the examination would be dismissed, or at least be less invasive. Western journalists also embraced this conviction. For example, the *Washington Post* photographed Canadian sprinter Irene Piotrowski putting on lipstick before competing. The caption under the image reads, "Just checking—Irene Piotrowski, Canadian sprinter, applies some makeup before reporting to yesterday's sex check."[76] Taken together, the picture and caption suggest that outward displays of femininity, enhanced with makeup, could help one prove her womanhood. Other accounts highlighted

"I think you will agree, Ladies, we have now come up with the perfect solution to the sex-test problem."

A 1972 *Punch* magazine cartoon satirizing the IOC's sex testing policy. Drawn by Ken Mahood. Courtesy of *Punch*.

similar beliefs. For example, *Punch*, a weekly British humor magazine, jokingly inferred that heterosexual intercourse verified femaleness. In a 1972 cartoon drawn by Ken Mahood, a bare-chested, presumably naked, IOC member is shown in bed with a line of female athletes outside his door. "I think you will agree, Ladies, we have now come up with the perfect solution to the sex-test problem," comments the overseeing Olympic official.

Accordingly, applying makeup or having sex could help women convince doctors and sport authorities of their womanhood. Although *Punch* approached the topic with humor, such insinuations nevertheless illustrate the social importance of gender in the medical determination of sex. But for Piotrowski and other female athletes, neither makeup nor sexual intercourse saved them from the exam.

Testing continued in the 1967 Pan American Games, held in Winnipeg, Canada. Commenced in 1951, this international event gathers all North and South American countries with a recognized NOC, every four years to compete in Olympic events and other sports that are popular throughout the two continents. According to Max Avren, the chief Pan-Am physician, organizers of the 1967 Games opted to implement sex control in track and field because men "were perpetuating a fraud" by participating in women's events. Consequently, three female doctors checked the anatomy of approximately one hundred athletes to deter male masqueraders.[77] US shot putter Maren Seidler, who was sixteen years old at the time, recalled having to undergo the exam. "You had to go in and pull up your shirt and push down your pants," she explained. "Then they just looked while you waited for them to confer and decide if you were OK."[78] Undoubtedly, the physical examinations were uncomfortable and humiliating. However, Eastern European countries, including the Soviet Union, did not compete in the Pan American Games. Therefore, while the successes of the Soviets exacerbated gender concerns, the fears of masculinized women in athletics extended beyond Cold War politics.

Despite the fact that sex control occurred in events that did not include Soviet athletes, Eastern Europeans, specifically the Soviet women, nonetheless continued to serve as scapegoats. As such, several competitors faced criticism for the timing of their retirements. For example, Tamara and Irina Press, who had won five gold medals for the Soviet Union in the 1960 Rome Olympics, faced allegations when they abruptly dropped out of the 1966 European Athletics Championships. Although they cited their mother's illness as the reason, many insinuated that the newly conceived physical exam was the actual deterrent. Furthermore, after a year of abstaining from athletics, Tamara announced her retirement. "I have devoted more than 10 years of my life to sports," she explained, "and I would like (to cede) my place . . . to young sportswomen . . . to help my successors."[79] Her sister, Irina, did not publicly comment, but she also never participated in an event that mandated a sex check.

Along with the Press sisters, many noted the sudden absences of Rumanian high jumper Ilona Balaş, Itkina, and Soviet long jumper Tatyana Schelkanova. According to IAAF president David Burghley, the sex test not only circumscribed womanhood but also "has been successful in frightening the doubtful ones away."[80] Tellingly, few in the West condemned Italian long jumper Maria Vittoria Trio for her refusal to undergo the examination and subsequent withdrawal from competition.[81] From the perspective of the West, the control served to remove only the "Communist record holders and title contenders."[82]

In order to increase surveillance, the IAAF instituted a chromatin test for the 1967 European Cup Track and Field Event in Kiev, Soviet Union, thereby replacing physical inspections. The control, also labeled the Barr body test or the buccal smear test, was a relatively new innovation that used cells from a person's mouth to identify the presence of X chromosomes.[83] Although scientists noted that no single qualifier could absolutely identify sex, and also

"Cinderellas. Athletic sisters who are queens of the track world. Irina (left) and Tamara Press, congratulate each other after both scored world record triumphs in the pre-Olympic tryouts at Moscow's Lenin Central Stadium," 1960. Courtesy of the Associated Press.

warned that humans did not always fit neatly in XX or XY chromosomal constitutions, the IAAF implemented the method to determine competitors' sex. The federation checked the chromosomal composition of all female participants and barred anyone who did not possess XX chromosomes. While believed to surpass "nude parades" and "manual examinations" in efficiency and accuracy, problems quickly surfaced.

Polish sprinter Ewa Kłobukowska, who had passed the visual examination in the 1966 European Championships, was discovered to have a "mosaic" of chromosomes.[84] She was stripped of her medals and barred from competition. Polish Olympic Committee president Włodzimierz Reczek protested the decision and proved foreshadowing in his opposition. "There are generally no accepted criteria of sex for women athletes," he noted, "and the lightminded [*sic*] arbitrariness in the interpretation of the results of examinations may harm the examined persons."[85] Despite his concerns, many international sport bodies viewed Kłobukowska's biology as justification for increased policing. Brundage, who had assumed the IOC presidency in

1952, agreed. He reasoned, "In view of the sex developments at the recent European Championships in Budapest and the action of the I.A.A.F., should we not have something in our rules on this subject?"[86] French doctor Jacques Thiebault, who would oversee the chromosomal check in 1968, seconded the idea. Regarding the rumors about the "so-called females who are as strong as oxen," he speculated that it "is inevitable that sooner or later the real representatives of the weaker sex will feel persecuted and will demand their feminine records be attributed to them."[87] To ensure that only "real" women participated, the IOC Medical Commission, first tasked with establishing anti-doping standards, eventually approved the introduction of sex testing in Olympic competition.

The IOC's Anti-Doping Controls

As Cold War concerns seeped into sex/gender verification discussions, the IOC concurrently debated anti-doping controls. Brundage publically recognized doping as an Olympic issue in 1960. Although concerns of performance enhancement had pervaded sport much earlier, the death of Danish Olympian Knud Enemark Jensen in the 1960 Rome Games pushed the IOC into action. After competing in a cycling race, which reportedly occurred in 104-degree weather, Jensen and two of his Danish teammates were hospitalized for heat exhaustion.[88] Jensen's questionable death in the hospital sparked an investigation, and the Danish team doctor eventually admitted that he had distributed Ronical, a vasodilator, to his riders. Although Jensen's autopsy also revealed traces of amphetamines, the Italian authorities failed to publish the medical results and punishments were not allocated.[89]

Seven years later the IOC received further motivation to research the implications of drug use. In the Mont Ventoux stage of the 1967 Tour de France, English cyclist Tommy Simpson swayed, staggered, and eventually collapsed on the side of the road. He died en route to the hospital from a combination of amphetamines and alcohol.[90] Despite the lack of immediate sanctions in the wake of these two fatalities, Jensen's and Simpson's posthumous legacies served as incidences that encouraged the IOC to assume an anti-doping stance.

Concerned with the possible widespread use of amphetamines in the Olympics, Brundage first organized a four-person committee in 1961 to assess the situation. He named Arthur Porritt (New Zealand) the chair and appointed Ryotaro Azuma (Japan), Josef Gruss (Czechoslovakia), and Agustin Sosa (Panama) to the doping committee.[91] Importantly, all four IOC members had medical backgrounds: Porritt was the president of both the British Medical Association and the Royal College of Surgeons of England; Azuma was a physician who specialized in physiology; Gruss was a gynecologist and obstetrician; and Sosa was a physiologist. The group also regularly collaborated with Giuseppe la Cava (Italy), a leading member of the International Federation of Sports Medicine. In the early 1960s the IOC attempted to deal with scientific and medical issues internally, combing the membership for physicians to lead the fight against performance enhancement.[92]

The newly formed doping committee immediately experienced difficulties. As outlined by sport historian Thomas M. Hunt, the IOC faced four interrelated problems in its early quest to abate doping. Foremost, some Olympic officials remained indifferent to the subject and consequently prioritized alternative issues. The complexities of amateurism, for example, consumed Brundage. Second, scientific difficulties in the detection of prohibited substances, coupled with the costs of such controls, worried the international federations. As a third deterrent, ethical and medicinal ambiguities regarding the definition of doping hindered implementation of anti-doping measures at early Olympic contests. Finally, Cold War politics and the fragmented nature of the international sport system served as dual obstacles. Notably, the IOC, the International Federation of Association Football (FIFA), and the IAAF instituted their own rules, regulations, and punishments.[93]

Nevertheless striving to resolve the issue of doping, the IOC next established its Medical Commission with Porritt as the head of the committee. However, Porritt's relative indifference toward the issue led to little action from the commission while under his tenure. He believed doping should remain under the surveillance of the international federations and not the IOC. As an example of his disinterest, at the 1964 Tokyo meeting Porritt recommended the IOC take three minimal steps to diminish doping in the Olympics: issue a formal declaration condemning the use of drugs, implement sanctions against individuals who promote drugs in sport, and request that NOCs require their athletes to undergo examinations. While recognizing doping as a dilemma, Porritt opted to avoid outlining direct policies. Yet when he stepped aside and Prince Alexandre de Mérode of Belgium assumed the reins, the IOC Medical Commission not only garnered control of doping tests but also assumed responsibility for the maintenance of sex/gender and sexuality norms.

Prince Alexandre de Mérode

As anti-doping needs increased, the IOC adjusted the composition of the medical commission. Whereas the earlier doping committee was comprised of individuals with medical and scientific backgrounds, by the late 1960s the IOC had awarded a nonmedical-person control and invited non-IOC members to join the group.[94] Perhaps most influentially, de Mérode succeeded Porritt in 1967. The Belgian aristocrat remained at the helm of the organization until his death in 2002, instituting anti-doping policies and gender verification measures for over three decades.

De Mérode was born to a noble family in 1934. He studied classics at Collège de Godinne, philosophy at St. Louis University Faculty of Brussels, and law at Louvain University. In addition, he served as president of the Belgian Supreme Council for Physical Education, Sport, and Outdoor Life. In 1964 he was elected to the IOC, and during the Tokyo Olympics that year, his first as an IOC member, de Mérode became obsessed with the threat of performance enhancement.[95] One year later he used the Tokyo experience and reported to the IOC on this issue, appearing to have borrowed heavily from a paper written by Belgian doctor Albert Dirix. This maneuver allowed de Mérode to both "take credit" for recognizing the seriousness of the situation and present himself as a doping expert.[96]

These tactics eventually helped de Mérode replace Porritt. When considering retirement, Porritt initially recommended that Sosa serve as his successor. IOC chancellor Otto Mayer suggested Brazilian physician Ferreira Santos.[97] However, due to de Mérode's explicitly expressed concerns regarding performance enhancement, IOC secretary Johann Westerhoff added his name to the list of candidates. In a letter to Porritt, he wrote, "I myself was thinking about Prince de Merode who, although being no medicine [sic], has showed much interest into the matter." To rectify de Mérode's nonmedical background, Westerhoff suggested, "We could always appoint some medicines from abroad as advisors of this committee."[98] Porritt agreed but emphasized that "it would obviously be wise to have some medical opinions on this subcommittee even if they have to be co-opted from outside the membership."[99] Therefore, when Brundage appointed de Mérode, he also added Professor Arnold Beckett (Great Britain), la Cava, physical education teacher Árpád Csanádi (Hungary), Dr. Pieter Van Dijk (Holland), Dirix, gynecologist Eduardo Hay (Mexico), Professor Ludwig Prokop (Austria), and Dr. Jacques Thiebault (France) to the committee.[100]

Doping scholars Paul Dimeo, Thomas Hunt, and Matthew T. Bowers have articulated two theories as to why Brundage awarded de Mérode the position and overlooked medical experts. On the one hand, they reason that Brundage wanted a public figure, not a scientist, to serve as the chair. Accordingly, a scientist would have underscored the serious nature of doping and thereby increased public scrutiny. On the other hand, the authors argue that Brundage did not believe that the IOC Medical Commission was important. "He was therefore happy to hand it over to someone he saw as a mediocre talent," they explain."[101] As an additional possibility, sport historian Alison M. Wrynn points out that, of the original doping committee, most members had either died or resigned; de Mérode was the sole person left, and he lobbied for the position.[102] Regardless of the reasons why, the Belgian prince assumed leadership of the medical commission and shaped both doping controls and sex/gender verification throughout the second half of the twentieth century.

* * *

Although sex/gender nonconformity had previously concerned sport organizers, the tremendous successes of the Soviet women exacerbated the anxieties. During the Cold War the United States and the Soviet Union viewed each other as threats. However, instead of deploying military force, the two nations engaged in a variety of cultural battles to demonstrate superiority. Notably, the superpowers interpreted the status of their women and their successes in sport as significant measures of national prowess. These two factors became intertwined when the Soviet Union rejoined international competitions.

The Soviet Union returned to the Olympics in 1952 and a medal count ensued. Quickly, the Soviet Union surpassed the United States, largely due to the performances of the Soviet women. While US physical education and sporting programs typically prioritized the training of men, the Soviet Union viewed female athletes as equally capable, which produced medals. Moreover, because the Soviet government expected its women to engage in physical labor, the society accepted training, muscularity, and power as appropriate qualities of femininity. Soviet women thereby excelled in many sports, including track and field, while US women remained limited by Western gender norms.

The USSR women's unprecedented victories and muscular physiques worried many sport organizations, most notably the IAAF. To combat fears of inauthentic women, male imposters, and female dopers, the IAAF instituted compulsory testing in the late 1960s. The deemed success of the policy quickly encouraged the IOC to follow suit. In the 1968 Grenoble Olympics the medical commission implemented sex testing.

3 Is the Athlete "Right" or "Wrong"?

The IOC's Chromosomal Construction of Womanhood, 1968–1972

IN 1968 THE IOC Medical Commission simultaneously introduced sex tests and doping controls into the Olympics. The measures were intended to scientifically confirm the separation of men and women in athletic competition as well as to guarantee the authenticity of participants. Fearful of masculinized women and the hazards of drugs, the commission tested female athletes' chromosomal patterns in order to determine sex and analyzed urine samples for traces of prohibited substances. According to Arthur Porritt, former chairman of the medical commission, such actions were necessary to deter female Olympians, particularly those from the Eastern bloc, from consuming male hormones. "There is a very simple test to determine if the athlete is right or wrong," he explained.[1] His conflation of sex tests and doping controls illustrates the significance of sex and gender in the medical commission's policies. Chromosomal and doping regulations attempted to distinguish between the "right" athletes, women deemed appropriately feminine by Western standards, from the "wrong" athletes, those deemed inappropriately masculine from the East.

To remove the "wrong" athletes from competition, the IOC Medical Commission mandated a chromosomal test for female participants in the 1968 Olympics. Selected women underwent verification in the Grenoble Winter Games; all female participants underwent the control in the Mexico City Summer Games. The commission embraced this check, known as the buccal smear test or Barr body test, because it was a relatively new, inexpensive technique that identified chromosomal composition. Moreover, by using a buccal smear test, the members suggested that an Olympian's chromosomes dictated her sex. The medical commission implemented the buccal smear test and permitted only 46,XX women into competition. Female athletes with any other chromosomal composition were banned. Believing the method successfully prevented male imposters, the commission extended it into the 1972 Sapporo and Munich Olympics.

In enacting a buccal smear test, the medical commission ignored the scientific community's concerns regarding the sole use of chromosomes in sex determination. Many experts pointed out the multifaceted nature of sex and warned the IOC about the problems of using only one qualifier. Several leading biologists, endocrinologists, and geneticists opposed the procedure; however, the medical community as a whole largely supported the effort to find some measure to justify sex-segregated sport. Such attempts to uphold dichotomous sex were not unique to the Cold War. Yet the assumption of female athletic inferiority, a belief in fairness, and the increasing importance of international sport all underlined the IOC's resolve to separate women from men.

Chromosomal tests bolstered a false demarcation of binary sex and promoted a gendered hierarchy in sport. While Olympic authorities viewed those who failed the sex tests as unintentional victims of inconsistent biology, the IOC Medical Commission attacked those who breached anti-doping controls as purposeful cheaters. However, any woman discovered to have transgressed either boundary was viewed as abnormal and consequently barred from competition. As USOC head physician Daniel F. Hanley aptly foreshadowed in 1967, with the introduction of the sex test the IOC "will establish a new definition of femaleness."[2] Through scientific regulations, the medical commission shaped Olympic womanhood along Western lines of gender and sexuality.

Historical Conceptions of Sex Classification

Although Cold War anxieties forced attention onto sex/gender difference, the desire to pinpoint the location of divergence between men and women was not a novel aspiration of the IOC. As sport scholar Kevin B. Wamsley notes, "Western social, political, religious, and economic institutions were built on the fundamental notion that men and women were clearly discernable entities."[3] Sport similarly embraced a dual-sex paradigm. Therefore, attempts to identify the reason, purpose, and moment of disparity between the sexes/genders predated Cold War politics. Notions of sex/gender difference were also consistently shaped by cultural beliefs and almost always used to maintain the status quo.[4] "Labeling someone a man or a woman is a social decision," explains feminist biologist Anne Fausto-Sterling. "We may use scientific knowledge to help us make the decision, but only our beliefs about gender—not science—can define our sex."[5] Scientists in the West shifted from a concentration on anatomical entities to a focus on chemical agency as the primary measure of distinction. Medical practitioners, who were also invested in a binary system, eventually interpreted scientific evidence to "cure" individuals who did not fit within the man/woman categorization pattern. Although concentrations, theories, and solutions changed throughout the nineteenth and twentieth centuries, Western scientific and medicinal allegiance to a binary system of sex was unwavering.

By the nineteenth century more than five hundred theories claimed to comprehend human sex differentiation. Of the numerous postulations, a great diversity of explanations existed, ranging from ancestral inheritance to environmental factors. For example, some people claimed that the position in the womb determined a baby's sex, while others argued that diet held sway—for example, a pregnant woman's poor nutritional habits guaranteed the birth of a boy. Numerous hypotheses initially existed, but attention to anatomical features eventually gained prominence. Anatomical studies reinforced a "separate spheres" ideology through measurements of brain formations, pelvis sizes, reproductive organs, and skull shapes. As Allen Petersen discovered in a historical analysis of *Gray's Anatomy*, anatomical studies cemented the longevity of a two-sexed model and reaffirmed the superiority of men's bodies. Disseminated as a canonical work of knowledge—from the mid-nineteenth century to the present—*Gray's Anatomy* positioned male anatomy as the standard and reaffirmed females' social role as dedicated to reproduction.[6]

With this attention on physical features, the gonads (ovaries and testes) emerged in the literature as the most significant factor of sex differentiation. As historian Alice Dreger explains, the late nineteenth century was the "Age of the Gonads." During this time, sex was "marked by one trait and one trait only, the anatomical nature of a person's gonads."[7] Dreger reasons that gonads gained recognition because Victorian gender beliefs stemmed from reproductive roles, regardless of an individual's actual or lack of reproductive capabilities. For example, one could appear feminine internally and externally yet be labeled a man due to the possession of testicles.[8] Despite a transition from general anatomy to the more specifically defined gonads, scientific interpretation remained embedded in social values. For example, Victorian-era scientists claimed that the testicles served as the seat of masculinity and fostered bravery, vigor, and longevity. The uterus initially signified femininity;

however, the discovery of the ovaries allowed medical authorities to shift the location of docility and subservience there.

Sex difference also became more linguistically defined. According to medical historian Thomas Laqueur, as the new terminology—the ovaries and the testicles—dictated different functions, structures that had previously been believed to be common to all, such as the skeletal and nervous systems, were also labeled along gender lines in the medical discourse.[9] Furthermore, authorities in the nineteenth century remained tied to what appeared before the naked eye, as they were unable to see molecular components. However, with the invention of the microscope, cellular and chemical components gained importance.

Equipped with the microscope, the study of sex differentiation shifted to the examination of sex hormones at the turn of the century. As progressive reformers challenged the social system, endocrinology emerged as another scientific tool to help maintain the social order. According to Fausto-Sterling, "Scientists defined some bodies as better and more deserving of rights than others."[10] Endocrinology also remained rooted in the preexisting beliefs of dualistic differentiation. Scientists labeled hormones as specifically sexual in nature, disregarding the full-body utility of the chemicals. This consequently rendered all of their other functions invisible. As health technology professor Nelly Oudshoorn explains, these endocrinologists thereby defined "sex" hormones as binary as well as specific in origin and function.[11] Consequently, the notion of "male" hormones and "female" hormones emerged. This development would later prove significant in the dialogue surrounding female dopers.

By the middle of the twentieth century, geneticists also posited that sex was irrevocably cemented at conception by nuclear elements. Whereas endocrinologists claimed that hormones constructed sex, geneticists argued that chromosomes determined development. Despite the momentary impasse, the two camps eventually agreed that both genes and hormones worked in tandem to define a person as man or woman. In other words, if genetic variables commenced the process, hormones completed the course.[12]

While this scientific gridlock was short-lived, the discovery of female sex hormones in men raised doubts over the specificity of endocrine function. This shocking finding also fostered concerns about the use of gender pronouns for human hormones. For accuracy, some adjusted the accepted classification system. For example, they used "ambosexual" hormone or the "so-called" female sex hormone as replacements. Others demanded a complete overthrow of the categorizations.[13] As a result, the words "estrin," "estrogen," "androsterone," and "testosterone" were introduced. Despite the classifications, each name remained attached to certain genders, another important development in the later perception of female dopers. As Oudshoorn explains, "Although scientists abandoned the concept of sexual specificity, the terminology was not adjusted to this change in conceptualization."[14] Furthermore, for the sake of monetary gain, pharmaceutical companies demanded specialization in the 1940s and pushed the classification further along a dichotomous path. Even if scientists viewed all organisms as a chemical combination of male and female, they nevertheless upheld the interpretation of the human body as dimorphic.

Finally, twentieth-century medical practitioners also maintained a dual-sex paradigm by studying "mixed-sexed" and transgender people. Some physicians "corrected" their patients by forcing adaptation into one of two socially circumscribed categories. Perhaps most notably, sexologist John Money sought to treat intersex individuals by incorporating environmental factors with biological status. Indeed Money was progressive in his field and equipped with a more innovative notion of social gender, but his treatments never embraced difference. Instead, he recommended prenatal solutions, psychological adjustments, and surgical alterations.[15] As radical feminist Janice Raymond wrote about Money, "Under the guise of science, he makes normative and prescriptive statements about who women and men are and who they ought to be."[16] In addition, male-to-female transgender soldier Christine Jorgensen captured attention in the wake of World War II. While she gained fame and recognition, her public transition also provoked anxieties regarding the collapse of society's sex/gender categories. According to historian Joanne Meyerowitz, despite the possibilities opened by transgender individuals for sex/gender blurring, Jorgensen's more immediate impact "was to reinforce traditional norms of gender."[17] Twentieth-century attempts to "fix" intersex and transgender people thus further privileged certain types of bodies and undermined the possibility for a sex/gender spectrum.

The Significance of Chromosomes

Scientists continued to search for concrete measures to identify sex difference. In 1948 University of Western Ontario micro-anatomist Murray Barr discovered a darkly stained mark within the nucleus of neurons while analyzing the nervous system of cats. With assistance from graduate student Ewart Bertram, he recognized that the darker stains were readily observable on some neurons and not apparent on others. The two scientists noticed that the appearance of the marks seemed to correspond to the sex of the animal. While the cells of the female felines exhibited the darker stain, the cells of the male cats did not. Barr and Bertram's corresponding report in *Nature* explained that "the morphological distinction . . . between the neurons of the mature male and female cat is so clear that sections from the brain, spinal cord or sympathetic ganglia of animals of both sexes may be readily sorted into two groups without prior knowledge of the sex."[18] The two scientists also suggested that similar marks exist in human cells.

With this study the identification of the Barr body, also known as sex chromatin, became the main signifier of sex. Although various chromosomal constitutions illustrate the fallacy of a clear chromosomally delineated definition of sex, sport officials used the discovery to create a sex check. In later Olympic competitions the IOC Medical Commission employed the Barr body test to analyze chromosomes and determine the presence of sex chromatin—and thus of a woman. However, according to health scholar Fiona Alice Miller, "The interpretation of the Barr body as a marker of the female sex chromosome constitution was erroneous."[19] While Barr and Bertram initially believed that the dark stain identified two XX chromosomes—one sex chromatin per pair of sex chromosomes—scientists Susumu Ohno and Theodore S. Hauschka verified in 1959 that the Barr body actually identified only one X chromosome.[20] This finding dramatically altered previous perceptions of sex determination. For example, before 1959 an individual with XXY was read as a woman; after the discovery the same person was identified as a man. Or a chromosomally XO person previously labeled a man was recorded as a woman after 1959. The changes in classification caused by Ohno and Hauschka's findings show the imperfect nature of determining sex through chromosomal composition.

Barr gained international recognition for his discovery, and his name was later attached to the test implemented in sport; however, he warned that the existence or nonexistence of a Barr body stain should not be the sole tool used in the determination of sex. In a 1956 *Lancet* article he begged physicians to act with "caution and diplomacy" when labeling sex and to use the chromosomal check sparingly. His request for restraint stemmed from the frequent situations where "the body cells are at variance with the obvious sexual anatomy." Pointing out the incongruence to a patient would only cause unnecessary anguish. Barr concluded, "The presence or absence of sex chromatin . . . is a minor detail in the femaleness or maleness of the whole person."[21] In spite of his request, Barr's method was later accepted by the governing bodies of sport, including the IAAF and IOC, for it seemingly supported a clear-cut sex division.

Almost four decades after his discovery, Barr explicitly protested the use of the Barr body test in sport. In 1987 he wrote to Roger Jackson, president of the Canadian Olympic Committee, and asked for the abandonment of the control. After identifying himself as the "senior person responsible for the discovery of the sex chromatin," Barr requested that chromosomal checks be discontinued, because "buccal smear testing in the area of athletics is totally inappropriate." In addition, he described the regret he had experienced as a result of the Barr body test's widespread adoption. "Its use in this way has been an embarrassment to me," he explained, "and I request that it be stopped."[22] His plea was disregarded and the verification method was continued. The Barr body test remained essential in the process of separating men and women in elite competition.

Chromosomal Control of Women

As Ohno and Hauschka revealed their interpretation of the Barr body test, medical practitioners assessed the major occurrences of the 1960 Rome Olympics. Accounts in leading Western journals, notably *JAMA: The Journal of the American Medical Society* and the *British Journal of Sports Medicine,* expressed concern about the treatment of athletes. From the US perspective, the major problems in Rome were dysentery and overeating. According to the British, doping served as the largest obstacle in need of a solution.[23] Yet when the IAAF implemented physical examinations in 1966, questions of sex determination appeared in the medical discourse. The failure of Ewa Kłobukowska in 1967 sparked further debate. Although authorities responded with a range of opinions and recommendations—and questioned the sole employment of the Barr body test in the detection of womanhood—most agreed with the IAAF and IOC as to the necessity of some type of verification system to maintain fair play in sport.

When reports of muscular Eastern European athletes spread through the popular media, details also seeped into the medical dialogue. The first *JAMA* article that discussed Soviet female athletic prowess appeared in 1960. Raymond G. Bunge, professor of urology at the University of Iowa, highlighted the gender concerns that plagued sport and proposed a simple solution. In "Sex and the Olympic Games," Bunge implied that the demands for sex control stemmed from Cold War concerns. "Probably the whole business arises from an offended American pride," he reasoned, hinting at the USSR women's greater capabilities in track and field. With the Soviets in mind, Bunge explained how the assumption that sex exists in a binary "does not always fit the products of Nature's capricious deviation." In addition, because physicians occasionally "do some head scratching about the assignment of sex for these unfortunate individuals," he outlined the various methods used to identify sex and described the problems with such tactics. First, according to Bunge, acts of sexuality failed to determine sex, for "the simple signs of the brothel are not enough." He then turned to social signifiers and asked, "Is the given name 'Mary' or 'James' enough?" Or, if an Olympian "look[s] like a woman, is that enough?" His inquiries demonstrate the influence of gender in the establishment of sex. To "forestall this knotty problem," Bunge advocated the implementation of the buccal smear test, a proposition that became reality in track and field seven years later.[24]

Prior to the IAAF's introduction of the Barr body test, *JAMA* published an editorial on the topic in 1966 titled "Introducing the, Uh, Ladies." The piece described the difficulty of separating men from women, particularly when male adolescents donned female clothing. More problematically, and erroneously, the report concluded that "certain 'lady' contestants in track and field have, over the years, turned out to be men."[25] The editorial agreed with the need for a sex check to identify the real ladies—those not designated by quotation marks—and suggested that the IAAF replace its visual/physical examinations with a buccal smear. This was a direct contrast to the publication's earlier position regarding the inadequacy of chromatin verification. In 1959 the editorial board had supported using a variety of factors when determining sex.[26] Seven years later, however, *JAMA* argued that implementing the Barr body test in sport assured "both dignity and integrity" of competitors.[27]

Similarly, Bunge echoed his earlier postulations in a 1967 *JAMA* article. He jokingly suggested that the IOC alter event titles to conform to chromosomal sex. For example, he advised that the men's and women's events be altered to "the XXY or the XXXY or the XXXXXY 100 meter dash, the pole vault, the mile run, etc." Although he was kidding, Bunge did outline a more serious consideration. "Out of this bewildering dilemma I offer the Olympic Committee a suggestion," he wrote. "Eliminate from competition all those who have a contradiction in the morphological criteria. . . . Allow competition only among those athletes who have no contradiction." While Bunge's words were admittedly harsh, he did also recommend that the IOC establish two sets of Olympic Games: "one for the 'normal' men and women and another for the contradictive group."[28] According to Bunge, the structure of "normal" sport needed a clear division of sex.

Others disagreed with the singular use of the Barr body test to denote classification. University of Glasgow pathology professor Bernard Lennox argued that the decision to segregate based upon chromosomal counts stemmed from a problematic Western emphasis on sex difference. He explained that while the divisions of sexes in nature served to prevent self-fertilization, "we are conditioned to exaggerate it, and we emphasize it by external additions of clothing, behavior and the like." Lennox further reasoned that because approximately 5 percent of the population was born with intersex conditions, utilization of chromosomal counts proved misleading and oftentimes inaccurate.[29] Writing in the same year, Keith L. Moore, anatomy expert and one of Barr's postgraduate students, argued that scientific innovations showed that no single criterion neatly distinguished man from woman. Chromosomal analyses did not identify one's "true sex." Therefore, he argued, women with chromatin-negative nuclei and "abnormal" chromosome complexes should not be prohibited from competition. Moore also noted the futility of the test, for "medically, there is no doubt about their femininity." Although he may have employed "femininity" as a synonym for "sex," his word choice is nonetheless significant. Moore also argued that ineligibility would be valid only when a Y chromosome and male-like characteristics appeared in women.[30]

Finally, also concerned with female masculinization, Hanley, the leading medical authority of the USOC, disputed Bunge's assertions of prohibition. In his view, women with sex-linked chromosomal variances should be permitted in Olympic competition. "If you are throwing out everybody with any chromosomal abnormality at all," Hanley reasoned, "then you are wrong." He postulated that a visual examination would provide more accurate results than the Barr body test. In his view, the current microscopic control would provide the "same conclusion that any near-sighted college boy can come to from a block away."[31] Similar accounts focused on the outward appearances of the athletes, inferring that female masculinization was the actual issue, not chromosomal "abnormalities."

The medical community may have disagreed with the IAAF and the IOC regarding the significance of chromosomes, yet all three structures sought to identify a division between men and women. Collectively, the governors of sport and the leading medical authorities used similar discourses that shaped the interpretation of what constituted a "normal" woman. It was in the 1968 Grenoble Winter Games that the IOC first experimented with determining womanhood.

The Grenoble Winter Olympics

After World War II French communist and capitalist systems experienced an intense struggle for power and prestige. Sport in France also evolved into a divisive arena. While some people supported Olympic organizations, others esteemed the communist *Fédération Sportive et Gymnique des Travailleurs* (the Gymnastic and Sports Federation of Workers).[32] Yet when Charles de Gaulle spearheaded the new Fifth Republic in 1959, he assumed control of sport in his quest to fashion France into a significant world power. Sport in the educational system was reconfigured to serve as the primary foundation for future leaders and world-class athletes. De Gaulle also created the Municipal Offices of Sport to act as the umbrella organization for school sport; Sport for All, a mass participation initiative; and elite sport. To further enhance both France's governmental and athletic reputation, as well as to gain economic, political, and symbolic profit, the country bid for the 1968 Winter Games.[33] By hosting the Grenoble Olympics, France also showcased its postwar gender norms.

After the war the French embodied a new way of living. According to historian Kristin Ross, the country transformed "from a rural, empire-oriented, Catholic country into a fully industrialized, decolonized, and urban one."[34] A quick, almost haphazard campaign of modernization sparked dramatic changes in individuals' private and public interactions. Importantly, a postwar governmental obsession with cleanliness and purity led to the controlling of domesticity. The idea that "an efficient, well-run harmonious home is a national asset" gained prominence, which helped normalize Western gender norms.[35] A model housewife ideal promoted gender conformity in France, which was showcased in the Grenoble Winter Olympics through sex testing.

Pre-Olympic Doping and Sex Controls

Alexandre de Mérode and the members of the IOC Medical Commission discussed the possibility of requiring doping and sex checks for all Olympic participants in Grenoble. As one of its first orders of business, the committee issued a press release that emphasized the likelihood of establishing medical controls in upcoming Olympic contests. Although it was rather unclear in terms of what methods would be used in the future, the press release explained that the medical commission intended to institute a variety of tests. First, the organization planned to change the entry form so that all athletes who signed it agreed to submit to any examination "thought necessary in the interests of both his health and future." Furthermore, the commission noted that it would provide a list of drugs and establish a procedure to test athletes in time for the Mexico City Summer Olympics. Finally, the press release explained that doping tests would be carried out on a random basis while the sex test would be completed on the three winning female competitors of some events, to be determined at a later date.[36]

To better understand existing control methods, the medical commission also sent a survey to the international federations asking each to identify its current practices. The circular letter requested information regarding any rules or measures previously used to combat the "very controversial prob-lems" of sex determination and doping.[37] Several international federations had already instituted rules to curb drug use in sport, including the organi-zations that oversaw archery, cycling, soccer, track and field, volleyball, and weightlifting. Others requested guidance from the IOC.[38] Only the IAAF had a sex determination policy in place. The international federations prioritized anti-doping measures and largely overlooked sex controls, highlighting both the widespread fear of performance-enhancing substances and the specific concern of female masculinization in track and field.

The medical commission also used the 1967 *Tercera Competencia Deportiva International* (Third International Sports Competition) as a forum in which to practice overseeing doping and sex controls. Originated in 1965 and con-tinued through 1967, the annual festival first served as an opportunity for athletes to adjust to the high altitude of Mexico City.[39] As noted in the *Wash-ington Post*, the event sought "to dispel the idea that thin air at Mexico City's altitude will slow down competitors in the Olympics," in hindsight a humor-ously incorrect assumption.[40] Angst over the city's high altitude surfaced before the IOC announced candidates for the 1968 Summer Games. Athletes and physicians initially worried that the location would increase fatigue. To alleviate such concerns, the organizing committee compiled research, mostly from the field of cardiology. With an increase in scientific studies, the medical commission left questions of altitude in the hands of non-IOC experts while it concurrently garnered control over sex and doping tests.[41]

As the research progressed, the suggestions of altitude detriment were re-placed by recommendations for altitude acclimation. In other words, studies showed that athletes would benefit if allowed to adjust to the altitude before competition. The IOC therefore needed to determine the ideal length of time for acclimation. Avery Brundage and IOC vice president David Burghley were largely responsible for shaping the policy. For these two men the issue centered more on ideology than science. They believed Olympians were amateurs with employment outside of sport; accordingly, amateurs could not miss work for altitude training. The IOC thus permitted only six weeks in special training campus, with no more than four weeks occurring during the three months that preceded the games.[42]

The Third International Sports Competition ran for two weeks in 1967, from October 15 to October 29. Along with the Olympic hopefuls, more than one hundred physicians attended to better understand Mexico City's unique atmosphere.[43] The IOC Medical Commission also supervised the introduc-tion of dope and sex controls; however, the international federations carried out the actual tests. The IOC's managerial, rather than controlling, position allowed some sport leaders to take the two matters less seriously than others. Nevertheless, with "the experience gained in Mexico," the medical commission determined that "a sound basis has been found for the carrying out of dope and sex checks in Grenoble."[44] The training opportunity offered in 1967 encouraged the medical commission to finalize its procedures and proceed for the Grenoble Games.

At the December 1967 medical commission meeting, the group concluded that dual measures to curtail sex/gender fraud and doping must be implemented for the Grenoble Winter Games, prior to its previously planned start for the Mexico City Summer Games. In January 1968, mere days before the opening ceremonies scheduled for February 6, de Mérode reported the medical commission's conclusions to the IOC Executive Board. Specifically, he outlined the methods for the tests. For the female competitors, a Barr body test would be used to identify sex chromatin. If the chromatin was unidentifiable, a full chromosomal analysis would occur next, followed by a hormone assessment. Finally, recognizing the expenses involved, the commission decided that only 50 out of the 250 female athletes would be tested, selected through a lottery system. However, de Mérode also made it clear that the commission intended to check all women's sex in the future.[45] With approval from the IOC Executive Board, the commission ordered sex testing for roughly 20 percent of Grenoble's female Olympians.

In conjunction with its decision to require "medical proof" of sex, the IOC Medical Commission also generated a list of prohibited substances. The committee banned the ingestion of alcohol, amphetamines, cannabis, cocaine, ephedrine, opiates, and vasodilators for the Grenoble Olympics. Although anabolic steroids were of concern, the medical commission lacked the knowledge and ability for accurate testing and therefore eliminated such substances from the original prohibited substance list.[46] Fears of female steroid users subsequently proliferated. For example, writing an editorial in the same year that the prohibited substance list appeared, Monique Berlioux, director of the IOC, confirmed the necessity of sex tests for the Olympics and criticized the use of steroids by women. Accordingly, because "hermaphroditism does not exist" and "one is born a man or a woman," maintaining sex segregation through the tests was an imperative of the Olympic movement. While Berlioux believed sex tests were essential, she did concede that "nature can play some funny tricks," acknowledging the possible existence of a biological spectrum. For that reason, speaking on behalf of the IOC, she explained, "We are grateful for this initiative, which will make it possible to put an end to the cheating, which takes place, whether intentionally or not."[47]

In this view, biological variation created fraudulent women. Although Berlioux perceived potential sex test failures as "unfortunate girls," she interpreted female dopers as unscrupulous athletes who purposefully altered their biology for gold medal victories. Attempting to win by the means of a drug "is worse than an act of dishonesty, it is an outright injustice," she argued.[48] Correspondingly, Jacques Thiebault, French Medical Commission member and head of the Grenoble medical controls, envisioned doping checks as a means to curtail an "evident attempt of fraud" whereas the role of sex testing was to "confirm a default in nature."[49] As illustrated through such claims, the IOC and its medical commission viewed gender transgression and drug use—specifically the ingestion of steroids—as dual and overlapping threats. Through the sex tests and doping controls, many hoped that only a specific type of woman would gain entrance into the Olympics.

"Research into Femininity": Sex Verification in Grenoble

To fulfill these aspirations, the medical commission instituted the two checks in the 1968 Grenoble Winter Games. To curb drug use in the Olympics, the group oversaw the analysis—the international federations actually conducted the tests—through gas chromatography and infrared spectrophotometry, for a total of eighty-six checks. In the eighty-six specimens, no doping substances were found.

The anti-doping measures proved relatively unproblematic to implement, but the incorporation of sex tests raised several issues. According to Thiebault, the very name "sex control" sparked confusion, for it applied to female participants only. He tellingly suggested that the term "research into femininity" be used instead. In his view, femininity entailed "a group of characteristics peculiar to women." Although the French doctor failed to elucidate his reason for the name alteration, his choice seemingly implies an underlying concern with outward expressions of gender performance.[50]

In addition to the misleading label, the sex tests faced several logistical problems. While the medical commission had wished for the examinations to be completed before the competition, not all female athletes arrived in France with enough time for that to happen. Furthermore, as planned, only one out of every five female participants underwent chromosomal verification. For the small percent of women tested, the medical commission attempted to perform the tests "with the greatest respect for human rights and with absolute secrecy." A different report noted that the controls occurred in such a secretive manner in order "to avoid all embarrassment."[51] Though the IOC sought to preserve the dignity of anyone who should fail its parameters, the possible disqualification of a woman with a different chromosomal makeup supported the belief that "real" female Olympians needed protection.

The sex tests also upheld white norms of femininity. Many people in the United States interpreted the new requirement as an unnecessary annoyance, specifically referencing white Western athletes who subscribed to conventional feminine ideals. For example, Shirley Povich of the *Washington Post* posited that by mandating the exam for eighteen-year-old American skier Karen Budge, "the IOC will be a whopping loser." According to Povich, although "the muscular Russian and Polish babes were not quite as feminine as they declared in the Olympic registry," Budge was a "peachcake" and had "blue orbs that would melt an entire ski slope." Moreover, she had the capability to "set off a whole cantata of wolf whistles."[52] Such accounts favorably interpreted outward presentations of white hetero-femininity. The highlighting of sexual appeal compromised athleticism and helped reaffirm sport as a masculine enterprise. Furthermore, although never mentioned explicitly, only white athletes were held up as representative of the ideal Olympic competitor, in both the Winter and Summer Games.

Finally, some people involved in the testing found the selection process too arbitrary. Under the supervision of de Mérode and Hay, the Swedish baron Gustaf Åkerhielm and two French doctors blindly drew fifty names for sex control. The results included fourteen Eastern European athletes, a proportion that upset many in the West.[53] For example, US ski team coach Bob Beattie noted, "The whole business of this testing is mad. . . . They're picking girls at random."[54] Likewise, in the words of one anonymous Olympic official, the indiscriminate selection "did nothing to solve the problem since it still left too many of the girls unchecked." This "problem" would best be solved if they tested "the most obvious" of the athletes.[55] One can assume "the most obvious" implied the women who did not subscribe to Western femininity—likely a reference to the muscular, powerful Olympians from Eastern European countries. The medical commission did not disagree. In his concluding report to the committee, Giuseppe la Cava argued that "it was a mistake to determine by lot the individuals subjected to the examination." His reasoning stemmed from the capricious nature of the selections, which had "no logical or biological function." Instead, la Cava proposed the medical commission test the top six competitors in each event to eliminate unfairness.[56]

Despite these concerns, no female athlete failed the sex test in Grenoble.[57] As Thiebault recounted, "Happily for us there has been no doubtful case because I still wonder how we would have acted if a young woman (with a fairly famous name) had become a problem."[58] However, Austrian Olympian Erika Schinegger, world champion skier and national hero, had opted to withdraw from the Grenoble Olympics rather than publicly undergo the sex test. Weeks before the 1968 Winter Games, the Austrian team visited the University Hospital in Innsbruck for a routine check. "I was told my tests had not proved satisfactory, that I could no longer compete as Erika," Schinegger recalled. "I was asked to sign a declaration that I was withdrawing from the sport for personal reasons." The doctors informed him that he possessed internal male sex organs. After sex-reassignment surgery, in 1968 Schinegger returned to the men's Europa Cup tour as Erik.[59] Perhaps because the failure occurred outside the Olympics, and Schinegger's transition reified a binary classification of sex, Thiebault was able to dismiss the adversaries of sex testing. He suggested that the IOC continue the practice in the Mexico City Summer Games.

The Mexico City Summer Olympics

As Western gender norms shaped Olympic protocol, the polarized ideological struggles between the United States and the Soviet Union influenced other countries. According to historian Julia Sloan, Mexico and other similarly positioned "Third World nations" were unable to escape the enveloping weight of the international disagreement. In presenting a more nuanced view of the traditional Cold War narrative, she argues that Mexico interpreted the global conflict as an example of aggression orchestrated by imperialist states to dominate countries that were less developed. Sloan posits that Mexico envisioned the turmoil "not as a contest between communism and capitalism, but as a contest between the nations that were internationally dominant and those that were dominated."[60] This sentiment underlined Mexico City's bid as well as the country's marketing of the 1968 Summer Olympics.

In the 1960s Mexico struggled in both domestic affairs and international perceptions. Despite two decades of substantial economic growth, dubbed the "Mexican miracle," political fractures plagued the country. A tacit understanding between the United States and Mexico had allowed Mexican authorities a degree of autonomy in exchange for guaranteed internal stability. Thus the ambiguous nature of the Mexican Federal Penal Code allowed the ruling party, the Partido Revolucionario Institucional (PRI), to pass the "Law of Social Dissolution" and punish acts of disorder, subversion, and treason.[61] With all opposition essentially silenced, the PRI maintained only a pretense of democratic leadership, creating a volatile situation that would come to a violent head mere days before the Olympic opening ceremonies.

International opinions concurrently marginalized Mexico as a "developing" nation. To combat this image, Mexican authorities looked to the prestige and power afforded by sport. In the 47th Session of the IOC in Helsinki, Finland, representatives of Mexico City placed a bid for the 1960 Games, hoping to bring the Olympics to Central America for the first time. Although Rome, Italy, eventually earned the honors, Mexico City gained esteem through its organization of the 1955 Pan American Games. The focus on sport continued unabated as the government poured resources into new facilities. For example, according to Mexican Olympic Committee president Marte R. Gómez, by 1960 the country had invested one hundred million pesos in its state-of-the-art "City of Sport."[62] Although Mexico's governmental spending would later be questioned, the IOC recognized the country's commitment and awarded Mexico City the 1968 Summer Olympics.

The Organization of the 1968 Summer Olympics

When Mexico City defeated Buenos Aires, Argentina; Detroit, United States; and Lyon, France, members of the IOC reacted with mixed support. According to historian Eric Zolov, an implicit ethnocentrism underlined the hesitancy of some outsiders to wholeheartedly embrace the city, while many Mexican citizens responded with celebratory unease. Both groups wondered if it was viable for a financially unstable country to stage the Olympics. The combination of ethnocentrism from abroad and skepticism from within encouraged the leaders of Mexico City to control all images surrounding the event. Zolov argues that the Cultural Olympiad, a yearlong scheduling of cultural events, enhanced this aim through the conveyance of five specific themes for foreign consumption. First, the official logo of the 1968 Summer Games depicted Mexico City as a thriving, cosmopolitan destination. To curb the image of Mexico as a "developing" nation, such demonstrations of modernity were abundant. Almost in contrast, a second aim was to illustrate Mexico's authenticity through a range of folkloric exhibitions. Third, promoters deployed bright colors to portray the country as both festive and exotic.

As a fourth ideal, organizers deployed iconic images of doves to represent Mexico's role as peacemaker in a time of international turmoil. This attempt now seems hypocritical in light of the Tlatelolco massacre that occurred in Mexico City just ten days before the opening ceremonies. Concerned with governmental oppression, irresponsibility, and spending—epitomized by the enormous Olympic budget—students had gathered in the Plaza de las Tres Culturas in protest on October 2, 1968. This peaceful gathering erupted in deathly violence.[63] Never one to admit the intimate relationship between the Olympics and politics, Brundage responded the following day that the games must continue.

Finally, according to Zolov, "liberated women" were strategically used to enhance the country's representation as modern. Because many considered Mexico a society of machismo, one in which women were denied mobility and rights, the organizers used the Olympics as a forum to highlight a new, modern woman. Officials recruited and showcased middle-class, lighter-skinned female volunteers to present a specific image.[64] The most notable example stemmed from the torch-lighting ceremony, where Norma Enriqueta Basilio served as the first woman to ever light the Olympic cauldron. This creation and conveyance of a modern woman mirrored the IOC's beliefs about appropriate female Olympians.

Women's Medical Examination in Mexico City

Although Thiebault, the French sex control authority, granted approval for the Olympic sex test procedure, Brundage attempted to delegate authority to the international federations. He was concerned about the legality of the IOC mandating sex and doping controls, as well as the associated expenses. De Mérode, on the other hand, wanted control. As a result, in the months leading up to the Summer Olympics the two clashed in a series of circular letters. On August 26, 1968, Brundage informed the international federations and the NOCs that it was not the intention of the IOC to carry out the tests. However, all Olympians would be required to comply with the regulations. In his view, the international federations would enforce sex testing policies and anti-doping procedures.[65] De Mérode immediately responded that the "absolute confusion" caused by Brundage's misinformation "is a serious blow to the work we [the medical commission] are trying to achieve."[66] He further reasoned that "this change of opinion brings us back to the question of how much we can depend on the decisions of the IOC." Worried about undermining the efforts of the medical commission, Brundage later agreed that all testing in Mexico City would be carried out under the supervision of the committee, according to its regulations.[67]

For the Mexico City Olympics the IOC required that "all women athletes participating in the Games will be controlled" by the medical commission. Led by Eduardo Hay, a professor of gynecology and obstetrics, 803 female Olympians underwent a sex check. According to *Chicago Tribune* reporter Marion Lay, the reactions from those being tested ranged from carefree nonchalance to severe stress. Moreover, in response to the long wait outside the polyclinic, "some athletes suggested that if doctors were good-looking enough, one might skip the test and prove her femininity by seducing him."[68] Such sentiments again illustrate the connections between heterosexuality, gender, and sex.

No woman officially failed the test. Although all female Olympians received "femininity certificates," documents that verified their womanhood, Berlioux remained suspicious. "We should remember that the controls did not in fact lead to any disqualifications," she noted. "On the contrary, certain 'female' competitors disappeared from the scene."[69] While the games remained free from "inauthentic" women, the IOC disqualified two athletes and one team for doping violations. Swedish modern pentathlon competitor Hans-Gunnar Liljenwall had absorbed too much alcohol, resulting in the disqualification of the entire team, and a wrestler had inhaled a cotton-wool swab soaked in ammonia. The two disqualifications did not mean that doping was curbed in the games; rather, the lack of violations stemmed from the limited nature of the medical commission's testing, which notably did not include a steroid check.

Post-Olympics Doping Concerns

Despite the barring of only two athletes by the IOC, later popular reports of the 1968 Mexico City Games described Olympians' rampant use of performance-enhancing substances. On the forefront an investigative piece in *Sports Illustrated* highlighted the universal trend of drug use in elite competition. Penned by Bil Gilbert, the report chronicled the extensive dependency on special pills, formulas, and shots for improved performances. Furthermore, he argued that if not banned, drug usage would only grow exponentially.[70] Likewise, according to writer Jack Scott, drugs and sport was "becoming as common among athletes as the wearing of socks." In Scott's *Chicago Tribune* article, Bill Toomey, the 1968 gold medalist in the decathlon and the winner of the AAU's Sullivan Award, admitted that he had used drugs to assist his Olympic performance. Decathlon teammate Tom Waddell verified Toomey's account and further claimed that more than a third of the US track and field team routinely ingested steroids prior to competition.[71] In response to the *Chicago Tribune* article, Sam Goldberg, a US decathlon hopeful, affirmed the commonly held notion that "no decathlete could win an Olympic medical without the aid of steroids and/or amphetamines." He also explained that "the same idea exists, but to a slightly lesser degree, as far as securing a berth on our American Olympic team."[72] All of the athletes who stepped forward articulated nationalism as the leading factor in the decision to dope. As weight lifter Ken Patera noted, "When I hit Munich next year, I'll weigh in at about 340, maybe 350. Then we'll see which are better—his [Soviet champion Vasily Alekseyev's] steroids or mine."[73]

Anxiety over steroid use also increased with regard to female Olympians. For example, after placing sixth in the discus in Mexico City, Olga Fiko-tová Connolly told Charles Maher of the *Los Angeles Times* that she did not foresee a medal finish for herself at the 1972 Munich Games. Connolly was a Czechoslovakian discus thrower renowned for her Olympic gold medal effort in the 1956 Games, as well as for her public love affair with US discus thrower Harold Connolly. According to the *Los Angeles Times* story, when she discovered that 90 percent of European female finalists in the Mexico City Games ingested steroids, she opted to forgo her chances of success rather than follow suit. "I don't like track any more . . . because of the drug business," she said. Connolly's decision did not stem from medicinal concerns, but from fears of masculinization. "Steroids make them [female competitors] more muscular, far more so than women used to be," she explained.[74] In conjunction with her public, heterosexual love life, Connolly embraced Western gender norms. With an abundance of such reports, the IOC Medical Commission opted to increase its vigilance for the 1972 Winter and Summer Olympics.

The 1972 Sapporo Winter Olympics

In the late 1930s Japan was poised to serve as the first Asian country to host the modern Olympics. Before Sapporo's and Tokyo's successful bids for the 1940 Winter and Summer Games, respectively, the Olympic movement had remained rooted in Europe and the United States. The 1937 Japanese invasion of China had revoked the country's bid, and the outbreak of World War II eventually canceled the 1940 Olympics. Although neither the 1940 Winter nor Summer Games happened, Japan's successful bid relied upon an important discursive paradigm that held long-lasting implications for the Olympic movement. The campaign presented Japan as the embodiment of oppositional tensions, which included being geographically Eastern and Western, old and new, and modern and traditional. In the interwar years this strategy of blended conventions resonated with the IOC; however, it also allowed the predominantly European authorities to mark Japan as different. Furthermore, as anthropologist William W. Kelly illustrates, all later Olympic Games hosted by Asian cities were similarly constructed as dissimilar from the European events, both culturally and politically. Therefore, when the Summer Olympics reached Japan in 1964 and the Winter Olympics in 1972, the Japanese organizing committees sought to use the forum as signifiers of the country's rebirth and selective modernization.[75]

After experiencing the devastation of World War II, Japan hoped to alter its image from a tarnished, defeated country to that of a nation of economic prosperity and confidence. Banned from the 1948 Olympics for siding with the conquered Axis powers, Japan returned in the 1952 Helsinki Games and started to use international events to help construct a new image. As historian Sandra Wilson explains, the 1964 Tokyo Olympics, along with the 1970 World Exposition in Osaka, showcased "deliberately-crafted versions of Japan's past, present and future," designed to persuade both domestic and international audiences of the country's flourishing position.[76] Innovative satellite technology in the 1964 Games permitted live global broadcasts for the first time in Olympic history and bolstered these dual aims. For example, the marathon race was run throughout Tokyo on a course strategically devised to visually highlight the city's urban change.[77]

While science, technology, and urban renewal proved to be the emphasized trifecta of modernity in the wake of World War II, Japanese sport also experienced subtle changes in the postwar period. Comparable to overarching social ideologies, sport in Japan both mirrored and resisted conventions from the West. As sport scholar John Horne notes, Japan concurrently appropriated European pastimes, such as baseball and football, and also maintained sporting hegemony over its Pacific neighbors.[78] Japanese women now saw increased opportunities for participation, including at the Olympic level. Female competitors excelled in the 1964 Tokyo Olympics; however, representations of women's achievements remained rooted in gender norms. As Japanese scholar Rio Otomo argues, sporting narratives shaped gold medal achievements as "self-sacrificial deeds for the nation;" moreover, the athletes were presented as dutiful daughters of fatherly coaches rather than as individual sporting victors.[79] Although Japanese sporting gender norms appeared to complement those of the West, concerns regarding masculinized female athletes continued in the 1972 Sapporo Winter Games.

The Medical Commission's "Sex Control" Guidelines

In the 64th Session of the IOC, merely two years after the conclusion of the 1964 Tokyo Olympics, the executive board approved Sapporo as the host city for the 1972 Winter Games. After the perceived successes of the dual medical checks in Mexico City, the IOC also maintained the necessity of sex tests and doping controls and continued to debate the question of oversight. Brundage, still wary of the legality and expenses involved, remained convinced that the IOC should delegate responsibility. He wanted the international federations to examine all competitors. As a result, in the 68th Session of the IOC in

1969 de Mérode reiterated that each international federation was required to carry out its own alcohol, dope, and sex tests, with the assistance of the medical commission. Because confusion failed to dissipate, the commission drafted two official pamphlets—one on anti-doping measures and one labeled "Sex Control"—in order to provide additional guidance for the Sapporo and Munich Games. The pamphlets were made available during the 72nd Session of the IOC, mere days before the opening ceremonies of the Winter Games.

The medical commission's 1972 "Sex Control" pamphlet provided stipulations for all female Olympians. First, any competitor registered as "being female" was required to take a sex control examination prior to participation.[80] The pamphlet dictated that all tests must occur in the presence of at least one member of the medical commission, which at the time was comprised of eight men and one woman.[81] Second, any athlete who had previously undergone a check and possessed a "sex control certificate," granted by either the medical commission or an international federation during world or continental championships, was exempted. Third, the samples derived from either the buccal mucous membrane or hair roots were screened for X chromosomes and Y chromosomes. Finally, the medical commission mandated a silent disqualification should a sample prove irregular. The pamphlet explained that "neither the fact of this examination nor its results will be made public out of deference to the human rights of the individual."[82] Any alternative chromosomal combination besides XX resulted in ineligibility.

Veiled in conventions of fair play, the guidelines constructed Olympic womanhood along binary notions of Western gender ideals. According to the *Sapporo 1972 Olympic Winter Games Official Report*, the purpose of the control measure in Japan was to deter muscular competitors from entering women's competitions. The report explained, "Women athletes are commonly required to undergo an examination to confirm their sexual identity because of the large number of individuals, who, although appearing to be female, have the physical characteristics of males."[83] This statement does not relay fears of chromosomal "abnormalities," but instead focuses on the speculation of masculine traits in women Olympians. Such an overt postulation begs the question, what exactly are "male" and "female" characteristics? According to Susan K. Cahn, female athleticism threatens a hierarchical status quo that depends upon a belief in natural and irrevocable gender difference. In the West, "not only have men dominated the playing fields, but athletic qualities such as aggression, competitiveness, strength, speed, power, and teamwork have been associated with masculinity."[84] To preserve athleticism as a male characteristic, sport authorities sought compensation through sex control measures.

Presumably, the Sapporo organizers wanted to eliminate any woman who transgressed Western gender boundaries. Equipped with the decrees of the IOC Medical Commission pamphlet, the Sapporo Olympic medical authorities administered checks on the 217 female participants registered in the three permissible sports: luge, skating, and skiing.[85] Although no "abnormalities" were reported, the sex control measures did not escape criticism.

The Danish Protest

In the midst of the Sapporo Olympics, Brundage received an alarming report regarding the IOC's use of chromosomal verification. Written by five Danish medical doctors, "A Memorandum on the Use of Sex Chromatin Investigation of Competitions in Women's Division of the Olympic Games" criticized sex control and called for the IOC to abolish the practice. The authors—two psychiatrists, two geneticists, and one gynecologist—disliked the policy and provided justifications for its termination.

Foremost, the authors noted that although no medical or legal delineation of sex existed, "the international olympic [*sic*] committee has made its own definition." The five Danish authorities did acknowledge that three types of sex could be outlined—chromosomal sex, somatic sex, and psychosocial sex; however, none provided an unambiguous classification system. Accordingly, chromosomal sex, the preferred measurement of the IOC, used the sex chromosomes, while somatic sex incorporated both gonadal anatomy and secondary sex characteristics. Psychosocial sex related to the self-identification of the individual. The authors argued that relying solely upon chromosomal sex unfairly barred women with a variety of naturally occurring "abnormalities," including ovarian dysgenesis, pure gonadal dysgenesis, and testicular feminization, more commonly known as Morris syndrome. The medical doctors explained that "the test discriminates . . . in a way that may lead to serious psychological disturbances in the individuals discriminated against." More directly, they concluded that the IOC's sex control was "irresponsible from a medical point of view, and unethical."[86]

After reviewing the report, from which the president of the Danish NOC quickly distanced himself, Brundage advised de Mérode that the medical commission should consider the "disquieting" information.[87] In a circular letter the IOC president suggested to the chairman that because the technical test proved unreliable, "maybe the eye of a 25 year old would be better."[88] Brundage's proposition implies that the underlying purpose of sex control was to deny access to any unattractive female competitors. In other words, the IOC's intent was to prohibit women who did not abide by the gender ideals of the West.

Upon learning of the Danish protest, the international federations requested that de Mérode meet with the authors of the report. The president of the medical commission listened to the concerns of the professionals and admitted that "it was practically impossible, scientifically, to define the sex of an athlete." Nevertheless, he maintained his belief that sex testing was a necessity. According to de Mérode, the aim of the control was not to determine the sex of the examined, but to ensure that no woman possessed a physiological advantage.[89] He also reasoned that "practical" issues raised by the IOC outweighed the professors' "scientific side." Brundage agreed.[90]

Eduardo Hay, the overseer of the exam in 1968, similarly defended the objective of the sex test in 1972. In his view, because of the need for fair play, the IOC could not accommodate individuals with different chromosomal types.[91] He thereby vocalized the necessity of gender conformity for entrance into women's Olympic events, a belief he upheld for years. As Finnish geneticist Albert de la Chapelle later reflected about Hay, "He is a charming person, but he still does not quite know what the whole thing is about."[92] Hay's repeated emphasis on femininity is telling; according to such assertions, muscular female athletes must be controlled. As he illustrated, the IOC was apprehensive about powerful Olympians who did not abide by contemporary norms. Thus changes would not be forthcoming in Munich.

The 1972 Munich Summer Olympics

The separation of Germany into the Federal Republic of Germany (FRG), supported by Great Britain, France, and the United States, and the German Democratic Republic (GDR), supported by the Soviet Union, created considerable animosity. Disturbed by the division, and still Western in orientation, the IOC recognized the FRG NOC in 1951 and denied the GDR application, limiting participation in Helsinki to the West Germans. After a brief period of dual recognition and joint team efforts, the IOC relented and granted the German Democratic Republic the right to enter a separate team in the 1968 Mexico City Olympics. From that point forward, the two nations competed under separate flags and sought to demonstrate superiority through athletic capital.

The masterminds of the Munich bid, West German Olympic Committee president Willi Daume and influential politician Hans-Jochen Vogel, sought the lauded host city position as a way to resituate West Germany at the forefront of international affairs. Before the Munich Games, the country's global ventures had remained primarily limited to the North Atlantic Treaty Organization, European pursuits, and sporadic exchanges in cultural diplomacy. Daume and Vogel believed that the return of the Olympics to Germany would encourage urban regeneration, stimulate civic conciliation, increase tourism, and "overlay residual images of the recent past with new narratives about the country's political, economic, social and cultural acumen."[93]

Yet, similar to the larger German population's burden of its Nazi past, the Munich Olympics Organizing Committee's (MOOC) recognized the 1972 Olympics' encumbering position. Promoters sought to both remember and dissociate from the tragedies of Nazi Germany. The eleven-year span from 1958 to 1969 served as the acme of public demand for somber reflection and exacting retribution; however, according to scholars Kay Schiller and Christopher Young, "By 1965, the year in which the Munich Olympic bid was conceived, a paradoxical mix of heightened sensitivity and moral ambiguity toward the past had clearly been established."[94] Hence, the 1972 Munich Games embraced an apocryphal vision of the country's heritage and presented a purposeful narrative about a newly modern, albeit divided, Germany.

Despite the MOOC's efforts to convey a positive image of a new West Germany, the 1972 Munich Olympics were marred by a horrifying massacre. In the midst of the games, the Palestinian terrorist organization Black September took eleven Israeli athletes hostage. After a failed rescue attempt, all eleven were killed. On September 6, the day after the "Munich Massacre" occurred, Brundage announced, "The games must go on," in a speech that many observers criticized as insensitive. Although the decision was controversial, the Olympic Games followed the predilection of its president and commenced after a memorial and moment of silence. Along with the scheduled competitions, sex control continued undeterred.

Sex Control "Failures"

With the 1972 "Sex Control" pamphlet's stipulations previously implemented in Sapporo, the required chromosomal checks ran smoothly in Munich. Unlike past sample-collection procedures, the MOOC suggested that international federations use hair roots for examination; rather than through a cheek swab, physicians located chromosomes on hair follicles. According to the Official Report of the Munich Olympics, "The sex of a person can be diagnosed without difficulty from the hair root just as certainly as by the usual methods." While perhaps scientifically innovative, the purpose of the hair root inspection appears to contradict de Mérode's previous assessment that sex control measures sought to prevent unfair advantage, not denote sex classifications. This inconsistency again suggests that the IOC Medical Commission, and consequently the international federations and organizing committees, did not know nor agree upon the fundamental reasoning for sex testing. Nonetheless, under the watchful eye of the medical commission, the international federations conducted 960 sex tests and validated the authenticity of 114 "sex control certificates."[95] Despite the ease in implementing the process, the commission quickly faced a worrisome situation. For the first time, whispers of failures surfaced.

Because the IOC proved stringent in its nondisclosure policy, the actual number of women who failed the sex test remains unknown. However, rumors marred most Olympics. In 1993 an Olympic official offhandedly remarked that from 1968 to 1988 there had been at least one or two disqualifications at every Olympic Games except one.[96] Scholars have also attempted to estimate the total number, basing their approximations on the ratio of chromosomal "abnormalities" within the larger population. For example, gynecologist John S. Fox has suggested that as many as one in every four hundred competitors were wrongly excluded.[97] Yet the total tally remains unclear. Some further speculated that when faced with an unexpected test result, questioned athletes may have preferred to withdraw rather than submit to clinical examinations that would permit eligibility. According to Hay, this happened approximately a dozen times from 1968 to 1980.[98]

Moreover, Hay's estimation only accounted for those who failed at the international level. Some local and regional organizations proactively embraced the Barr body test to detect possible issues in young athletes. For example, British geneticist Martin Bobrow described a situation in which coaches arranged checks because they were "reluctant to put years of work into bringing promising youngsters on and then have them fail a test at a later stage."[99] De la Chapelle similarly detailed his experiences with two girl athletes, a skier and a swimmer, who "failed" the buccal smear test required by their local associations. The "perfectly normal-looking young ladies," both of whom had testicular feminization, were told to disappear from sport, without further examination. "There must be hundreds if not thousands of women who have been silently shuffled aside this way," de la Chapelle reasoned.[100] The patients identified were not only prone to experience emotional suffering, depression, and suicidal thoughts but were also possibly informed in an insensitive fashion.[101] As de la Chapelle succinctly surmised, "What goes on at the large international games is just the tip of the iceberg."[102]

More concerning from the perspective of Olympic officials was the rumor that a male masquerader had successfully evaded detection in volleyball. For Olympic volleyball in 1972, the eight highest-ranked teams competed in two pools of four. After round-robin play the top two squads in each division advanced to the semi-finals. The Democratic People's Republic of Korea

(DPRK), Japan, the Republic of Korea (ROK), and the Soviet Union earned the four positions, with Japan and the Soviet Union easily moving into the finals. In the consolation match for third place, the DPRK swiftly defeated the ROK in three sets. According to various insinuations, however, the DPRK team included a male player who helped the squad earn the bronze medal. The DPRK supposedly devised a complex scheme whereby the person who underwent the sex test was a woman carrying the passport belonging to the man who participated in the games.[103] After the match the ROK Olympic Committee filed an official complaint and requested that the player undergo further testing. Although the International Volleyball Federation (FIVB) supported the protest, it was denied by the IOC Medical Commission.[104]

Regardless of the accuracy or exaggeration of this tale, rumors that three additional women failed the chromosome check surfaced after the closing ceremonies of the Munich Games. In response to these suspicions, de Mérode explained in a press release that "scientifically the examinations are irreproachable" and that "from an administrative point of view everything is perfectly in order."[105] Although most names still remain concealed, the IOC's handling of the so-called failures is important. Whereas official policy publicized all doping violations, the IOC Medical Commission refused to release the names of any woman it deemed irregular. According to commission member Hay, the IOC published and circulated reports of doping breaches as a tool to deter others from following suit. In cases of sex control abnormalities, however, "care must be taken for the result to be kept secret," he explained. Furthermore, "her malformation should not be publicised since she is not at fault."[106] With this arrangement the IOC shaped male Olympians who doped as competitive cheaters and female Olympians who did not pass the sex test as irregular monstrosities. Yet fears of female dopers and the anxieties fostered by sex control failures further conflated doping and sex control.

* * *

In the 1961 edition of *Olympic Review*, Marie-Thérèse Eyquem, the general superintendent of women's sports for France, penned an article dedicated to the status of female participation in international contests. Renowned for her feminist and socialist leanings, she condemned the sexualization of female athletes in the piece. However, she simultaneously embraced contradictory views, demanding that while women compete, they try to maintain their elegance and beauty. Eyquem deplored the "inaesthetical aspect of a graceless woman." Moreover, concerned with doping scandals, the French pioneer of women's sport also denounced "a particularly revolting form of doping—that of women athletes who take male hormones."[107] Eyquem's disdain paralleled that of the larger population and also seemed to mirror the thoughts of the medical commission.

The IOC introduced doping and sex tests in 1968. Both measures served to eliminate inauthentic competitors. While anti-doping controls checked for traces of prohibited substances, sex verification barred any woman who did not possess an XX chromosomal composition. Although the medical community opposed the IOC's singular use of chromatin for sex determination, many scientists agreed that a control method was necessary to uphold fairness in sport. As a result, in the Grenoble Winter Olympics one in five female athletes underwent the exam, and in the Mexico City Summer Olympics all women were tested. The anxieties and controls continued in the 1972 Sapporo and Munich Games.

The IOC Medical Commission viewed female drug users and sex test failures as inauthentic, unnatural women. Although the commission defined dopers as cheaters and labeled ambiguously sexed athletes victims of biology, the IOC nevertheless conflated the two as detractors of true womanhood. This practice was heightened in the 1976 Montreal Games as East Germany gained international sporting prestige.

4 "East Germany's Mighty Sports Machine"

Steroids, Nationalism, and Femininity Testing

IN THE 4 X 100-METER MEDLEY RELAY finals in 1976, seventeen-year-old East German swimmer Kornelia Ender touched the wall 6.6 seconds ahead of US swimming star Shirley Babashoff. With this convincing difference, Ender and the German Democratic Republic team handed the United States its only non–gold medal Olympic finish since the medley relay was first introduced in the 1960 Rome Games. The gap not only surprised the US squad but also ensured Ender a fifth medal. She became the first female swimmer to win four gold medals in a single Olympics. Babashoff, on the other hand, walked away with only one gold, four silvers, and suspicion.[1]

Consumed by Cold War fears and expecting a better performance from its team, the US press immediately conflated sex and gender, gender and sexuality, and sex testing and doping controls when describing the German Democratic Republic's feats. The media described the East German women as masculinized, nonheterosexual cheaters. For example, Bill Shirley of the *Los Angeles Times* labeled the East German squad "the world's first bionic swim team," while additional reports referred to the 5' 9", 163-pound Ender as the "king-sized Kornelia."[2] It should be noted that Babashoff, a US swimming favorite, measured in at 5' 10" and 160 pounds.

Discarding any similarities between the teams, US athletes also offered remarks about their competitors' appearances. Wendy Boglioli, who placed third in the 100-meter butterfly, commented, "Kornelia is phenomenal, but personally I wouldn't want to look like most of the East German swimmers. Sports shouldn't come to having a woman looking like a man." Male swimmer John Naber agreed, noting, "Our American girls don't want to make the sacrifice to lift weights. . . . They wanted to go on dates instead, and I can't

The 1973 World Aquatics Championships 100-meter freestyle medalists. From left to right: Shirley Babashoff (United States, silver); Kornelia Ender (East Germany, gold); and Enith Brigitha (Netherlands, bronze). Courtesy of the German Federal Archives, German News Service.

blame them."[3] The GDR female Olympians repeatedly passed all sex testing and anti-doping measures, including the new steroid check, yet many in the West remained unconvinced.

During the 1976 Innsbruck Winter Games and the 1976 Montreal Summer Games, nationalism underlined the calls for improved control measures. East Germany's debut, as well as the country's sudden increase in victories, led many to decry a loss of fairness in sport, in terms of both doping and gender violations. After having competed with West Germany under the Unified Team of Germany flag since 1956, the German Democratic Republic participated as a single nation from 1968 to 1992. Once on its own, the country quickly moved up in the medal count. Later accounts verify that the head of the GDR sport federation, Manfred Ewald, had implemented a regime of systematic doping.[4] Suspicions prompted Western sport authorities to call for increased policing of Eastern nations, veiling its nationalism and hypocrisy under the guise of fair play. The USOC purposefully ignored similar doping habits within the United States in order to help the country secure medals.

Ewald's requirements were a clear and tragic violation of human rights, yet both arrangements breached the Olympic charter. Furthermore, the rapid ascent of the GDR female athletes in the 1970s fostered fears of doped, gender-transgressive women.

Although sex and doping checks attempted to combat such skepticism, albeit differently, medical authorities, athletes, and reporters alike viewed the two controls as a single tool to eliminate women they considered inappropriate from competition. This confusion allowed many to view all muscular female Olympians as substance-enhanced, masculinized frauds. Such accusations not only excluded women found to have genetic differences but also helped deny strength and power as acceptable characteristics for female athletes. The coverage of sex testing and doping control in the 1976 Games helped reaffirm conventional Western femininity as the preferred incarnation of gender and heterosexuality as the expected embodiment of sexuality for women athletes.

Lord Killanin and the Rise of Steroids

After serving the Olympic movement for two decades, Avery Brundage ended his career as IOC president in 1972. His successor, Lord Killanin (Michael Morris), the head of the Olympic Council of Ireland, assumed the position following the Munich Olympics. During Killanin's reign, political dissension worsened; as a result, his term was marred by nationalistic embroilment, protests, and boycotts. Although he oversaw a difficult and short presidential term, Lord Killanin did affect the Olympic movement in two significant ways. First, he softened Brundage's interpretation of amateurism with a more moderate view. He recognized the need for some Olympians to obtain athletically generated finances.[5] Second, Killanin increased the medical surveillance of competitors. In a 1978 speech at the University of Sussex, he articulated his belief that the tendency for nations to use fraudulent competitors—"abnormal" women and dopers—"is the most serious affecting international sports and the athlete today."[6] During his tenure the IOC heightened sex checks and anti-doping measures, which included the addition of a steroid test.

History of Testosterone

The use of anabolic steroids, a synthetic form of testosterone, was not new in the 1970s. Throughout history, various forms of artificial testosterone were believed to strengthen one's capacity for work and to enhance one's sexual experiences, which helped foster a cultural lore around the substance.[7] According to scholar John M. Hoberman, "Testosterone became a charismatic drug because it promised sexual stimulation and renewed energy for individuals, and greater productivity for modern society."[8] Synthetic forms of testosterone elicited promises of hormonal rejuvenation, illusions of sexual excitement, and, perhaps most importantly to Killanin, fears of superhuman athletes.

Anecdotally, a farmer in the Neolithic Era first recognized the importance of testes—later identified as the production site of testosterone—when he castrated a sheep and noticed improvements in the domestication of the animal. The first deliberate testicular experiment did not occur until the eighteenth century. Rooted in the scientific tradition whereby gonads determined sex, in 1787 Scottish surgeon John Hunter removed a testicle from a rooster and implanted it in a hen. Although the appendage adhered, Hunter did not perceive any changes in the recipient; therefore, he opted not to publish his findings and discussed the results only in lectures. Almost a century later, Arnold Adolph Berthold noted that a "bloodstream substance" in roosters affected the species' appearance and behavior. Unfortunately for the German physiologist and zoologist, his theory was not widely accepted by his contemporaries.[9]

Perhaps the most bizarre case in the history of testicular research occurred at the end of the nineteenth century. In 1889 French physiologist Charles Édouard Brown-Séquard published the results of an auto-experiment in which he injected testicular extracts from guinea pigs and dogs into himself. He reported amplified strength, greater mental capacity, and a larger appetite, as well as relief from constipation. Brown-Séquard also noted an increase in the arc of his urine stream.[10] Importantly, the seventy-two-year-old Harvard professor publicly declared "that he had drastically reversed his own decline by injecting himself with a liquid extract." Brown-Séquard also provided samples of the liquid, free of charge, to any physician willing to test the substance, thereby sparking a wave of international experiments aimed at curbing a variety of disorders, from cancer to hysteria.[11] By the end of the century, more than twelve thousand physicians had administered such fluids to patients, and the predecessors to modern pharmaceutical companies sold it as the "Elixir of Life."[12]

As knowledge of the supposed capabilities of testicular extracts proliferated, medical authorities grew increasingly interested in its strengthening potential. In an 1896 paper, Austrian physicians Oskar Zoth and Fritz Pregl proposed that injecting athletes with testicular-derived substances would enhance their performances. The two had inoculated themselves with extracts and measured increased strength in their middle fingers.[13] Similarly, by the early 1900s Viennese physiologist Eugen Steinach had developed the

"Steinach operation," a partial vasectomy that claimed to increase hormonal production for the "middle-aged" and "listless." According to medical doctor Jennifer L. Dotson and scholar Robert T. Brown, "It was apparent to researchers that some substance circulating in the blood was responsible for their findings."[14] However, it was not until 1929 that a more specific framework was established, which paved the way for the synthesis of testosterone.

In 1929 German biochemist Adolf Butenandt isolated the first sex hormone, producing estrone in crystalline form. With the discovery, experimentation on human subjects accelerated. Three research teams, each subsidized by competing pharmaceutical companies, raced to isolate and manufacture the driving force behind testicular secretions. The foundation for modern androgen therapy was therefore laid by several scientists. In 1931 Butenandt separated steroidal androgens from urine.[15] Four years later, Karoly G. David, Elizabeth Dingemanse, Janos Freud, and Ernst Laqueur isolated what they eventually named "testosterone" in crystalline form from the testicles of bulls. The four scientists coined the term from a combination of "testicle," "sterol," and "one," the suffix of "ketone." Finally, also occurring in 1935, Butenandt and his colleague Günter Hanisch, as well as Leopold Ružička and Albert Wettstein, chemically synthesized testosterone.[16]

With testosterone isolated and synthesized, research on its potential flourished in the 1940s United States. In 1945 US microbiologist Paul de Kruif published *The Male Hormone*. De Kruif endorsed testosterone in his breakthrough monograph, claiming it increased libido and boosted athletic performance. Although poised at mid-century to be the preeminent therapy for rejuvenation and stimulation—and an aid for athletic enhancement— testosterone failed to hold sway in the public consciousness. The resistance stemmed from the ignorance and biases of physicians regarding sexuality and from the general prudery of the US population.[17] Despite the opposition to testosterone therapy in the United States, body builders on the West Coast embraced steroids as a tool to build muscle mass. With the spread of anecdotes that described gains in strength, athletes increasingly dabbled with synthetic variants to improve individual performance.[18] As a result, steroids and sport became intimately linked.

The Medical Commission and Steroid Testing

Although the IOC recognized this connection, amphetamine controls proved a greater concern for its medical commission in the early 1960s. The lack of an effective steroid test also deterred its addition to the prohibited substance list. In its 1972 *Doping* brochure the commission explained that steroids "cannot be detected with certainty." Arthur Porritt and his successor, Alexandre de Mérode, both feared that the inability to detect synthetic testosterone might challenge the legitimacy of the new anti-doping regulations.[19] Therefore, when Raymond Brooks discovered a successful method for detecting synthetic testosterone, the medical commission labeled steroids a prohibited substance.

In the early 1970s Brooks, a professor at St. Thomas's Hospital in London, worked on applying radioimmunoassay—a technique that measures antigens, such as hormone levels, by using antibodies—to steroids. He effectively created a test in 1974 that identified orally ingested steroids. The method required two to three days for complete analysis. Despite the time gap required, the first steroid check occurred at the 1974 Commonwealth Games in Christchurch, New Zealand.[20] Nine athletes tested positive, but no names were released nor punishments dispensed.

With this breakthrough the medical commission added anabolic steroids to the list in April 1975 and commenced its detection in the 1976 Montreal Games. The IOC did not introduce the new technology in the Innsbruck Winter Olympics, because the medical commission felt that summer athletes were more likely to use anabolic steroids than their cold-weather counterparts.[21] The Olympic authorities may have viewed its winter athletes as less inclined to dope; however, anxieties regarding the sex/gender of Eastern bloc female lugers, skiers, and skaters still surfaced.

The 1976 Innsbruck Winter Olympics

In 1970 the IOC selected Denver as the host city for the 1976 Winter Olympics. With the decision the Colorado capital edged out Sion, Switzerland; Tampere, Finland; and Vancouver, Canada. Preparations commenced immediately. Two years after accepting the bid, the Denver populous grew disenchanted with the prospect of hosting the games. Concerns stemmed from the expansion of expenditures asked of the city and state, as well as the projected environmental impact.[22] Led by local politician and later governor Robert "Dick" Lamm, Denver citizens succeeded in securing a referendum regarding the ability of the city and state to provide the necessary finances to the Denver Olympics Organizing Committee (DOOC). On November 9, 1972, voters resoundingly approved an amendment to the Colorado constitution prohibiting the use of further state funds, which forced the DOOC to withdraw its acceptance.

Upon learning of the Colorado referendum, the IOC scrambled to secure a replacement. The executive board sent a circular letter and questionnaire to all NOCs to identify possible candidates. In an effort to keep the Olympics in the United States, the USOC offered Salt Lake City as an alternative. However, the city also proved unable to guarantee the required funds. The USOC next suggested Lake Placid as a potential site. Perhaps annoyed with Denver's abrupt rejection and frustrated with the USOC, the IOC offered the games to Innsbruck, Austria, a small city that had previously hosted the Winter Olympics in 1964.[23]

With less time for planning, combined with the IOC's underlying fear that the Winter Olympics were marred by gigantism, professionalism, and commercialism, the Innsbruck Olympic Organizing Committee (IOOC) deemed the upcoming 1976 Winter Games the "Unpretentious Games." Headed by Karl Heinz Klee, the IOOC was determined to limit its budget to the equivalent of $40 million, approximately one-third of the projected budget for the upcoming Montreal Summer Olympics.[24] Although the IOOC achieved austerity, Cold War entanglements continued to undermine the games.

Nationalism was rampant in the 1976 Winter Olympics. Although it touched nearly every aspect of sport, Cold War biases proved most overt in the figure skating events. According to the Associated Press, the "ugly business of political dealing and bloc voting is still alive and festering."[25] As a result, US and USSR skaters alike cried partiality, claiming they did not get "a fair shake" from the communist bloc and capitalist bloc judges, respectively. From the political standoff US skater Dorothy Hamill emerged as "a fantasy of grace" to win the women's gold, earning unanimous first-place votes from the nine judges.[26] The nineteen-year-old Chicago native embodied the Western ideal of femininity: white, conventionally feminine, and romantically (publicly) involved with Dean Martin Jr. As such, she was idolized as a Western icon of beauty, grace, and appropriate athleticism. For example, before her performance in the free program, a member of the audience held up a sign that read, "Which of the West? Dorothy!" Referring to Cold War politics and playing upon *The Wizard of Oz*, the sign maker was asking which Western athlete would defeat East Germany's Christine Errath for the gold: Hamill.[27] Such positioning of Eastern and Western female athletes as gender foils occurred not only on ice but in other sports as well. Consequently, Western norms continued to underline the sex test in Innsbruck.

Checking Sex in Innsbruck

While social assumptions remained present in the sex check, new protests regarding the control method surfaced. More than one thousand doctors and nurses were on site for the 1976 Games, which included the handful who separated "the Jacques from the Jills."[28] University of Innsbruck Hospital endocrinologist Eva Marberger oversaw the test and examined the chromatin of 241 female Olympians. Gender expectations not only shaped the analysis but also influenced the surrounding discourse. For example, Marberger noted that although it was likely she would identify some cases for further examination, one group would pass without difficulty—the figure skaters. "They are the typical females," she explained.[29] The socially sanctified nature of the sport, along with the gender performances required for the different events, likely led Marberger to this conclusion. It was the winter sports that required greater strength that were believed to lead to problems. Many adopted the fair play rhetoric and argued that women who competed in these more physical events needed protection from masculinized women. "It's a matter of philosophy," contended USOC physician Daniel Hanley. "Men are muscular and stronger. A man with feminine tendencies would not have an advantage. A woman with male tendencies definitely would."[30] Female athletes similarly embraced the biological advantage ideology. Downhill skier Nicole Spiess commented, "If a girl is a boy, it makes a lot of difference . . . but if a boy is a girl it doesn't matter." [31] These statements downplayed female athleticism and upheld a binary notion of sex.

However, not all female Olympians agreed. For the first time since the onset of compulsory testing, some athletes publicly protested the policy. The rise of the women's liberation movement in many Western countries, and its focus on equality, seemed to spark the objections. For example, British figure skater Erika Taylforth opposed the women-only nature of the test and cited women's lib advocate Billie Jean King for support. "Can you imagine what Billie Jean King would do if she came to the Olympics?" she asked. "She would raise quite a fuss," suggesting the sex imbalance of those tested.[32] Similarly, Canadian figure skater Barbara Berezowski argued that if women must undergo the exam, men should too. "Why not?" she reasoned. "Everyone is equal."[33] An anonymous Canadian luge racer also argued for equity, wondering, "If the women must take the sex tests, why not the men?"[34] Though some competitors wanted equivalence, the IOC Medical Commission remained steadfast in its decision to solely check those who participated in women's events.

Therefore, throughout the Innsbruck Olympics, fifty-nine Alpine, fifty-eight Nordic, fifty-four figure skating, forty-four speed skating, and twenty-six luge athletes underwent the buccal smear test. All passed. Curiously, two South Korean athletes opted to forgo the test and still participated in the games. Speed skater Lee Nam-Soon competed in four events, finishing twenty-fifth in the 500-meter, 1,000-meter, and 1,500-meter races, and twenty-fourth in the 3,000-meter race. Figure skater Hyo-Jean Yoon concluded her event in seventeenth place. While the medical commission noted their nonappearances in the final Innsbruck report, the committee did not clarify why the two Olympians declined the exam nor explain how they were able to participate without certification. One possibility is that Lee and Hyo finished competing before the medical commission realized the oversight. The commission repeatedly described difficulties in requiring athletes to undergo testing forty-eight hours prior to the start of their events. As Lee participated in the 1980 Lake Placid Winter Olympics—finishing fourteenth in the 500-meters and twenty-sixth in the 1,000-meters—the absences do not appear to be examples of fraud.[35]

Finally, the conflation of anti-doping controls and sex checks also appeared in Innsbruck. Although each control fell under the authority of the IOC Medical Commission, they maintained different purposes. According to the Innsbruck Olympics *Final Report*, the medical department was divided into three sections—medical care, doping checks, and sex checks—"the functions, localities and staff of which were severely separated."[36] Yet not everyone recognized the separate aims and instead focused on the singular effort to police femininity. Perhaps most notably, several accounts suggested the sex check served to prohibit steroid-enhanced women. For example, the Associated Press incorrectly reported that sex testing assessed women's hormones. The account, which appeared in several international newspapers, noted, "A smear is taken from inside the jaw and if laboratory tests of the smear show a preponderance of male hormones, the competitor is declared ineligible."[37] The belief that sex control caught female dopers became increasingly apparent when the East German women captured international attention in the 1976 Summer Olympics.

The Success of the GDR Sport System

At the close of World War II the Soviet Union helped establish the German Democratic Republic as a socialist state within the eastern zone of occupied Germany. Although the Soviets relinquished control in 1949 to the Socialist Unity Party, headed by Wilhelm Pieck, East Germany remained a satellite territory to the Soviets. As German scholars Werner W. Franke and Brigitte Berendonk explain, "In the 1960s, the GDR was a relatively obscure country with a Cold War image and dominated by the 'Iron Curtain' surrounding it."[38] To absolve this representation, the German Democratic Republic attempted to utilize sport, specifically the Olympics, as a tool to gain international prestige.

East Germany competed as its own Olympic nation for the first time in 1968. Earlier contests required the Eastern and Western divisions of Germany to participate as a single entity. Upon the German Democratic Republic's introduction in Mexico City, the small nation of seventeen million people immediately gained international recognition for earning twenty-five medals. The country's success continued for decades. As Bill Shirley reported in the *Los Angeles Times*, by 1972 "the East Germans even had the Soviet Union and the United States looking nervously over their shoulders as they demonstrated the marvels of socialism by sweeping 66 medals, only 30 less than the superpowers."[39] When contrasted with population, the German Democratic Republic's success was astonishing.

To proactively combat questions of illegal enhancements, the German Democratic Republic invited US journalists and athletes to examine its sport system in advance of the Montreal Games. The visit left many in awe. In an article titled "East Germany's Mighty Sports Machine," Michael Getler described GDR youth sports and commented that the country's success "amounts to an extraordinary phenomenon that extends well beyond the world of sports into the realm of international politics, mass psychology and sociology."[40] Swimmer Donna de Varona also noted the country's "excellent organization." The gold medalist was amazed not only by the national dedication to exercise but also that "women are equal."[41] Unlike in many Western countries, the German Democratic Republic demanded its female athletes undergo training equivalent to the males. Equality also extended into medicinal treatments.

After the fall of the Berlin Wall, researchers recovered a variety of documents that detailed the steroid dosages given to thousands of East German Olympic athletes for almost two decades. In 1966 physicians started to administer Oral-Turinabol, an androgenic-anabolic steroid, to male Olympic

Table 2. Medals Earned in the Summer Olympics and National Populations, 1968–1988

	German Democratic Republic		Russian Soviet Federative Socialist Republic		United States of America	
	Medals	Population	Medals	Population	Medals	Population
1968	25	17,084,000	91	128,000,000	107	200,706,000
1972	66	17,043,000	99	131,437,000	94	209,896,000
1976	90	16,786,000	125	134,690,000	94	218,035,000
1980	126	16,737,000	195	138,291,000	*Did not compete*	
1984	*Did not compete*		*Did not compete*		174	235,825,000
1988	102	16,666,000	132	146,343,000	94	244,499,000

Population rounded to the nearest thousandth. US Department of Commerce, "United States Census Bureau," http://www.census.gov; "Population Statistics: Historical Demography of All Countries," http://www.populstat .info; "Olympic Statistics and History Database Online," http://www.databaseolympics.com.

potentials. This alone was not an atypical practice; steroid use was widespread among athletes in strength-dependent events, including those from the West.[42] However, the German Democratic Republic commenced a state-sponsored program of steroid administration, which incorporated women Olympians in 1968.

By 1974 steroid consumption for GDR athletes was a requirement, not a choice. Many female competitors later reported being forced to ingest "blue pills," with devastating health and psychological ramifications.[43] "They did not care at all about the dangers or the damage," alleged Andreas Krieger, former GDR shot-putter. "We were the guinea pigs in some huge experiment that was undertaken to build the prestige of . . . the communist system," he explained. Krieger, who competed as Heidi and finished first in the 1986 European Championships shot put, listed chronic pain, depression, and severe mood swings as consequences of the state-sponsored androgenic abuse. Furthermore, confusion regarding sexual identity, compounded with the virile effects of steroids, convinced Krieger to undergo sex-reassignment surgery in 1997. "I had no sympathy with my body, it had changed beyond all recognition," he explained. "It was as though they had killed Heidi."[44]

Hundreds of athletes, male and female alike, experienced significant post-career health ailments due to systematic doping, which included breast and testicular cancer, depression, heart disease, and liver tumors. Women also described issues with fertility and reproduction, citing miscarriages and children born with deformities.

The 1976 Montreal Olympics

Cold War disputes also extended into the host city selection process. For the 1976 Summer Games, Los Angeles, Montreal, and Moscow emerged as the top three candidates to secure the bid. Although Moscow ended the first round of voting ahead of the other cities, the lack of a majority required a revote. Upon the removal of Los Angeles as an option, Montreal acquired seventeen additional votes—the exact number previously cast for the US city—to defeat the Soviet Union. The Soviets unhappily interpreted the turn of events as an example of capitalist countries working together to defeat communist nations.[45] According to the Telegraph Agency of the Soviet Union (TASS), the country's official news agency, IOC members failed to expand the Olympic movement and instead voted "from their personal political likes and dislikes."[46] Others similarly suspected that the IOC shied away from having to select one superpower over the other. "They didn't want to get involved in a power struggle between the two blocs," reasoned Los Angeles committee member Warren Dorn.[47] Montreal therefore earned the right, or as some would later venture, the burden, of hosting the 1976 Summer Olympics.

In his speech before the IOC Executive Board, Montreal mayor Jean Drapeau promised austerity and frugality for the twenty-first Olympiad. He estimated that the costs would peak at Can$125 million. However, divisive nationalism and ambitious aspirations marred the planning and preparations, eventually pushing the final price tag closer to two billion. The city was left with tremendous debt. As historian and former Olympian Bruce Kidd explains, the clashes between French-speaking Quebeckers and Canadian liberals polarized the country and delayed the necessary organization. Moreover, it was only in 1973 that the provincial government (reluctantly) guaranteed its financial help, which allowed just three years for facility construction.[48] Drapeau also rescinded his commitment to thrift and instead proceeded grandiosely. According to historian Allen Guttmann, "He planned for the Olympic Games as if he were a Roman emperor rather than an elected official."[49] These compounded issues ensured that the legacy of the Montreal Olympics was to serve as a warning of mismanagement.

Sex Control in Montreal

When compared to the governmental difficulties, the Montreal medical services team was organized with ease. Directed by Carroll A. Laurin, orthopedic surgeon and professor at McGill Medical School, the Montreal Medical Planning Committee met five years before the games to begin organization. In the midst of planning, the group was forced to adjust to changes made to the Olympic Charter. The IOC combined part of Rule 26, the "Eligibility Code," and Rule 29, the "Participation of Women," in 1975. Previously, Rule 26 outlined several requirements for eligibility, including the bounds of amateur status and an anti-doping clause. According to the guideline, all athletes were required to undergo a doping test. Anyone found guilty would be disqualified. Rule 29 listed the sports permissible for women and noted that "female athletes may be subjected to medical proof."[50] Under the new Rule 27 of the 1975 Olympic Charter, the "Medical Code," the IOC outlined four regulations:

A. Doping is forbidden. The IOC will prepare a list of prohibited drugs.
B. All Olympic competitors are liable to medical control and examination, in conformity of the rules of the Medical Commission.

C. Any Olympic competitor refusing to take a doping test or who is found guilty of doping shall be eliminated.

D. Competitors in sports restricted to women must comply with the prescribed tests for femininity.[51]

This combination of sex and doping controls further conflated the purpose of the two policies in the minds of Olympic officials and Olympic audiences.

With the simultaneous introduction of doping controls and sex testing in 1968, the US media had already interpreted the medical commission's implementation of these scientific measures as a means to prohibit masculinized women. The combination of Rule 26 and Rule 29 only exacerbated the confusion. These accounts depicted doping and sex/gender transgression as parallel forms of deviancy, thereby constructing nonconventionally feminine women as both chemically enhanced cheaters and manly frauds. Yet the reports also hinted at the impossibility of locating the exact boundaries of womanhood.

Gendered Interpretations of the Medical Controls

The underlying concern most frequently repeated in the Western discourse was the fear of female masculinization as a signifier of nonheterosexuality. The US reports regularly pointed out the masculinizing effects that female athletes supposedly experienced through the ingestion of steroids. Increased bulk, the development of facial hair, and the deepening of voice were the most highlighted implications. As sociologist Rebecca Ann Lock notes, being accused of looking like a man was a grave insult in the United States. She argues, "What these kinds of insults reveal is that femininity is aligned with heterosexual attractiveness and one is read as ugly when one's muscularity is close to that of a man's."[52] The assumption also suggests that sexuality can be read on the body.

To combat the perceived transgressions of female dopers, the US media described the Eastern European athletes with disdain and highlighted the heterosexuality of the American competitors. As previously noted, the 1976 East German women's swim team received the most derision. For example, Rod Strachan, described by the *Chicago Tribune* as "a handsome University of Southern California swimmer," commented that the German Democratic Republic swimmers did not look feminine. "They're quite a bit bigger than most of the men on the American team," he said. "They could go out for football at [the University of South California]. They've got some big guys there."[53] The US public also read the squad's unparalleled and seemingly in-

The 1972 Olympic 4 x 100-meter medley relay silver medalists. Left to right: Renate Vogel, Christine Herbst, Kornelia Ender, and Roswitha Beier. Courtesy of the German Federal Archives, German News Service.

stantaneous successes with doubt. Shirley reported that "the explosive power of the teenagers, as well as their uncommonly rapid improvement, has made some people suspicious."

The competitors' appearance was the central cause of concern. As Shirley explained, "The girls' size—reportedly they average two inches taller than their opponents—also has caused talk and at least one official complaint."[54] This reference to the Olympians' sizes parallels Lock's interpretation of compulsory heterosexuality. She argues that popular media interpret size in terms of muscles. "In these instances," Lock explains, "the accused or tested dopers are insulted because of their muscularity."[55] Furthermore, rapid growth seemed to be an issue only for the GDR female competitors. When Australian swim star Shane Gould grew five inches in a short period of time, she experienced no similar condemnation. The US doping discourse during the Cold War aligned Western femininity with attractiveness.

Some reports also noted that athletically spurred masculinization hindered heterosexual social relationships. Neil Amdur of the *Chicago Tribune* pointed out that many US women refused to adopt serious weight-training methods, because "the effects of seeing themselves with broader shoulders would create further complications in a social life already inhibited by rigid practice schedules."[56] Such accounts envisioned heterosexuality as a marker of femininity. These assertions not only privileged Western sex/gender norms but further reasserted sexuality as binary and heterosexuality as natural.

As anxieties over sex incongruities and drug use consumed the public imagination, many turned to the medical commission for guidance. For example, *Chicago Tribune* writer Jack Scott suggested doping was a widespread occurrence. While he described the use of doping in weight lifting and throwing events (discus, javelin, and shot put), Scott did so without judgment and did not criticize male dopers. However, of female competitors he reported that "the most serious and dangerous use of drugs by females is the taking of male hormones." Fortunately, though, according to the report, the "new infamous sex test" was designed to detect the practice.[57] Scott fused together the purposes of the dual measures and interpreted sex testing and doping controls as a single method to detect unnatural female Olympians. In the same vein, journalist Kathleen Burns explained, "At the Olympics, women are required to take the sex test to see if male hormones are present in their systems."[58]

Misunderstandings also stemmed from Olympic sources. As recorded in the *New York Times*, Olympic reports suggested that the sex test worked to discourage female athletes from ingesting steroids. Accordingly, the reason the former Olympians from the Soviet Union and Rumania retired unannounced was out of fear that they "would not have passed because they had been taking male hormones."[59] The reports were not only inaccurate, but they also hinted at the underlying significance of nationalism.

Nationalism in the 1976 Olympics

Sportswriters, concerned with the medal count and troubled by muscular women, masked their nationalism through calls for fair play. Accounts criticized the science of the Eastern bloc and its powerful female Olympians. Accustomed to the US team securing a majority of Olympic medals, journalists were shocked when countries from Eastern Europe challenged its gold medal stranglehold. For example, when the Soviet Union sprinter Valeriy Borzov earned the title "the world's fastest human," the US press was appalled. In response to the accomplishment, *Los Angeles Times* columnist Jim Murray bewilderedly asked, "I mean, can you believe Volga Boatman winning a sprint?"[60] He further noted, "Russians are supposed to win things where you grunt a lot, or get a hernia. Or where you time them with a sun dial." His nationalistic sentiments surfaced when he posited that "they gave Borzov the standard doping test but that ain't about to satisfy me. I want to check him for wires and valves and reset buttons. . . . This guy wasn't born, he was programmed."[61] Murray's postulation illustrates the nexus of nationalism and doping in Olympic history. To combat the Soviet and East German challenges, Americans condemned the Eastern Europeans as analytical, machine-like, and stoic. US sports reporters saved the most severe criticisms for the Eastern European women.

The West cited foul play and condemned the Eastern bloc countries for utilizing illegal substances. Without self-inspection the reports criticized the Eastern Europeans for pushing the limits of human performance and risking the athletes' health for the sake of gold medals. In this line of thought the Eastern European countries were guilty, not the United States. Therefore, increased policing was necessary. While nationalism underlined almost the entirety of the US discourse, two pieces from Murray provide the most striking examples. Veiled in humor, yet seeped in nationalism, he derided the Eastern European countries and painted its women as masculinized, fraudulent cheaters.

The first piece described the contents of a hypothetical time capsule from the next century. Titled "100 Years from Now," the article predicted the status of the sporting world in the year 2076. First Murray posited that in the 2076 Olympic Games, the planet Krypton angrily boycotted the 46th Olympiad because the planet Telegony was permitted to enter under the name of Greater Uranus—a satire of the political boycotts that plagued the Olympics during the Cold War. He then speculated about the continued importance of the sex tests and anti-doping controls in the Games. According to the time capsule, the East German housewife "Lotta Bulk" won the unisex shot put with a throw of 287 feet. Murray explained that "the 900 pound East German is the first to throw the 16-pound shot overhand." Couched in humor, Murray's column illustrates the nationalistic interpretation of the Eastern European women. He ended the piece by suggesting that his hyperboles were actually rooted in truth: "If any or all of these things are true, nothing has changed."[62]

The second piece similarly used nationalistic satire to demean the women from the Eastern bloc. Titled "The New Order comes to the Vorld [sic] of Sports," the article described a hypothetical interview with the fictitious head of the German sports medicine ministry. Speaking in broken English, the fabricated doctor described his chemical experiments. The article played upon the robotic stereotype of the Eastern European competitors and pointed to the inauthenticity of their bodies and performances. With regard to female competitors, the GDR doctor explained that he could successfully enlist King Kong in the women's division. He suggested, "My poy, ve could get King Kong certified for de girls' figure skating or der female half of der gold dances! Nothing is impossible for German engineering! All ve need is a few parts from

Krupp und a Punsen purner!"[63] These two articles represent the sentiment that appeared within the United States. Nationalistic undertones discredited the Eastern European women's femininity and sexuality, and helped US sport authorities call for increased controls under the guise of fair play.

Ridiculing the Eastern European women was not solely a US venture. Similar accounts surfaced throughout the West. For example, writing from Fiesole-Firenze, Italy, Leo Campagnano asked, "As far as women athletes a question is in order. Are they really women[,] these Russian and East German athletes who have no esthetical marks of women, who walk like men, and have a decided masculine face? It is true they are wonderful performers, but are they women? Or are they a third sex?"[64] Campagnano's questions highlight the importance of gendered appearances in the determination of sex. The discourse surrounding the 1976 Montreal Olympics vilified the Eastern European women who did not abide by conventional Western notions of femininity.

The "Nymphet Syndrome": Olga Korbut and Nadia Comăneci

Not all Eastern European Olympians received such harsh criticisms from abroad. Those who exhibited femininity, as prescribed by the West, often earned praise for their gender-appropriate athleticism. Perhaps most notably, gymnasts Olga Korbut and Nadia Comăneci gained worldwide admiration for their circus-like feats and elfin-like appearances. Before the 1972 Munich Olympics, gymnastics was largely considered a male activity. However, Korbut, Comăneci, and their teenage contemporaries not only feminized the sport in the 1970s but also altered the judging criteria. In the wake of the "sprites'" performances—which dramatically increased the sport's popularity—judges started to award more points to the high-risk routines best suited to prepubescent, flexible, and lightweight bodies.[65] In other words, to succeed in gymnastics, one had to be petite and powerful. Gymnastics was a women's sport executed almost entirely by girlish athletes, which allowed the West to embrace the Eastern European "pixies." Unlike the bulky East German swimmers, the gymnasts fit comfortably within society's gender norms.

Korbut became an internationally recognized superstar in the 1972 Summer Olympics. The seventeen-year-old "sprite . . . from a Disney movie" earned three gold medals, one silver, and "the hearts of millions of TV viewers."[66] With her "ponytails flapping like flags" and body "bending like a pretzel," she finished first in the balance beam, floor exercise, and team competition and second on the uneven bars.[67] While all her performances proved unprecedented and dynamic, it was on the uneven bars where Korbut gained the most recognition. During this event she debuted the "Korbut Flip," a difficult act that entailed completing a back flip from the high bar before re-grasping the lower bar. Many in the West positively contrasted Korbut's pigtailed, girlish countenance against her impressive strength and dangerous feats. For example, the *Los Angeles Times* depicted her as a "tiny Russian doll with an impish smile," then described how her flip stole "the spotlight from a bevy of taller and more conventionally graceful performers." Similarly, according to the London *Times*, "For many Britons the brightest flowering of the Olympic spirit was the petite Russian gymnast." Perhaps in the most succinct fashion, the *New York Times* labeled Korbut an "84-pound powerhouse."[68] Korbut's girlish yet powerful physique assisted her rise to fame; however, four years later she lost her throne to a fourteen-year-old Rumanian gymnast.

Comăneci usurped Korbut as the "queen of the Olympic gymnasts" in the 1976 Montreal Games.[69] The 5-foot-tall, 86-pound "elf in a ponytail" earned three gold medals and one silver, which included an unprecedented perfect 10.0 on the uneven bars. She continued to amaze with an additional six perfect scores. Similar to the descriptions of Korbut, many in the West simultaneously discussed Comăneci's petite size and her physical prowess. Murray first described her as a "tiny, big-eyed Romanian schoolgirl," then noted she performed like "Peter Pan on a balance beam, Tinker Bell on a wire, a marionette to delight all ages, part Shirley Temple, part Dresden doll."[70] Such comparisons to a Dresden doll, a delicate porcelain figurine, regularly appeared in the popular media. This likening highlighted Comăneci's fragile appearance, thereby tempering her impressive strength.

The 1970s "nymphet syndrome" granted the gymnasts power, albeit in a controlled, socially approvable fashion. As US journalist Janice Kaplan adeptly noted, "We like our female athletes in huggable packages. When they are cute, they are not threatening."[71] The childlike appearances of the gymnasts reassured the public of women's appropriate place in sport. Unlike the disdain awarded to the Soviet throwers and the East German swimmers, the West was enamored by the "little dolls with pigtails."[72]

* * *

Although most of the US media condemned the German Democratic Republic, demands for Olympic victories remained prevalent. Shortly after the Montreal Games the USOC approved the formation of a medical panel to study the application of scientific advances to athletics. Headed by Dr. Irving Dardik, the committee was to look into areas considered "taboo."

The United States never adopted a doping program to the same degree as the GDR; however, as Hunt explains, the regimen implemented in East Germany "was the sort of attitude that characterized the connections within the Olympic movement between nationalist forces and the increasing popularity of performance-enhancing drugs."[73] In other words, nationalism spurred doping violations in several countries. Thus one could argue that it was the GDR's requirement of female doping that alarmed many in the West.

The successes of Kornelia Ender and the East German women fostered doubts about the authenticity of their performances. As they secured more and more medals, the conflation of sex testing and anti-doping measures increased. Even with the two controls in place, many people continued to complain about a loss of fairness in sport, frequently pointing to the Eastern Europeans' muscular physiques. The GDR female athletes' muscles and size were repeated targets for criticism. Yet not all Eastern competitors experienced disapproval. Korbut and Comăneci delighted Western audiences with their pigtails, flips, and twirls. The two executed incredible athletic feats while remaining girlishly feminine. Their international acceptance, which occurred concurrent to Ender's lambasting, suggests that appearance, not performance, was the root of the sex/gender anxieties.

The simultaneous condemnation and infantilization of the Eastern bloc athletes occurred at a time when Cold War anxieties were somewhat lessened. Through the 1970s the Soviet Union and the United States curbed hostilities in détente, greatly reducing ideological and propagandist conflicts. Yet after this brief glimmer of mollification, the 1980s saw a dramatic resurgence in international dissension. Against a backdrop of heightened nationalistic embroilments, the 1980 and 1984 Olympic Games emerged as even more significant political forums.

5 The US vs. USSR

Gender Testing, Doping Checks, and Olympic Boycotts

IN 1973 MEMBERS OF THE US track team traveled to Minsk, in the Soviet Union, to square off against the USSR national squad. The two countries had started an annual series in 1958 as a means to promote athletics and encourage friendly rivalry. As Cold War tensions heightened, the USA-USSR dual meets gained increasing political significance and evolved into a forum for both diplomacy and propaganda. For example, the Soviet Union boycotted the 1966 matchup in protest of the US entanglement in Vietnam. The United States returned the favor and skipped the 1980 track meet in response to the USSR's involvement in Afghanistan. Furthermore, the international competitions also highlighted the physical prowess of the two superpowers, which each nation interpreted as corollary to their overall global influence. Prior to the 1973 Minsk meet the Soviet Union had outscored the United States in seven of the ten contests; the Soviet women bolstered these victories by regularly trouncing the US women.[1] With such repeated and notable losses, the United States turned to individual athletes and singular accomplishments to demonstrate its superiority.

Consequently, fourteen-year-old Mary Decker emerged as an overnight sensation. Too young to compete in Munich, she garnered attention in Minsk for winning the 800-meter race, finishing ahead of USSR runner Nijolė Sabaitė, the event's 1972 Olympic silver medalist. Although the Soviet Union handily defeated the United States, 216–163, the American public celebrated the surprising victory of its newly discovered 86-pound phenom. US reporters contrasted her youth, slight stature, and pigtails against the power, muscles, and strength of the Soviet athletes. Jill Gerston of the *New York Times* explained that Decker gained worldwide admiration when the "pig-tailed sprite spurted the last five yards to beat the bigger and more experienced Russian women." Dave Distel of the *Los Angeles Times* similarly suggested that her "story is something for Disney writers."[2] Significantly, the teenage runner routed the more muscular Soviets while upholding Western gender norms. Decker continued to impress, setting six world records in 1982.

Synchronous to Decker's rise in athletics, Cold War animosities elevated. In 1979 a group of Iranian students overran the US embassy in Tehran and held fifty-two Americans hostage for 444 days. The Soviet Union entered Afghanistan one month later to bolster Afghans' unstable communist government. As a result, all US-USSR sporting contests in the 1980s shouldered political meaning. Before the 1980 Lake Placid Winter Olympics, the United States declared a boycott of the 1980 Moscow Summer Games. Shortly thereafter the Soviet Union announced its decision to forgo the 1984 Los Angeles Games. With the embargoes, the interceding Sarajevo Olympics gained importance as the only games in which both the United States and Soviet Union competed for eight years. Through athletic contests and strategic boycotts, the Olympics again served as a nonmilitary forum for the two superpowers to exert international dominance and demonstrate political views.

Against this backdrop of political impasse, Decker embodied and espoused nationalistic femininity. Her athletic successes, girlish appearance, and vocal condemnations of Eastern European runners seemed to prove that women could excel in track and field without succumbing to masculinization. As the *Los Angeles Times* explained, Decker was "America's big chance to prove that you don't have to look like a piano mover or nightclub bouncer to win a women's running event at the international level." With a return of international anxieties, many in the West embraced the belief that "'Little' Mary Decker . . . repulsed the Red Menace."[3] As illustrated in Decker's career, politics touched all corners of the Olympics, including in the interpretation of gender tests.

"Fem Cards": The Certification of Femininity

To help guarantee womanhood, the IOC used a certification process. Some governing bodies had previously required documentation to help validate the sex/gender of their women competitors. In 1946 the IAAF requested female track and field athletes show a medical certificate, signed by a "qualified medical doctor," prior to participation. The IOC embraced a similar policy in 1948. Yet, with the start of compulsory on-site testing, the requisites for certification altered. In 1966 the IAAF implemented a physical examination for all female athletes in area games or continental championships, after which those who "passed" received an official IAAF certificate. Two years later in Grenoble, the IOC also provided "identity cards" to female Olympians who had "no abnormality" present in the chromatin check.[4]

As sex testing expanded into other sports, the IOC Medical Commission questioned the acceptability of using the international federations' documentation systems. Some members of the commission believed that anyone who possessed an authorized certificate should be allowed to skip the Olympic exam. Others feared that passing the screening to the international federations in non-Olympic events created opportunities for fraud. For example, Giuseppe la Cava argued that unethical competitors could easily obtain the necessary documents from disorganized committees. Eduardo Hay momentarily solved the problem by ensuring that the Mexico City laboratory had the ability to test a large number of women. Therefore, all female competitors underwent the test in 1968 and received femininity certificates—dubbed "fem cards" by athletes—valid for future Olympic competition.[5]

Despite Hay's efforts to diminish opportunities for fraud, worries about the certification process surfaced in 1972. Many international federations incorrectly assumed that if they enacted a control in an area, continental, or world championship, participants would be allowed to forgo the test. Adding to this misperception, a complete list of acceptable certificates or documented competitors did not exist.[6] The South Korean volleyball team's protest cast further doubt on the certification process. Although the medical commission dismissed the ROK's assertion that the DPRK's squad included a male participant, the complaint did convince the committee that the photographs glued to the IOC's identity cards were too easily replaceable. The commission consequently refused fem cards to all Munich volleyball players and added height, weight, and a signature to all other certificates.[7] Even with these additions, however, problems continued.

For the 1976 Montreal Olympics, the medical commission decided to accept femininity certificates granted by the IOC as well as those provided by international federations during continental championships, continental games, and world championships.[8] However, the group adjusted its criteria during the games in two significant ways. First, the commission disallowed documents authorized by the International Basketball Federation (FIBA). FIBA's credentials did not explicitly reference the control, which rendered them invalid. To cover participants in future competitions, the medical commission directed FIBA to add the phrase "the athlete has passed the femininity test" to the papers.[9] Second, the committee rejected the documents provided during the 1973 European Cup semifinal events due to an organizational oversight. The IAAF had not required the winners to produce their

Miss/Mrs .... PATINO
Mlle/Mme

First name(s)/Prénom(s) Maria José Martínez

of/de .... Spain .... (Country/Pays)

born/née .... (date)

On the occasion of the
A l'occasion des

... World Championships
(Games or Championships/Jeux ou Championnats)

held at/tenus à Helsinki on/le .. 1983 ....

the above mentioned athlete underwent an approved medical test, the result of which was sex-chromatin positive. This satisfies the I.A.A.F. requirements for competition in Women's athletic events.

L'athlète mentionnée ci-dessus a subi un examen médical approuvé, et la chromatine sexuelle s'est révélée positive. Ceci répond aux règlements de la F.I.A.A. pour concourir aux épreuves féminines.

CERTIFICATE No. 5341

I hereby confirm that this Certificate is issued in accordance with the report of the official Medical Panel of the within-mentioned Games/Championships.

Je confirme par la présente que ce certificat est délivré conformément au rapport du Comité médical officiel des Jeux/Championnats mentionnés ci-contre.

Athlete's signature/Signature de l'athlète

General Secretary, I.A.A.F.
Secrétaire/Général, F.I.A.A.

María José Martínez Patiño's "Femininity Certificate," granted in 1983.
Courtesy of María José Martínez Patiño, University of Vigo, Spain.

identification cards upon receiving medals; although women were ineligible without certification, the medical commission claimed that deception could have occurred.[10]

After the Montreal Olympics the IAAF protested the IOC's control of certification. In particular, the track and field organization disliked the medical commission's refusal to accept the European Cup fem cards. IAAF president Adriaan Paulen argued that the commission's denial served "to negate completely the considerable work" of the federation.[11] Lord Killanin agreed. He contended that such redundancy wasted money, which was a significant concern for the 1980 Olympic organizing committees.[12] With prodding from Killanin, the medical commission asked the international federations for a list of competitions during which female participants received femininity certificates. Of those that responded, seven required femininity control only during Olympic competition: the International Canoe Federation, International Federation of Gymnastics, International Fencing Federation, International Hockey Federation (field hockey), International Rowing Federation,

Nancy Hogshead with her uncle at the 1984 Los Angeles Olympics. Her gender verification card (left) is almost as big as her Olympic credentials. Courtesy of Nancy Hogshead-Makar.

International Skating Union, and International Swimming Federation. In contrast, the FIBA, FIVB, IAAF, International Handball Federation, and International Luge Federation conducted their own testing outside the games.[13] With this information, the medical commission reluctantly agreed in 1979 that all femininity certificates granted by an international federation during a world championship would be accepted in Lake Placid and Moscow.[14]

The 1980 Lake Placid Winter Olympics

As the medical commission weighed the advantages and disadvantages of accepting non-Olympic femininity certificates, the IOC Executive Board faced a Cold War quandary. Only the United States put forward a bid for the 1980 Winter Olympics. The Canadian cities of Vancouver and Garibaldi had originally demonstrated interest in jointly hosting the games; however, the financial concerns highlighted by the 1976 Summer Olympics convinced the two to abandon the effort. The Montreal Games cost an unprecedented amount, nearly bankrupted the city, and took thirty years to pay off. When the Vancouver-Garibaldi committee officially withdrew its bid in 1974, Lake Placid remained as the lone candidate. In an anticlimactic announcement, the IOC selected the US city as the location of the 1980 Winter Games.

With a population of twenty-seven hundred year-round residents, one hundred less than in 1932, Lake Placid became the smallest city to ever host the Winter Olympics. According to organizer J. Bernard Fell, the greatest challenge for the city was to prove the "Lake Placid claim . . . that small dedicated communities with appropriate winter sites can still play host to the world's athletes."[15] Unfortunately, without the assurance of local, state, or federal governmental funding, the Lake Placid Olympics Organizing Committee (LPOOC) faced substantial financial difficulties. The city's standing infrastructures required several improvements as well as the addition of new facilities—a large concern for a small community.[16] By 1979 the price tag for the 1980 Olympics had exceeded $200 million, six times the original estimate.

Aware of Montreal's staggering debt, the US government initially refused financial assistance for the Olympics, thereby casting doubt on the capabilities of the LPOOC. Fearful of another last-minute withdrawal from a US host city, Olympic officials asked Innsbruck to serve as a substitute should the LPOOC falter.[17] The US Congress eventually voted to provide support when the organizing committee threatened to terminate its bid. To ensure the LPOOC's success, the government reluctantly agreed to supply $47 million for sport facilities; $22 million for athletes' housing, which was later converted into a federal detention center after the games; and $12 million for security. Even with this aid, the LPOOC amassed almost $6 million of debt. The medical controls required by the IOC increased this encumbrance. President Killanin recognized that "there was no doubt that the programme was expensive"; however, he continued to emphasize its necessity.[18]

From Sex Control to Femininity Test

The LPOOC was not alone in its dismay of the ever-increasing expenses associated with hosting the games. Moscow's Organizing Committee (OCOG-80) also feared the exorbitant price tag. In one of the rare instances of US-USSR camaraderie during the Cold War, the two cities pointed to the expansion of medical controls as a significant burden and requested financial assistance. The LPOOC "is *most concerned* with the truly astronomical cost of providing the drug testing program," Fell explained. "This concern is shared equally by the representatives of the [OCOG-80]." According to the LPOOC's estimations, doping tests cost approximately $800 per athlete, which totaled roughly $1 million. With such a high-priced budget, Fell reasoned, "It seems both reasonable and equitable to request that the IOC, the party requiring . . . the drug testing program for the Olympics, assume the responsibility for payment of the cost of providing such program."[19] OCOG-80 president Ignati Novikov agreed. He asked the IOC to allocate $1.5 million to the committee for medical equipment. Killanin denied both requests.[20] In compromise, the medical commission agreed to reduce the number of doping controls required and increase the number of medical certificates accepted. The LPOOC therefore tested only the first four competitors in each event, plus one selected randomly, for illegal substances and accepted fem cards from the international federations.[21]

The LPOOC spent $975,000 to curb drug use and $9,250 to detect any sex/gender abnormalities.[22] Following the guidelines outlined in Rule 27, the committee tested for anabolic steroids, central nervous system stimulators, painkilling narcotics, psychomotor stimulants, and sympathomimetic amines and checked 1,155 women for chromatin abnormalities. The medical commission also approved the medical certificates of 160 female athletes, allowing them to skip the exam.[23] Despite the attempts to alleviate costs, USOC physician Daniel Hanley publicly argued that doping controls and sex testing procedures were complicated, expensive, and unnecessary. For, when completed on women, the results "are the same as what any nearsighted college boy could have told you with a glance across the street."[24] In his estimation, outward appearances could verify sex, rendering both tests moot.

Others agreed. Perhaps most noticeably, the LPOOC medical services team changed "sex control" to "femininity test" to better identify the objective. The press also displayed unease over unfeminine winter athletes. For example, as *Washington Post* reporter Ken Denlinger explained, the Lake Placid medical tests served to ensure appropriate participation. First, he noted, women passed through "Femininity Control," whereby female competitors underwent "an uncomplicated sex test." Denlinger reasoned that such a process was necessary to determine what "one assumed was obvious," again referencing outward appearance and physique. Furthermore Dan Perl, pathology professor and director of the cytogenetic lab used during the games, argued that femininity control was "for their own protection."[25] Many conceded that the IOC's regulations were necessary to preserve femininity and ensure a level playing field.

Political Entanglements in the
1980 Lake Placid Winter Olympics

Not only did Cold War mandates of femininity impact the Lake Placid Olympics, but the 1980 Winter Games also occurred against a backdrop of increasingly volatile international relations. The 1979 Soviet invasion of Afghanistan and the country's refusal to remove its troops troubled the United States. From the US vantage, the incursion served as a violent resurgence of communist intent. The Soviet Union viewed its actions as those of a stronger country assisting a faltering neighbor under its sphere of influence.[26] Despite the differing perceptions, both countries utilized the Olympics as a tool to acquire foreign support and invalidate the other nation.

In the wake of the 1979 Afghanistan controversy, US president Jimmy Carter sought to improve his public persona. Facing reelection, he feared that the country's confidence in his leadership was diminished due to the enduring Iranian hostage crisis, the Soviet's demonstration of military hostility, and domestic stagflation.[27] Therefore, on January 20, 1980, mere weeks before the scheduled commencement of the Lake Placid Games, Carter articulated an ultimatum for the Soviet Union: remove troops from Afghanistan within one month or the United States would lead a boycott of the 1980 Moscow Summer Olympics. The US president reasoned, "Aggression destroys the international amity and goodwill that the Olympic movement attempts to foster. If our response to aggression is to continue with international sports as usual in the capital of the aggressor, our other steps to deter aggression are undermined." Carter later reflected, "I did not want to damage the Olympic movement, but at the same time it seemed unconscionable to be guests of the Soviets while they were involved in a bloody suppression of the people of Afghanistan."[28] Upon reviewing the president's declaration, the House of Representatives endorsed the boycott the following day. The Senate provided the necessary approval one week later. Carter's congressionally supported ultimatum—which was not championed by the USOC, at least initially—heightened international tensions during the Lake Placid festivities.

To garner support for the United States' position, Secretary of State Cyrus Vance gave a speech to the IOC two days before the Lake Placid Opening Ceremonies. He described the underlying purpose of the Olympic movement, pointing out that the IOC strove to foster international accord through sport. According to Vance, the question before the Olympic officials was "whether the Games should be held in a country which is itself committing a serious breach of international peace." Vance posited that to do so would be "wholly inconsistent with the meaning of the Olympics." He therefore suggested that the IOC transfer the Summer Games to a different location or postpone the event. If those options proved impossible, he noted, the IOC had canceled the Olympics in the past. "By upholding the principles of the Olympics when they are under challenge," Vance reasoned, "we will preserve the meaning of the Olympics for years to come."[29] His speech was met with irritated silence. IOC president Killanin later recalled, "I had the feeling as these words came down from the rostrum that there were a lot of white knuckles gripping the arms of chairs to conceal anger."[30] All seventy-three IOC members voted to reject Vance's proposals.

Tensions between the two superpowers thereby increased during the 1980 Winter Olympics. Any event that pitted the United States against the Soviet Union was engulfed by political and ideological beliefs—from the US perspective, none more so than the hockey semifinal match. On February 22, the US men's hockey team, comprised of young, collegiate amateurs, beat the highly ranked Soviets, 4–3. Earlier the Soviet Union had defeated a National Hockey League all-star team, 6–0, and the US Olympic team, 10–3, in exhibition matches. The team had also outscored its Olympic opponents, 51–11. Dubbed the "Miracle on Ice"—a reference to commentator Al Michaels's famed question, "Do you believe in miracles?"—the surprising victory revitalized the United States and provided the country with a brief moment of nationalistic pride. The triumph also weakened domestic support for the president's proposed boycott.[31] As Carter recalled, "I was hoping this victory and the gold medal were an omen of better days ahead. But that was not to be."[32]

Despite his hope for better days, the US president maintained the ultimatum. When the Soviet Union did not remove its troops by the end of February, Carter reiterated his plan to boycott the Moscow Games. Technically, neither the White House nor Congress held direct power over the USOC. A privately funded organization, the USOC maintained the right to send US athletes abroad for participation in Olympic events, without governmental approval. Therefore, as historian Allen Guttmann explains, "Since he had no *legal* right to command the USOC to comply with his wishes, the president resorted to threats and intimidation."[33] Carter foreshadowed an end to all financial support and a possible increase of taxes should the officials opt to authorize US representation in Moscow. On April 12, 1980, the USOC voted to boycott the Summer Olympics, by a margin of two to one.

After receiving the (reluctant) approval of the USOC, President Carter sought to expand the boycott. The British Parliament and Prime Minister Margaret Thatcher agreed to reject Moscow's invitation; however, the British Olympic Committee defied its government and voted to send athletes to the Summer Games. By the opening ceremonies eighty other nations opted to compete and sixty-two boycotted. Among those that refused participation were Western allies Canada, Israel, and West Germany. Although only 5,929 athletes participated, far fewer than in the previous three Olympics, the US-led boycott was largely deemed a political failure.

The 1980 Moscow Summer Olympics

Cold War tensions increased when the Soviet Union won the bid for the 1980 Summer Games. The possibility of a communist city holding the Olympics had surfaced long before Carter announced his ultimatum. In 1970 the Soviet Union put forward a proposal to serve as host of the 1976 Summer Olympics. The IOC sidestepped an overt Cold War entanglement by selecting Montreal over Los Angeles and Moscow. The latter two reintroduced bids for the 1980 Summer Olympics but served as the only candidates, seemingly forcing the IOC into a Cold War conundrum. However, the lateness of the Los Angeles bid—which surfaced only in response to Moscow's initial position as the lone candidate and therefore required an extended deadline—along with the IOC's desire to appear apolitical, ensured a Soviet victory.[34] The Soviet capital edged out the US city, 39–20. With the nineteen-vote advantage, the games moved behind the Iron Curtain.

From the perspective of the West, sport in Eastern Europe continued to encourage inappropriate gender norms. In particular, many people feared that Soviet women too willingly embraced masculine characteristics, either through intense physical training or the consumption of anabolic steroids. The USSR sport structure may have initially started under dissimilar circumstances than those in the West; however, by the height of the Cold War, the Eastern and Western systems mirrored each other more than they differed. Nevertheless, sex/gender anxieties allowed Western officials and journalists to draw distinctions between Eastern and Western female athletes, which in turn encouraged the IOC to continue testing.

Women's Sport in the Soviet Union

Prior to World War II the Soviet Union promoted gender equality as a significant component of its communist regime. The state-controlled utilitarian system advocated sport participation for all citizens, men and women alike, as a tool to improve both individual health and collective military force. Specifically, the Soviet Union encouraged women's participation in sport in order to foster greater worker productivity, ensure military preparedness, and promote new "ideologically correct" forms of physical activity.[35] When contrasted against the West, Soviet women in the 1920s and 1930s experienced much greater support for full athletic participation. As historian Kateryna Kobchenko explains, "The concept of sports specifically for women was almost redundant because almost all sports, except for boxing and wrestling, were considered to be suitable for women." Indeed USSR female athletes demonstrated substantial physical prowess and more muscular physiques than their Western counterparts. Purposefully established as dissimilar from the "bourgeois ladies" of the West, Soviet norms of femininity celebrated "masculine" traits in women.[36]

However, ambivalence trickled into the nation following the war. As a result, Soviet gender affinities started to align more closely with those of the West. When Leonid Brezhnev assumed power from Khrushchev as general secretary in 1964, he initiated several reforms, one of which provided substantial financial support to athletic organizations and fostered the Soviet Union's dominance in the Olympics. Women's sport faced contradictory ideologies as the general secretary simultaneously promoted and discouraged female participation.[37] For example, Brezhnev highlighted certain sporting achievements, specifically those earned in gymnastics, while concurrently banning other physical activities. Most notably, in 1973 the USSR Sports Committee, a state-run sport organization, outlined a resolution that impeded women from competing in events that enticed male voyeurs or harmed female reproductive organs. Notions of femininity thus changed. During the Brezhnev era, *zhenstvennost* signified a supposed athletic inner beauty possessed by female athletes, comprised of compassion, grace, and motherhood.[38]

Although the Soviet press showcased *zhenstvennost* as the preferred form of womanhood, this celebration of femininity did not exactly mirror that of the West. In an assessment of Cold War media accounts, scholar Stefan Wiederkehr found numerous similarities between the East and West. For example, all outlets underreported women's sporting experiences and also implemented linguistic devices that downplayed female achievements. However, one significant difference stemmed from the treatment of "nonfeminine" women. In the Western presses, reporters contrasted "ugly" women of the Eastern bloc against the conventionally feminine, "pretty" women of the West. Journalists from the East ignored all incidences of nontraditionally feminine women.[39] The continued reporting of "ugly" female athletes in the West likely supported the medical commission's efforts to bolster its femininity testing and doping controls in Moscow.

Moscow's Femininity Test

To comply with the sex and gender mandates of the IOC, the OCOG-80 established a medical services team. Comprised of eighteen doctors and sport specialists, the group was placed in charge of both femininity control and doping checks. The laboratory for the femininity tests was housed in the doping control center, which further conflated the purpose of the different exams. The OCOG-80 Medical Services examined 995 competitors and recognized 200 femininity certificates.[40] Although the IOC Medical Commission did not publicize the number of failures, rumors of seven disqualifications surfaced.

Speaking without the permission of the IOC, Ludwig Prokop informed the London *Times* of the supposed sex test failures. He reported that "some women athletes from third world nations did not have the right set of chromosomes required to be counted as women." Furthermore, Prokop noted that the disqualified Olympians were likely unaware of their chromosomal constitution, because the IOC used "sophisticated methods not available to developing nations."[41] This account highlights the Western orientation of sex control. The committee attempted to draw a line not only between men and women but also between Olympians from "developed" and "developing" countries. If Prokop's count was true, the femininity test likely barred less affluent women of color.

Alexandre de Mérode promptly denied Prokop's report, saying, "The story is crazy and completely untrue."[42] He also sent a telegram to Prokop asking him to recant his account. "IOC medical commission members are not allowed to make any other statement," de Mérode reminded Prokop. "I am sure it must be [a] mistake of [the] journalist trying to find bad publicity. Will you confirm it to this journalist?" Prokop responded that it was indeed a case of miscommunication.[43] However, in a later account Hay admitted that the OCOG-80 Medical Services team uncovered three inconclusive cases in Moscow. Of the three, two athletes did not pass further examination and were subsequently barred from competition.[44]

The "Unfortunate Case" of Stella Walsh

The death of a former Olympic athlete gave the IOC Medical Commission unexpected support for its continuation of femininity control. Stella Walsh, the winner of the 100-meter race in 1932, was active in track and field for most of her life, competing in various national, international, open, and senior competitions. At one point in her long and illustrious career, she held forty-one national records and twenty world titles. Walsh eventually retired from athletics and remained in Cleveland where she was a beloved member of the community. As an example of the city's reverence for her sport accomplishments and civic involvement, Cleveland mayor Carl B. Stokes officially christened April 13, 1970, "Stella Walsh Day." She was also enshrined in seven different halls of fame and named one of the state's "My Favorite Ohioans," alongside astronaut Neil Armstrong, Senator John Glenn, comedian Bob Hope, and the first-in-flight Wright brothers.[45] But Walsh's sudden death caused a furor and encouraged some to question the legitimacy of her accolades.

On December 5, 1980, Walsh was killed in a convenience store parking lot. When two men attempted to steal her purse, she refused to acquiesce and was fatally shot in the chest. Upon learning of the homicide, Clevelanders grieved and established a memorial for their "Polish Flyer." Days after the homicide—and before Walsh's burial—two local television stations aired segments that questioned the track star's sex. WKYC-TV Channel 3 and WEWS Channel 5 both claimed that a physical inspection conducted by the coroner showed the runner had abnormal genitalia. Many local citizens were outraged by the scandalous reports. "I am saddened by Ms. Walsh's death and find it contemptable [*sic*] that such stories are circulating," wrote Congressman Louis Stokes. "Stella Walsh was an extraordinary human being whose memory must not be tainted by undocumented and unwarranted rumors." Mary Lou Sundheim of Shaker Heights, Ohio, similarly expressed anger, arguing, "This good and decent human being did nothing except serve her community and fellow human beings with generosity and grace." Along with the public criticism, Walsh's longtime friend Casimir Bielen filed a defamation lawsuit against WKYC and WEWS. Because the death was labeled a homicide, the Cuyahoga County coroner conducted an autopsy that included a chromosome test.[46]

The results provided salacious material for the national media and supposed confirmation for the IOC Medical Commission. On January 23, 1981, the Cuyahoga County coroner's office released the autopsy report. The practitioners found that Walsh had an abnormal urethra; no uterus; a tiny, nonfunctioning penis; and small, underdeveloped testes. A buccal smear test verified the presence of both XX and XY sex chromosomes. Recognizing the urge to sensationalize these conclusions, the coroners cautioned against making misleading pronouncements. Walsh's situation was "not black or white," reasoned deputy coroner Lester Adelson. "Nature is infinite in her manifestations." Furthermore, coroner Samuel Gerber noted that the buccal smear test did not exist in the early 1900s; as such, a doctor or midwife likely conducted a physical inspection when Walsh was born and classified her as female. More importantly, according to Gerber, "Socially, culturally and legally, Stella Walsh was accepted as a female for 69 years."[47]

Adelson's and Gerber's efforts to quell a scandal failed. The media ignored the pleas for sensitivity and instead printed ignominious accounts about the Olympian's "questionable" sex. For example, Dan Balz of the *Washington Post* described the "seamy and controversial story," then surmised that "the question is, was Stella Walsh a Man?" Fellow *Post* writer Victor Cohn reported that "famed Olympic medalist Stella Wasn't a 'She.'" Canadian journalist Noel Jeffries of the *Globe and Mail* argued that Canada's Hilda Strike, the 100-meter runner-up of 1932, should be awarded gold, "in view of the revelation that Stella Walasiewicz . . . was in fact a male."[48] Although Clevelanders continued to support Walsh, the Western media tarnished her legacy.

Sport authorities also questioned Walsh's sex and debated her place in the record books. IAAF secretary John Holt noted that despite the discovery, the organization did not intend to take retrospective action against the deceased athlete. Her name remained on the list of former title holders simply because the IAAF did not conduct chromatin testing during her career. "It's rather different from the Klobukowska case," he explained. "We conducted femininity tests and she had her records taken away." The IAAF may have agreed to uphold Walsh's honors; however, Holt added that, in light of the autopsy, "Hilda [Strike] is quite entitled to consider herself to have been the world's fastest woman at the time."[49] Both the IAAF and IOC used Walsh as evidence that femininity testing stopped such controversies from occurring.

The IOC Medical Commission publicly expressed parallel sentiments. One week after the coroner's office released the autopsy report, Monique Berlioux sent Hay newspaper clippings that described Walsh's anatomical and chromosomal composition. She suggested he write a piece for the *Olympic Review* to ensure that Olympic stakeholders understood the situation.[50] Hay agreed and in April published an article that sought to articulate why the IOC allowed Walsh, "not a normal person from the femininity standpoint," to participate in the 1932 and 1936 Olympics. He pointed out that although "hermaphrodites" existed in ancient Greece, the "problem" such individuals posed did not surface until women entered the games. When female Olympians gained access, men maintained a biological and physiological advantage. "It would be unfair . . . to give this advantage to an athlete with masculine characteristics," Hay argued. Femininity control was therefore imperative. When considering Walsh, "it is obvious that she would not have been allowed to participate nowadays, since she would have . . . failed the femininity control." From the vantage of the IAAF and IOC, the "unfortunate case of Stella Walsh" illustrated the need for sex testing.[51]

The Caracas Scandal

The medical commission also received surprising support for its anti-doping controls. One year before the 1984 Olympics, Caracas, Venezuela, hosted the ninth Pan American Games. As the largest multisport event in 1983, the

Caracas Pan American Games served as the first international forum that implemented relatively accurate testing for both anabolic steroids and testosterone. The IOC did not test for exogenous testosterone until 1984. With the improved anti-doping measures, fifteen male athletes failed: eleven weight lifters, one cyclist, one fencer, one sprinter, and one shot-putter.[52] Perhaps more notably, twelve US track and field athletes abruptly flew home. A surprising number of last-minute injuries also occurred. The sudden departures and dropouts seemingly served to save the athletes from suspension. As Craig Neff reported in *Sports Illustrated*, the Caracas scandal was the "broadest, most heavily publicized drug scandal ever to hit amateur sports."[53]

With the sudden exodus of the US athletes and the disqualification of Jeff Michels, a top US weight lifter, many people questioned the bounds of doping. Previously perceived as an Eastern European corruption, the Caracas scandal illustrated the extent of doping in the West. As British reporter David Miller argued, the US public may be "neurotic with the suspicion of Russia," yet American athletes "are among the world's worst offenders."[54] Journalists investigated the sudden withdrawals and discovered that the USOC was not the only group "who had chosen the 'see no evil, hear no evil, speak no evil' approach to the problem."[55] The National Collegiate Athletic Association, National Basketball Association, National Football League, and other professional sport industries had also regularly turned a blind eye to drug use. As a result, USOC head F. Don Miller announced that there would be testing at all upcoming US Olympic trials. To save face for the impending Los Angeles Olympics, however, Miller did not publicly announce the discovery of eighty-six positive tests at the trials until after the 1984 Games. He also did not impose sanctions. Although the Caracas scandal cast doubt on the USOC, it helped showcase the IOC's newest testing techniques and the organization's seriousness regarding anti-doping control. However, to avoid legal issues, the medical commission weakened the doping controls in Sarajevo as it simultaneously strengthened the gender verification measures.

Femininity Testing in the 1984 Sarajevo Winter Olympics

As doping scandals surfaced and political protests increased, the Winter Olympics headed to Yugoslavia. The Sarajevo Games marked the second Olympics held in a communist-controlled state. In a surprise decision during the 80th Session of the IOC in Athens, the Yugoslavian bid defeated Gothenburg, Sweden—considered by many to be the lead candidate—and Sapporo, Japan. Not only was Sarajevo's victory unexpected, but the timing also proved significant; seventy years earlier, the assassination of Archduke

Ferdinand in Sarajevo had triggered World War I. The irony was particularly poignant because the Yugoslavian organizers promoted the city as an "intersection" between different worlds. Those responsible for the candidacy noted "Sarajevo closely knits the East and West."[56] With hostilities between the two superpowers increasing, a neutral location was clearly necessary. Moreover, when the United States announced its decision to boycott the 1980 Moscow Olympics, the Soviet Union mirrored the declaration by refusing to send its athletes to Los Angeles four years later. The 1984 Winter Games therefore stood as the lone Olympic opportunity for a competitive encounter between the two countries. Recognizing the international clout granted to sport, the medical commission continued to check competitors.

For both the 1984 Winter and Summer Olympics, the IOC utilized the new testosterone test developed by West German biochemist and medical commission member Manfred Donike. As a former cyclist who had competed twice in the Tour de France, Donike was concerned that athletes might employ synthetic forms of testosterone to gain an advantage. He therefore developed a method to accurately determine whether a competitor had used "exogenous" (unnatural or synthetic) testosterone. Due to legal concerns, the IOC altered Donike's measurements and checked for a ratio above six to one. In other words, in order to be detected as cheating, an athlete had to possess six times more testosterone than was considered normal. Some feared that this would do little to curtail the ingestion of synthetic substances.[57]

Related to this concern of testosterone enhancement, the medical commission pondered incorporating stricter checks for women. Once again returning to the question of femininity certificates, de Mérode argued that accepting documents from the international federations opened the door for cheating. He claimed that the IAAF had provided fem cards during local contests, violating the medical commission's rule that certification only take place in world championships. According to the chairman, because the IAAF had no control over the regional laboratories, tests, or certificates, "*déplorable*" incidents occurred at the 1980 Summer Games. He later argued that "supposed females" with IAAF certificates had been "caught" in Moscow.[58] Given the earlier reports from Hay and Prokop, it seems unlikely that the "supposed females" de Mérode referenced were male masqueraders. Rather, one can infer that the female Olympians "caught" were those from less affluent countries who did not have access to chromosomal testing. Nonetheless, to limit the possibility of fraud, de Mérode suggested that the medical commission be the sole organization permitted to examine and approve of women athletes. The IOC agreed in 1982 and declared that only the documentation provided by Olympic authorities would be accepted in Sarajevo.[59]

The FIVB and IAAF immediately protested the change in protocol. FIVB president Paul Libaud explained that his international federation followed the IOC Medical Commission's stipulations and permitted certification only during the World Cup and World Championship. Hence FIVB's certificates should be accepted during the Olympics.[60] Similarly, IAAF secretary Holt noted that the IAAF adopted "a very serious attitude" regarding its femininity program and suggested it was "in everyone's interest to avoid repetition of testing." To assuage the medical commission's concerns, he also described two improvements enacted in the IAAF's verification process. First, the international federation agreed to send an official "medical delegate" to all tests to ensure the exams were satisfactorily conducted. Second, if an IAAF medical delegate was not present, certificates would not be issued. The two measures further "safeguarded our system," Holt argued."[61] De Mérode proved unwavering.

In line with the medical commission's control over certification, the group maintained dominion over the determination of womanhood. The justifications for sex/femininity testing had varied throughout the previous two decades—altering from the need to unmask male masqueraders to the need to identify biological "abnormalities"; however, the underlying purpose remained unchanged. The IOC Medical Commission sought to bar any woman who did not adhere to conventional notions of Western femininity. "The sex tests are obligatory under Olympics rules," de Mérode postulated. "They are conducted on women only and are intended to prevent athletes who are biologically male from competing in women's events."[62] USOC medical director Anthony Daly explained that the regulations were intended to "protect Olympic female athletes against unfair competition."[63]

The medical commission thereby continued to proclaim the necessity of femininity testing, despite its rising cost. In the Sarajevo Olympics the organizing committee pooled the resources of the Sarajevo University Medical Centre, medical institutions of the Yugoslav National Army, Sarajevo first-aid services, health centers at Hadzici and Pale, the Institute for Sports Medicine, and the Red Cross. The IOC also awarded the Sarajevo medical committee "considerable financial investments" to ensure adequate testing for both doping and gender.[64] Despite the anxieties raised in the wake of the Caracas scandal, only one positive doping test was uncovered. Of the 262 women examined, no mention was made of any failures; however, that does not mean that women were not barred. As de Mérode reasoned, anyone who did not pass the femininity measures would "quietly disappear . . . without publicity."[65] While he avoided opposition in Sarajevo, de Mérode faced criticism in Los Angeles regarding the purpose and limitations of the chromosomal analysis.

The 1984 Los Angeles Summer Olympics

On January 20, 1981, former California governor Ronald Reagan gained control of the White House. He defeated the incumbent Carter and assumed the presidency in a time of national uncertainty and discontent. The prolonged war in Vietnam, sustained Soviet presence in Afghanistan, and continued hostage crisis in Iran, combined with the upheaval sparked by social movements and unrest fostered by identity politics, led to a "confidence gap" in the United States.[66] As historian Robert M. Collins explains, the coalescence of these anxieties caused "a palpable loss of confidence, a disturbing sense that the nation's drift might easily turn into permanent decline."[67] Reagan was thus determined not to mirror his predecessor's passivity.

The president therefore introduced changes to the economy. He increased interest rates to eliminate inflation, reduced income taxes to stimulate growth, and provided corporations with write-offs to encourage subsidization. One of his overarching beliefs was that the private sector should assume more responsibilities in the public realm. Deregulation initially fostered a recession and lowered the president's approval ratings; however, the 1984 Summer Games offered the White House an opportunity to showcase the virtues of the free market system.

Only Los Angeles submitted a bid for the 1984 Summer Olympics. Other interested cities decided to withhold their offers, recognizing that with the 1980 Summer Games awarded to Moscow, "Los Angeles had every chance of being chosen."[68] The single-city candidature extended Cold War hostilities and also granted the Los Angeles Olympic Organizing Committee (LAOOC) unprecedented leverage over the IOC. When California voters refused to finance the games through taxes, the IOC reluctantly agreed to share joint responsibility of any accrued debt. Furthermore, without state support, the organizers "were literally forced to turn fully to the private sector."[69] Due to novel media contracts and sponsorship deals, the 1984 Los Angeles Games earned a profit, a first in Olympic history. The monetary yield also boosted Reagan's domestic policies. As scholars Rick Gruneau and Robert Neubauer explain, the Olympics dovetailed with Reaganomics. "For Ronald Reagan the success of the 1984 Los Angeles Summer Games provided common-sense evidence of the superiority of the private sector over the ability of governments to solve problems and provide important services," they said.[70] The games both legitimized a neoliberal project in the United States and proved transformative in Olympic organization as private contracts replaced state funding.

While adjusting the economy, Reagan also introduced a more aggressive approach to end the Cold War. Many of his foreign policies involved directly confronting the Soviet Union and maintained the long-term goal of defeating communism entirely. For example, the administration orchestrated the Reagan Doctrine, a stance that allowed the United States to actively aid groups living under communist regimes that attempted to help eradicate the government. In his 1985 State of the Union Address, the reelected president declared that "support for freedom fighters is self-defense" and noted that he wanted to "support the democratic forces whose struggle is tied to our own security."[71] Although previous presidential doctrines had embraced defensive positions, such as the Truman Doctrine and the Nixon Doctrine, the Reagan Doctrine embodied a preemptive orientation.[72] Under the Reagan Doctrine, the United States provided assistance to anticommunist movements in Afghanistan, Angola, Cambodia, Grenada, and Nicaragua. The policy also prompted a significant shift in the United States' stance on communism, from an ideology of "containment" to that of "rollback." Not surprisingly, Reagan's efforts increased Cold War hostilities.

Thus the decision to hold the Summer Games in the United States allowed the Soviet Union to reciprocate the US's boycott of the 1980 Moscow Olympics. On May 8, 1984, the USSR NOC announced its decision to withdraw from the Los Angeles Games, citing security concerns as the primary factor. According to TASS, the Reagan administration encouraged an "anti-Soviet hysteria," which would create "unbearable conditions" for Soviet athletes and officials. "In these conditions," TASS reported, "the National Olympic Committee of the U.S.S.R. is compelled to declare the participation of Soviet sportsmen in the Games impossible."[73] Reagan, who initially supported Carter's boycott but later altered his position for political reasons, responded by calling the Soviet's position an unjustified and "blatant political act."[74] Ignoring the hypocrisy of this assessment, Reagan continued to try to persuade the Soviets to attend. The Soviet Union remained unwavering and opted to forgo the Los Angeles Olympics. As a result, fourteen Eastern bloc countries did not compete in 1984; without contestation from East Germany or the Soviet Union, the United States dominated almost all events.[75] Although women from the Eastern bloc did not participate, the medical commission maintained testing.

Nationalistic Femininity

The US press depicted certain American athletes as foils to the Eastern European women who remained home. For example, journalists lauded Mary Decker as reassuringly oppositional to USSR superstar Tatyana Kazankina. The Soviet runner had earned three gold medals in Montreal and was the first woman to run the 1,500-meter race in under four minutes. When Decker eclipsed the four-minute barrier in 1980, the first US female to do so, she finished seven seconds behind Kazankina. She was beloved, despite her inability to lower the Soviet's record. The US public appreciated that Decker stayed petite and attractive while the Eastern European runners seemed to increase in bulk and power. For example, as *Los Angeles Times* columnist Jim Murray explained, the American athlete did not present the typical characteristics of a world-class runner. Unlike Decker, most "women's international track and field stars are beginning to look like someone you might call 'Bubba.'" Murray further noted that while "90% of the adult female world wants to look like Bo Derek," an American model and actress, the Eastern Europeans were "working more towards looking like Bo Schembechler," a famous US football player and coach. The references to male figures illustrate the anxieties derived from female gains in strength, speed, and size. Due to this supposed masculinization, Murray concluded that "in a world of perfect '10s,' they're minus-3s."[76] Decker, on the other hand, was the ideal embodiment of femininity. America loved its pigtailed prodigy.

Further enhancing her persona, Decker also embraced and espoused the virtues of nationalistic femininity. She repeatedly disparaged both her competitors' appearances and physiques. For example, Decker repeatedly called Kazankina "Ted," for what she explained were "obvious reasons." She further claimed, "When I first ran against her as a young girl in Moscow years ago, I used to beat her in the 800. The girl I ran against now looks like her brother."[77] Decker also found other Eastern European opponents disturbingly masculine. Of the East Germans, she scoffed, "All I know is they have hair growing in places where normal women don't. And the runners I've seen look different than I do."[78] Her suggestion of "normal" and the contrast against herself are notable. Not only did the US public believe that Decker personified femininity, but she also envisioned herself as gender appropriate. As perhaps the clearest example of her disdain, she told Murray about an incident that occurred during a track meet in Hungary. According to the anecdote, Decker entered the locker room and immediately rushed out in horror. "I thought I told you I wanted a *women's* dressing room!" she had implored to officials. When told that it was a women's locker room, Decker was apparently "flabbergasted." As Murray recounted, "She had thought she wandered into a touring troupe of the Green Bay Packers by mistake."[79] Decker both epitomized and embraced feminine norms during the heightening of the Cold War. Consequently, "We are fools for Mary Theresa Decker. Hopelessly smitten," confessed US writer Rick Reilly in 1984. "She is what we like. She wins. She smiles. She is the girl we carry in our wallet."[80] For over a decade, Decker existed in the minds of many Americans as the perfect image of female athleticism. Yet even the US "sweetheart" was required to verify her sex for the 1984 Summer Olympics.[81]

From "Femininity Testing" to "Gender Verification"

For the 1984 Summer Games the IOC outlined two adjustments regarding femininity testing. First, the group approved a name change. The LAOOC used "gender verification" in place of "femininity control" to better relay the purpose of the chromosomal exam.[82] Second, the IOC lifted the embargo on non-Olympic femininity certificates. Frustrated with the medical commission's repeated refusal to accept its documents, the IAAF had turned to the IOC Executive Board. IAAF president Primo Nebiolo convinced IOC president Juan Antonio Samaranch to recognize his organization's femininity program. He highlighted the large number of track and field athletes in need of control and guaranteed that only the IAAF medical delegate issued cards. After hearing Nebiolo's reasoning and de Mérode's objections, Samaranch sided with the IAAF. The medical commission therefore begrudgingly accepted the IAAF's documents and extended the opportunity to FIVB, so as to avoid discrimination. Displeased with the IOC's decision, the commission refused to provide IOC-authorized fem cards to any athlete who used IAAF or FIVB certificates.[83]

For those without femininity certificates, the LAOOC medical services team conducted examinations at polyclinics in the University of California, Los Angeles (UCLA); the University of California, Santa Barbara; and the University of Southern California.[84] Graduate nursing students collected the buccal smear samples under the watchful eye of a medical commission member. Highlighting the intertwinement of gender and sexuality that consistently underlined the check, one nurse joked, "We have a waiting list of men who want to take our positions."[85] Presumably the male hopefuls aspired to verify the Olympians' womanhood through a different type of inspection.

The LAOOC contracted the Nichols Institute, a for-profit organization that specialized in diagnostics, for the chromatin analysis. The Nichols Institute conducted a total of 1,610 tests, of which less than 1 percent demonstrated questionable results. Most often the need to repeat an assessment stemmed from technique error. Yet chromosomal "abnormalities" did cause complications. As UCLA physician Gerald Finerman explained, "There are a number of different syndromes . . . and if a woman shows one, she cannot compete."[86] Approximately eight competitors demonstrated such syndromes. The LAOOC did not publicly report how many women failed the analysis;

however, according to Hay, five Olympians underwent an additional clinical evaluation and were allowed to participate. Yet, when informed of the distressing news, the other three refused to return for further examination.[87]

Without fully understanding the science behind nor the purpose of gender verification, female Olympians were divided about the compulsory check. "I had no idea there was such a thing as genetic difference," recalls US swimmer Nancy Hogshead-Makar. "My understanding was that [gender verification] was akin to drug testing."[88] Although her views regarding chromatin testing have changed—she now believes that the IOC's policies were discriminatory and unfair—Hogshead-Makar and most female athletes in the 1980s did not fully comprehend the complexities of human nature. Consequently, many interpreted the test as a necessary inconvenience. Others echoed the IOC's sentiments and assumed that those who failed were male masqueraders. Hurdler Deby Smith explained, "I'm happy to see them catch people who are doing this." Ostensibly "doing this" entailed men posing as women for athletic success. She further supported the test, arguing, "I prefer to know I'm competing against women." High jumper Pam Spencer agreed and believed it was "the only way the officials can cover all bases." Although she did note that "it's insulting in a way," she maintained that "overall, it's a good idea." Without understanding the nuances of chromosomal composition, most female athletes preferred to "take [it] in stride" in order to ensure fair competition.[89]

* * *

Politics marred the Olympics during the 1980s. Tensions intensified as the two superpowers reengaged in cultural confrontations. With the United States' declaration of a boycott in 1980, the Soviet Union reciprocated four years later. Regardless of the embargoes, the IOC remained dedicated to gender verification. The medical commission expanded testing even though the organizing committees complained about the increasing medical costs. In addition, the commission was convinced that some international federations provided unauthenticated femininity certificates to women athletes; therefore, the group briefly assumed control over all documentation. Finally, although some expressed frustration over the finances of testing, the death of former Olympian Stella Walsh seemed to provide justification for verification. With the continued checks, at least eight women produced irregular results in Los Angeles.

Due to the possibility of unfair disqualifications in 1984, controversy surrounding gender verification amplified. The IOC Medical Commission simultaneously—and seemingly contradictorily—declared the need for gender verification and noted the imperfection of the current methods. De Mérode repeatedly highlighted the obligatory nature of the tests and explained that the purpose remained "to prevent athletes who are biologically male from competing in women's events"[90] However, he acquiesced, saying, "It is not rare for women to have both sets of sex-linked chromosomes." Rather than admit defeat, though, de Mérode and the medical commission implemented slight alterations in the procedure. "The IOC has determined that the ratio should not exceed 30% male-to-female," he explained.[91] Under de Mérode the medical commission repeatedly argued that an arbitrary line had to be drawn to uphold sex segregation in the Olympics. Because no biological division existed, the IOC created its own. Upset with the continued iterations of femininity control, protesters turned their attention to the 1988 Calgary Winter Olympics.

6 "One of the Most Horrid Misuses of a Scientific Method"

The Development of a Protest

IN 1985 TWENTY-ONE-YEAR-OLD US swimmer Kirsten Wengler traveled to Kobe, Japan, for the World University Games, an international, multisport event organized specifically for the participation of university athletes. She underwent the requisite gender verification control; the Japanese medical organizers checked all female competitors for both X and Y chromatin. Many experts disliked the Y chromatin test due to the likelihood of false positives, of which some athletes inevitably fell victim, including Wengler.[1] After undergoing the exam, the US swimmer lined up to receive her femininity certificate; however, she was not issued documentation. "I remember sitting in a big room with my teammates. When they handed out the cards, they did not give me one," Wengler recalls. "Initially I thought it was a joke."[2] Then she was told to return to the laboratory.

The retest confirmed the presence of a Y chromatin. "I was crying and really freaked out," Wengler explained. "I thought I would never be able to have children and that something was wrong with me."[3] After much debate, she was allowed to compete in the University Games. One account suggested that her eventual inclusion occurred because the medical organizers were not prepared to conduct a gynecological inspection. Wengler argues that her admission actually stemmed from her appearance. "I think they realized I did not have other abnormalities," she said. "Visually, I did not look masculine. . . . I did not have the appearance of a male so they let me swim."[4] Her account supports the notion that anxieties about gender sparked investigations into sex.

When she returned to the United States, Wengler's parents, both employed in medical professions, arranged for her to undergo a more sophisticated

Kirsten Wengler swims the freestyle leg of the 400-yard medley relay.
Photographed by Travis Spalding, *Daily Texan*. Courtesy of Texas Student Media,
University of Texas at Austin.

test. This assessment found that Wengler was the victim of a false positive.
The abnormality supposedly uncovered in Japan was actually a protein that
resembled a Y chromosome. Although the young swimmer was obviously
relieved, she feared that others could face similar errors. In particular, Wengler worried for those who, in a comparable situation, would not have the
resources to coordinate a different examination. "She would probably go
home, never find out about the mistake, and feel inadequate for the rest of
her life," she said.[5] It is likely that some did experience such a fate.[6]

Spanish hurdler María José Martínez Patiño also had difficulties with
the gender verification control in Japan. Because she had forgotten her fem
card—previously granted to her in 1983 at the World Track and Field Championships in Helsinki, Finland—she had to repeat the chromosomal checkup.
This time she failed. Unlike Wengler, Patiño did not have medical backing.
"I tried to speak to the best doctors, but there was really no one there to
support me," she said in a later interview.[7] With the negative results, and
at the request of her team doctor, Patiño claimed injury and remained on

María José Martínez Patiño running hurdles at the Spain
Athletics Championships in Barcelona, July 1, 1984. Courtesy
of María José Martínez Patiño, University of Vigo, Spain.

the sidelines. She was devastated. "I spent the rest of that week in my room, feeling a sadness I could not share," Patiño recalled. "Growing up, neither my family nor I had any idea that I was anything other than normal." The following year, the team physician ordered her to again excuse herself, this time from the Spanish National Games. She refused.[8]

Her success in the 60-meter hurdles sparked an avalanche of international criticism. She was expelled from the athletes' residency, her sport scholarship revoked, and running times erased. "What happened to me was like being raped," Patiño explained. "I'm sure it's the same sense of incredible shame and violation. The only difference is that, in my case, the whole world was

María José Martínez Patiño in Adidas gear in Madrid, before
the 1985 World University Games. Courtesy of María José
Martínez Patiño, University of Vigo, Spain.

watching."[9] Despite the international ostracizing, she did receive support.
Finnish professor of clinical genetics Albert de la Chapelle reached out to
the Spanish hurdler. The two forced the issue to the forefront of both the
medical dialogue and the public conscious.

With Wengler's and Patiño's publicity, many observers began to more
openly question the acceptability of Olympic testing. One could argue that
these objections, as well as the assistance the two athletes received, stemmed
from Wengler's and Patiño's status as Western women. Protests surfaced in
the buildup to the 1988 Calgary Winter Olympics. Although the medical

commission carried out the chromatin checks in Canada, one of the doctors hired to conduct the exams withdrew, citing ethical concerns. When the protests did not abate for the 1988 Seoul Summer Olympics, the IAAF and IOC started to look for alternative methods. The track and field federation seemingly eliminated gender controls in 1992; however, the IAAF encouraged physicians' to inspect women's anatomy during doping surveillances. The IOC Medical Commission explicitly maintained gender verification, albeit with a new technique. For the 1992 Albertville Winter Games and Barcelona Summer Games, the group implemented polymerase chain reaction (PCR) testing, a DNA assessment tool. The IAAF and IOC may have disagreed over type of check, but each organization supported the notion that only certain types of women should be allowed to compete in elite sport.

IOC President Juan Samaranch

Before the 1980 Moscow Summer Olympics, Lord Killanin concluded his time as IOC president. After enduring the occupational strains for four years and then suffering a heart attack, which he blamed specifically on the stresses caused by various Olympic crises, the Irish nobleman announced his desire to serve as a one-term president.[10] "There's a lot of pressure on me to run again," Killanin explained in 1977, "but my ulcer says 'No, eight years is enough.'" He was resolute in this decision and stepped down. Killanin warned that any person who fulfilled the presidency should be able to withstand disapproval, for "there is one thing of which I can assure you—you will find it very lonely at times."[11] Spanish diplomat Juan Antonio Samaranch assumed power and, as forewarned by Killanin, faced criticism for his handling of gender verification and doping allegations.

Although mottled by several international scandals, Samaranch's presidency did oversee the first inclusion of women into the IOC. As his successor Jacques Rogge reflected in 2010, "People tend to forget that in 1980, when Samaranch was elected, that the IOC was a very conservative, men-only club."[12] When he assumed the reins from Killanin, not only had the IOC never recognized a single female member, but also only 18 percent of Olympians were women.[13] Samaranch pushed for advancement by admitting several women into the administration, expanding the number of women's sports in the Olympics, and increasing the percentage of female athletes. In 1981 he approved the election of two women, Flor Isava-Fonseca (Venezuela) and Pirjo Häggman (Finland), and three more within the next five years: Mary Alison Glen-Haig (Great Britain), Princess Nora (Liechtenstein), and Anita DeFrantz (United States). He also oversaw the addition of seventeen Olympic sports.[14] Yet his efforts did not extend into all aspects of female participation. Gender verification continued under Samaranch's reign, despite the increasingly vocal international protests.

Opposition from the Medical Community

The IAAF's and IOC's singular use of chromatin to determine womanhood sparked concerns almost immediately upon its introduction in the 1967 European Cup and 1968 Mexico City Olympics. For example, the organizers of the 1970 Edinburgh Commonwealth Games sought to comply with the IAAF's medical directives and requested the expertise of Scottish geneticist Malcolm Ferguson-Smith. The internationally acclaimed professor refused to give assistance, as he found the test inappropriate and discriminatory. In 1969 Ferguson-Smith informed the commonwealth officials that the buccal smear check "taken in isolation says nothing about the sex of the individual." He further highlighted three reasons why the method was inaccurate. First, a person's chromosomal composition does not always mesh with his or her social and legal sex. Second, seven out of every one thousand individuals possess "abnormal" sex chromatin. Finally, according to Ferguson-Smith, physical inspections would prove more suitable in identifying male masqueraders. He concluded that the IAAF and the IOC "have been wrongly advised and that it is not in the best interests of the individual competitors to have this test."[15] The Scottish geneticist contended that the Barr body test was incorrect in determining sex, not that determining sex was incorrect. Many from the medical community disliked the chromatin test; however, they advocated different verification measures in order to delineate a gender divide and prohibit biological advantage in sport.

In line with Ferguson-Smith's objections, the European Society of Human Genetics gathered in 1970 to discuss the "Determination and Differentiation of Sex" in Ghent, Belgium. At the meeting several renowned geneticists and endocrinologists concluded that the Olympic chromatin test was severely flawed. According to de la Chapelle, a member of the society, the group agreed that the procedure was "one of the most horrid misuses of a scientific method."[16] These initial instances did little to change the minds of the IAAF and IOC members. Ferguson-Smith, former Olympian Elizabeth Ferris, and de la Chapelle nevertheless continued to publicly oppose the control.

After learning of the IOC's unwavering reliance on chromatin, Ferguson-Smith voiced his opposition directly to the medical commission in 1976. He explained that not only did false positives inevitably occur but that also several genetic varieties existed. For example, from a sample of "normal-appearing males," the Barr body test labeled one out of seven hundred as female. The test also identified one out of two hundred women as male, which was of particular significance for the Olympics. Moreover, "the rationale . . . that these women should be ineligible is completely unjustified," Ferguson-Smith argued. If the medical commission truly worried about male imposters, he said, all competitors—both male and female—should undergo a medical examination that included a genital check.[17]

Medical doctor and former Olympic athlete Elizabeth Ferris joined Ferguson-Smith in opposition. A British diver, Ferris had earned a bronze medal in the 1960 Olympics. As a proponent of women's involvement in the Olympic movement, she expressed misgivings over the IOC's "prescribed tests for femininity." In a 1978 lecture at the first International Conference on Women in Sport, she disputed the purpose and results of the compulsory sex test. Ferris argued that rather than deter male imposters, "what has in fact happened is that *women* with rare, anomalous chromosome conditions have been the unfortunate victims of this weeding-out process." She implored the IOC to adjust its criteria. "There is a fundamental flaw in the underlying assumption in the way the Femininity Control Test was devised," Ferris said.[18] Eduardo Hay responded to her objections and noted that although sex differentiation studies remained imperfect, the IOC Medical Commission simply strove to prohibit the individuals with "sexual differentiation problems" that granted "physical advantage to these competitors." Embracing the fair play rhetoric, he argued that the buccal smear test was simple, valid, and "sportsmanlike."[19]

Albert de la Chapelle and Alexandre de Mérode

De la Chapelle concurrently challenged the medical commission's control. The Finnish geneticist proved to be the most vocal and persistent, to such an extent that de Mérode refused to attend the 1983 IAAF Congress because it was held in Finland, de la Chapelle's home country.[20] In 1982 de la Chapelle first contacted the chairman and immediately identified an issue that had confounded the commission from the onset of testing. "I have not been able to find a concise definition of what exactly is the aim of the 'femininity control,'" he noted. For over a decade, rationalizations for compulsory testing had fluctuated between catching male masqueraders and eliminating genetic advantages. According to de la Chapelle, the current methods failed to accomplish either goal. In addition, not only was the identification of abnormal chromatin "a flagrant violation" of human rights, but informing a person of the genetic anomaly "is likely to create serious, if not fatal, psychological damage."[21] De Mérode ignored the complaints.

In line with his refusal to meet with de la Chapelle—and travel to Finland—de Mérode eventually handed off the geneticist's multiple letters to Hay. More than one year after de la Chapelle's initial inquiry, the Mexican gynecologist offered a response. Hay contended that the femininity control targeted two groups. The medical commission incorporated testing due to the presence of female Olympians that "either by the use of drugs or the presence of congenital abnormalities, placed such athletes in an unfair advantage in relation with the normal athlete."[22] His supposition not only conflated gender verification and doping controls but also drew a line between "abnormal" and "normal" female Olympians. According to Hay, "abnormal" competitors were those who doped or who possessed genetic advantages. In his view, neither type belonged in sport. Hay may have recognized the inaccuracy of the chromatin test; however, he nevertheless believed it was necessary to maintain fairness.

Frustrated with de Mérode and Hay, de la Chapelle next wrote to IOC president Samaranch. In 1987 de la Chapelle adjusted his complaints and highlighted the inability of the chromatin test to uncover genetic advantages. In his estimation, the Barr body test failed to identify approximately 90 percent of the "hypermuscular" women competitors "who should probably not compete in the female events." Additionally, the check problematically barred the Olympians "who do not have any physical advantage over other females." He reasoned that the sex chromatin screening was "so inefficient and harmful that it should simply be dropped."[23] Although de la Chapelle articulated two reasons to abandon chromatin testing—it did not catch male masqueraders nor prevent biological advantage—the medical commission refused to recognize his arguments.

Thus when de Mérode finally responded to de la Chapelle, at the behest of Samaranch, he disagreed on almost every count. Foremost, the chairman argued that the IOC Medical Commission did not use the chromatin test to identify a person's sex/gender. "It is not our aim to issue decisions 'ex cathedra' concerning the masculinity or femininity of persons participating in the Olympic Games," he explained. Rather, the group sought to scientifically dispel the rumors and innuendos that were "besmirching sport," an unsubtle reference to the muscular women from the East during the Cold War. In addition, de Mérode noted, the commission used the chromatin test to ensure that no female competitors possessed an unfair genetic advantage. Abandoning the test would result in "a resurgence of scandals of which sport would be the victim," he argued.[24] The elimination of Olympic sex testing would not be forthcoming.

Arne Ljungqvist and the IAAF Medical Committee

Not all sport officials unquestioningly agreed with the IOC. Perhaps most notably, Swedish professor and former Olympic athlete Arne Ljungqvist challenged the validity of the buccal smear test. A high jumper in the 1952 Olympics, Ljungqvist retired from athletics to pursue a medical degree. With his training he eventually served as the IAAF's vice president (1981–1999), senior vice president (1999–2007), and Medical Committee chairman (1980–2004). In 1987 he also earned a position on the IOC's Medical Commission, despite the objections voiced by de Mérode.[25] In these various capacities, Ljungqvist repeatedly challenged the IAAF's and the IOC's sex/gender tests.

In the 1981 IAAF Medical Committee meeting, the group invited members of the IOC Medical Commission to discuss the growing criticisms of femininity control. After circulating an article written by Ferguson-Smith, Ljungqvist explained that sex determination involved a variety of criteria, including anatomic sex, genetic sex, psychological sex, psychosocial sex, and somatic sex. Due to the many factors involved, several doctors refused to make a "finite decision" of sex based solely on chromatins. Ljungqvist thereby concluded that the IAAF's and IOC's dependency on a singular criterion was "ethically and medically quite unacceptable." De Mérode disagreed. He acknowledged that academics found little biological difference between men and women; however, sport organizers dealt with the "practical aspects of male and female competition." While the IOC representatives concurred, the IAAF members sided with Ljungqvist. For example, Egyptian medical doctor Alaa Gheita believed using chromatin to prohibit male masqueraders was "ridiculous" and argued that participants could not cheat a physical examination. "Secondary organs could never be imitated," he remarked. Gheita also noted the lack of African facilities able to test for sex chromatin, alluding to the IOC's geographic bias.[26]

Although Ljungqvist proved unable to sway the medical commission, he continued to debate the acceptability of the Barr body test. For example, in 1986 he again informed the commission of the ethical and medical issues surrounding the chromatin check. This time around, Ljungqvist supported his position by highlighting the inability of the control to prevent unfair biological advantages. He explained that the current method failed to eliminate female athletes with congenital adrenal hyperplasia (CAH). Women with CAH typically appear masculine but possess XX chromosomes and would pass the exam. Ljungqvist argued that only a physical inspection would accurately demonstrate sex, which he agreed was currently unacceptable. Therefore, he suggested dropping all forms of sex/gender control. The medical commission refused. These disagreements planted the seed for later disputes between the IAAF and IOC regarding gender verification, but in the mid-1980s neither group was willing to forgo the exam. As de la Chapelle commented in 1987, "I am now quite pessimistic about achieving anything without a public scandal."[27] Patiño provided the necessary impetus.

María José Martínez Patiño

Unlike others who "failed" the chromatin test, Patiño dismissed the team doctor's plea for her to leave athletics. "I was told to feign an injury and to withdraw from racing quietly, graciously, and permanently," she said. "I refused."[28] As a result, she faced immediate criticism. However, due to her public plight, the medical community as a whole started to more vocally question the legitimacy of the procedure.[29] After two decades of unmediated sex testing, Patiño's story sparked changes in the protocol.

The international scrutiny forced upon Patiño produced a variety of responses from medical authorities. After contacting the Spanish hurdler, de la Chapelle wrote to fifteen internationally renowned geneticists and asked for their opinion on the Olympic sex/gender policy. All but three responded, and the twelve concurred that the test was scientifically unsound and ethically incorrect.[30] He also published a study that found gender verification "not only inaccurate but also discriminatory." According to de la Chapelle, the method practiced by both the IOC and the IAAF failed in two significant ways. Foremost, it barred women with chromosomal "abnormalities" unfairly, for these athletes did not possess advantage over other competitors. Second, the scientific technologies employed left the majority of individuals who should be excluded unidentified. In his view the participants who should be barred were men, women who consumed hormones, and women with natural conditions that increased strength and size.[31] While de la Chapelle influentially criticized the IOC and the IAAF for their dependency on chromosomal verification, he also suggested that sport authorities return to visual inspections to exclude "abnormal" females.

US medical geneticist Joe Leigh Simpson agreed that the singular use of the chromosomal test was inadequate and unfair. He also recognized the complexity of the subject, and, unlike de la Chapelle, posited that all verification measures would be unable to determine sex. In his view, "eliminating screening would probably have little or no practical effect, and it might restore a few personal dignities." Simpson later acquiesced that a visual examination would be the "lesser evil."[32] Similarly, Ferguson-Smith and Ferris argued that the Barr body test incorrectly banned individuals, including those with androgen insensitivity syndrome, gonadal dysgenesis, Klinefelter's syndrome, and mosaicism. Although the two outlined the flaws of chromosomal testing, they suggested increased vigilance in laboratories rather than the abolishment of the examination.[33]

Finally, famed sexologist John Money also criticized the IOC. Writing to pediatric endocrinologist and opponent of sex/gender testing Myron Genel in 1987, he argued that the Olympic position was an immoral "policing policy." In Money's view, requiring all competitors to showcase identical chromosomal counts was as impractical and idiotic as demanding that all athletes possess equal height, weight, intelligence, hormone levels, and lung capacity. Half jokingly, he suggested that sports

> copy the policy of wrestling and boxing: divide people into competitive championship classes, and run the Olympics like the Westminster Dog Show. There could be special classes for the adrenogenital syndrome; for the androgen-insensitivity syndrome; for the supernumerary Y syndrome; for Klinefelter's or Tuner's syndrome; for Marfain's [*sic*] syndrome; for eunuchs; for testosterone replacement syndrome; and yes, even for those who risk impaired health or a shortened life span by dosing themselves up with anabolic steroids.[34]

While Money clearly chided the IOC, he did articulate a more serious point. He concluded that the current gender verification policy was both "arbitrary and totalitarian."

Even though many medical experts found de la Chapelle's results compelling, others remained unconvinced. Hay was notably unmoved. After several direct conversations with this "chief guru of the sex chromatin business," de la Chapelle noted that Hay was "an extremely nice old gynecologist, but knows little about endocrinology and almost nothing about genetics."[35] It would therefore be years before the medical commission considered ending sex/gender policing.

Protest in International Competitions

Criticisms of the chromatin check also extended into non-Olympic contests. For example, the *Norges Friidrettsforbund* (Norwegian Athletics Association), or NFIF, agreed to host the 1981 European Cup women's semifinals in Bodø, Norway. As per the IAAF's regulations, the NFIF was responsible for overseeing femininity control. Although this had been a European Cup requirement since 1967, the NFIF Medical Committee experienced difficulty in organizing the check. Many Norwegian geneticists found the test anachronistic and consequently refused to assist. According to the NFIF medical committee president, identified as Dr. Leif Roar Falkum, the practitioners opposed chromatin verification for three reasons. First, they found the method unreliable and inaccurate. Second, the geneticists questioned the purpose of banning individuals with sex anomalies. They noted that all competitors possessed different advantages, such as varying levels of natural testosterone, yet only women faced expulsion. Finally, the protesters concluded that the test was unethical. As Falkum explained, one simply does not divulge to a person who is anatomically, legally, and socially considered female that she has XY chromosomes and is therefore genetically male. "Her only problem is that she is not menstruating," he argued. "That should be her only problem in the future too." For these three reasons the NFIF outlined an ultimatum: Bodø organizers would conduct physical examinations or would not conduct any examinations at all.[36] Without any agreeable alternatives, the IAAF permitted the clinical exam. Although the IAAF Medical Committee explained that this was an exception and not a precedent, other sport organizations started to question the validity of the gender verification.

Perhaps the greatest misinterpretation of the physical examination occurred during the 1987 Mediterranean Games. Presumably to avoid the controversial chromatin check, the Syrian organizers opted to implement a multifaceted test. According to several popular reports, medical authorities first assessed the athletes' outward displays of femininity. If appearances were inconclusive, the judges told the women to lift up their shirts.[37] The incidents at the Mediterranean Games were anecdotal and likely distorted by rumors. However, the accounts point to the unraveling of the IAAF's and the IOC's control, which continued in the Calgary Games.

Gender Verification in the 1988 Calgary Olympics

After putting forward two unsuccessful bids in 1964 and 1968, Calgary, Canada, won the right to host the 1988 Winter Games. As the Calgary Olympic Development Association (CODA) planned for the festival, objections to gender verification increased. For example, Murray Barr, the scientist who had made chromatin testing a reality, beseeched Canadian NOC president Roger Jackson to end its use in sport. "Since the sex chromatin is a Canadian discovery, what better time to put an end to its misuse than prior to the Canadian Winter Olympics of 1988?" he asked.[38] De la Chapelle similarly asked Samaranch to terminate the control, noting that "the inefficiency and harmfulness of the test is so great that [it] should be dropped before Calgary."[39]

Others called for medical geneticist Brian Lowry and physics professor Edward Bruce Challis to refuse assistance in the examination process. In 1986 Lowry had published a piece with colleague David I. Hoar in the *Bulletin of the Hereditary Diseases Program of Alberta*, in which the two authors described the inadequacies of the chromatin control. They suggested that physical inspections would be a better method in the determination of sex. According to the report, "The chromosomal sex is not the final answer to an individual's gender."[40] With this public condemnation of the Olympic policy, many people were surprised when Lowry accepted the IOC Medical Commission's request to oversee the control in Calgary. Both Lowry and Challis recognized the inherent flaws in chromosomal verification; however, they remained committed to the IOC. In a 1987 response letter to de la Chapelle, Challis noted that while "there is reason for concern . . . we do not see how a blank refusal to carry out the sex testing program in Calgary would obtain the ends that you desire." Despite initially agreeing to assist the IOC, Lowry withdrew his support at the last minute, alarmed that the local medical organization insisted upon using volunteers instead of trained professionals for the preparation of the buccal smear slides.[41]

Geneticist Joe J. Hoo and de la Chapelle proposed other ideas to persuade sport authorities to abandon testing. According to Hoo, a "total offensive" move was necessary to stop gender verification at the Calgary Games. He argued that those opposed to the practice should generate a written statement accessible to a lay audience, obtain signatures from medical authorities, and distribute the documents to the press.[42] De la Chapelle, on the other hand, opted to approach IOC officials directly. He wrote de Mérode and asked him to explicitly identify the purpose of the policy, as it still remained unanswered. De la Chapelle noted that suspicions rooted in social anxieties should not serve as the rationale. "Concern about incessant allegations in the Olympic Village and persistent rumors do not themselves form a basis of such decisions," he argued. Additionally, de la Chapelle demanded the test be stopped immediately, for "the present practice is inefficient, injust [sic], harmful and immoral."[43] Despite such vocal opposition from a variety of medical authorities, the IOC opted to maintain femininity testing for the 1988 Winter Olympics. In the Calgary Games the medical commission tested 296 female athletes with no published positive results.

The IOC's "Working Group on Gender Verification"

After the Winter Olympics the IOC agreed to consider the concerns voiced by de la Chapelle and the other leading medical authorities. In July 1988, one month before the start of the Summer Games, the medical commission formed the "Working Group on Gender Verification" to discuss matters related to the testing. Along with commission members de Mérode, Hay, and Ljungqvist, geneticists de la Chapelle, Simpson, and Kurt Götz Wurster attended the meeting.

Hay and de Mérode opened the workshop by defending the chromatin check as the most up-to-date and feasible method available that identified sex. The chairman also explained the motivation for the control. Accordingly, the medical commission did not intend to delineate sex/gender, but sought to eliminate male imposters. In refutation, de la Chapelle reiterated the ethical and medical problems with the test. He also noted that several national bodies conducted verification checks prior to international contests, which raised concerns about incorrect examinations and the traumatization of young athletes. To the group's knowledge, such pre-competition controls had occurred in Belgium, Germany, France, and the United States, and likely elsewhere. In conclusion, the three geneticists supported the abandonment of chromatin checks and favored the reintroduction of clinical examinations. De Mérode and Hay expressed interest; however, they also noted their inability to make such dramatic changes before the Seoul Games. Hence little was actually accomplished during the meeting.

The group dissipated under the impression that de Mérode would reconvene the workshop the following year.[44] He did not. As de la Chapelle exasperatingly surmised in a letter to Ferguson-Smith, "In other words, the whole thing is to be forgotten. Parenthetically, let me insert a word of admiration for the Prince de Mérode: this is exactly how one should handle an unpleasant affair. Just appoint a committee, convene it once, and let it die."[45] Because de Mérode—the chairman of the medical commission since 1967—remained at the helm of the organization, the group repeatedly upheld the necessity of sex/gender control. According to Ljungqvist, while some from within the IOC eventually questioned gender verification, "We didn't stand a chance of changing things while de Mérode remained in office."[46] As a result, it was the IAAF that led the way in ending the practice; however, one could argue it was a change in name only.

The 1988 Seoul Olympics

De Mérode and the IOC Medical Commission continued testing in the 1988 Summer Olympics in Seoul, South Korea. South Korean president Park Chung Hee was the first to envision his country as the host of the Olympic Games in the late 1970s. After Park was assassinated in 1979, his successor,

Chun Doo Hwan, articulated similar ambitions, albeit for different purposes. Following Park's death, South Korea faced great instability; after years of experiencing a military dictatorship, many citizens hoped for a return to civilian governance.[47] Worried about the potential international repercussions should South Korea succumb to political turmoil, in 1980 the United States dispatched forces to establish a de facto government, headed by Chun. The South Korean economy expanded under President Chun, which sparked labor shifts and social dislocation.[48] This subsequent rise in economic prosperity also increased political expectations, fostering criticism of Chun's military system. Finally, the administration faced hostilities from North Korea. According to political science scholar Jarol B. Manheim, these three factors prompted Chun to outline a bid for the 1988 Summer Olympics. The South Korean president believed that hosting the games would legitimize his rule by drawing world attention to the government, showcasing the recent economic prosperity, and casting a negative light on the North Korean threat. As Manheim explains, "The visibility afforded by a successful Olympic enterprise would proclaim to the world South Korea's new status as an industrializing country while providing a vehicle for credit-claiming at home."[49]

Organizing the Seoul Games

President Chun's desires materialized in the 84th Session of the IOC, when Seoul defeated Nagoya, Japan. With the winning bid the games moved to Asia for the second time. The Seoul Olympics Organizing Committee (SLOOC) hoped to utilize this connection and mirror the successes of the first Asian Olympics, held in 1964 in Tokyo. Specifically, SLOOC president Roh Tae Woo and President Chun interpreted the Tokyo Summer Olympics as a triumphant introduction of the newly modern Asia to the world. Although South Koreans maintained an embittered relationship with the Japanese, due to Japan's previous occupation of South Korea, Roh and Chun recognized and aspired to Japan's position in the global economy. Despite this eagerness to repeat the successes of the 1964 Games, however, the Seoul Games actually more closely emulated the 1968 Mexico City Olympics. The 1988 Olympics were marred by political unrest and student protests. Tensions raised by the organizers of the Olympics actually provided the impetus for direct elections in 1987, which led to the ousting of President Chun. SLOOC president Roh assumed governmental power, guaranteeing that the Olympics occurred in South Korea.[50]

Coupled with these domestic complications, the IOC also feared a second Soviet boycott. After the creation of two Korean nations in 1953, the Soviet

Union recognized the Democratic People's Republic of Korea, North Korea, as the only legitimate representation of Korea. The United States maintained a similar relationship with the Republic of Korea, South Korea. In view of these Cold War relationships, the Soviet Union initially wavered in the possibility of its participation. According to the head of the Soviet Olympic Committee, Marat Gramov, the IOC's selection of South Korea was "not an appropriate place," for the country possessed few diplomatic relations. "Frankly speaking," he commented, "we don't understand why the Olympic Games should be held in Seoul."[51] President Chun's conciliatory gestures toward Moscow, as well as newly empowered Mikhail Gorbachev's lessening of hostilities, eventually encouraged Soviet participation. On January 11, 1988, the Soviet Union agreed to attend the Seoul Olympics.[52]

The IOC also worried about the potential for a North Korean boycott. To reduce political differences, Samaranch suggested that five Olympic events—archery, cycling, table tennis, women's volleyball, and the first round of football—be held in Pyongyang, North Korea. The SLOOC adamantly opposed the proposal, pointing out that such a maneuver breached the Olympic Charter. North Korea also proved adverse to the suggestion and demanded it instead be named an official co-host of the games.[53] Unable to compromise, North Korea refused to attend the 1988 Olympics. The Seoul Games thus continued the pattern of boycotts, ongoing since 1972, and also marked the final showdown between US and USSR athletes, as the Soviet Union would cease to exist before the 1992 Barcelona Games.

Despite the growing opposition from the medical community, the IOC maintained gender verification in the Seoul Olympics. Under the watchful eye of the medical commission, the SLOOC conducted chromosomal analysis on 2,050 female athletes and exempted 255 participants who possessed an IAAF or IOC femininity certificate.[54] However, the growing disputes and Patiño's publicity did vex some sport officials. According to Ljungqvist, after the Spanish hurdler made international headlines, he "wanted to persuade the IAAF and the IOC to stop this idiocy."[55] Yet it would take over a decade of protesting for the IOC to change its sex/gender position.

The IAAF's "Workshop on Femininity"

When de Mérode did not schedule a second meeting, Ljungqvist organized an IAAF "Workshop on Femininity" in Monte Carlo, Monaco. According to the IAAF Medical Committee chairman, the meeting aimed to review gender verification practices, discuss the necessity of control, and outline alternative methods that were "acceptable from a scientific, human and practical point of view."[56] For two days in November 1990, experts from Belgium, British Columbia, Bulgaria, the Federal Republic of Germany, Finland, France, Mexico, the Republic of Senegal, Spain, Sweden, Switzerland, the United Kingdom, and the United States, as well as the reluctant chairman of the IOC Medical Commission, listened to a variety of presentations that discussed the benefits and problems of the current sex/gender policies in sport.

On behalf of the IOC, Hay reiterated the medical commission's opinion that the "control of femininity is necessary and well done." Dr. Peter Jenoure, senior physician of the Swiss Ski Federation, articulated the International Ski Federation's (ISF) comparable view that sex/gender testing remained essential for competition. According to Jenoure, the ISF's medical commission was considering introducing a multifaceted control, one that required a chromosomal check, gynecological exam, and blood testing. Similarly, French medical doctor Bernard Dingeon described a new method for gender verification, PCR testing, which the IOC would eventually adopt in 1992.

In contrast, US professor of medical psychology Anke Ehrhardt articulated the psychological aspects of the procedure and the "unintended discrimination" caused by current gender-verification procedures. US athlete Alison Carlson conveyed the lack of consensus among female Olympians regarding the policy and admitted that without education most of them "aren't impelled to give it much thought." However, she did note that although most Olympic athletes agreed with the underlying intent of testing, a revision of the current system "is sorely needed." Finally, de la Chapelle, Ferguson-Smith, and Ferris all argued for an end to the current practices.

At the workshop's conclusion the group outlined several recommendations for sex/gender control in future competitions. First, they noted that there was a lack of documented material regarding past procedures. The attendees therefore suggested more information be made publicly available; in particular, they requested reports on the number of women who had not passed previous tests, reasons cited for their failure, diagnoses, and final decisions enacted. Second, the working group attempted to answer the always nebulous question, why mandate sex/gender testing? Accordingly, the purpose remained solely to prevent male masqueraders. As such, they argued, gender verification should never preclude those born with chromosomal differences who are raised female. The IAAF participants recognized that several athletes had been unfairly barred in past competition. Furthermore, to eliminate linguistic inconsistencies, they proposed that the title of any assessment be changed to "Eligibility Test for Women's Competition."

Perhaps most important, as a fifth point, the IAAF workshop called for sport authorities to abandon chromatin testing. In their view, "the present

sex chromatin test is inappropriate and scientifically unsound." Instead they
suggested sport officials adopt a physical checkup to ensure the health of all
athletes, including men. The participants reasoned that such an examination would serve to determine if any athlete, male or female, suffered from
a condition that would lead to injury.[57]

The IAAF heeded the advice and terminated chromatin verification for
all international track and field events. For future participation, the IAAF
Medical Committee provided two guidelines. First, because the fundamental
purpose of the procedure stemmed from the desire to prohibit male masqueraders, the group reasoned that gender verification was moot with new anti-
doping requirements. The visual inspection of competitors during urination
collection eliminated the possibility for fraudulent sex. Hence the stipulation
did not terminate sex control but instead returned attention to supposed
anatomical differences. As sport scholar C. L. Cole argues, the IAAF "used
the conditions created through drug testing to visually inspect genitals."[58]

Second, to ensure the well-being of competitors, the IAAF replaced the
chromatin test with a "health check." With this new policy, the medical committee required a "simple physical inspection" for all athletes, both male
and female.[59] According to de la Chapelle, a proponent of the procedure,
the health check ensured sex delineation because "have you heard of people
who cannot tell a man from a woman?"[60] In other words, he suggested that
anatomical sex trumped all other qualifiers. Similar to the visual scrutiny
necessary for anti-doping tests, the physical examination further reinforced
the social belief in gendered bodily difference.

The IAAF's "Health Check"

The IAAF finalized its new "health check" policy mere months before the
start of the 1991 World Championships in Athletics, held in Tokyo. Confusion quickly followed and the IAAF faced immediate criticism. Several team
doctors complained that the protocol was not fully explained; difficulties
with administration and language only exacerbated the problem.[61] Others
protested the policy itself. Medical representatives from North America contended that the health check was a reversion to the "nude parades" of the Cold
War, and members of the Australian federation denounced the inspection
of men as "pointless."[62] British team doctor Malcolm Brown simply refused
to conduct the new test. As an "intimate exam," he said, "it is not appropriate for us, as team doctors, to do it."[63] Female participants voiced similar
opposition to the "peek-and-probe" examination. For example, Canadian
race walker Ann Peel found the inspection "offensive and demeaning" and

argued that it was "a step back in time for women."[64] Despite the confusion and discord, 422 female competitors underwent a physical inspection before the championships or were required to do so in Tokyo.[65]

The confusion, expenses, and cultural concerns precipitated by the health check in Tokyo convinced the IAAF to abandon the procedure in 1992. Recognizing the flaws of gender verification and the likelihood that "there will never be a laboratory test that will adequately assess the sex of all individuals," the governing body completely abandoned compulsory testing. The IAAF trumpeted its decision as groundbreaking; however, the group nevertheless maintained the right to check any "questionable" competitors on a case-by-case basis.[66] In other words, an examination could be required based upon an athlete's external (nonconventionally feminine) appearance or from a detection of "abnormal" genitalia. Thus the IAAF's "abolishment" of gender verification actually repositioned the scrutiny of sex/gender within anti-doping controls, physical inspections, and suspicion-based checks.

The Medical Commission Responds: PCR Testing

Before the IAAF announced its new policy, the IOC Medical Commission also discussed the possibility of relinquishing its control over sex/gender during a 1991 meeting in Albertville, France. There Ljungqvist detailed the proposals outlined by the IAAF Workshop on Femininity. Unconvinced, the commission voted to accept only one point: the prerequisite that athletes undergo a "health check" in their countries of origin. "The IOC Medical Commission was far more difficult to convince then the IAAF Council," Ljungqvist recalled. "It became clear to me . . . that it would be impossible to obtain a 'full victory' and that a step in the right direction was the maximum I could expect."[67] The commission moved to an opposite conclusion. While the group did recommend to the IOC Executive Board that all female Olympians should possess a "health and gender" certificate, it also lobbied for the introduction of its own novel form of gender verification: polymerase chain reaction testing. Unlike the previously utilized Barr body test, PCR assessed genetic material to determine sex/gender. The IOC adopted PCR for the 1992 Albertville Winter Olympics.

Although the Olympic authorities attempted to combat potential opposition with an innovative method, medical experts, national governments, and athletes alike questioned the legitimacy, legality, and ethics of the procedure. Many noted the technique's sensitivity to contamination and potential to cast false positives. For example, geneticist Simpson found the precarious nature of the process alarming. "With sex chromatin testing I was at least assured that in expert hands the test could do that for which it was designed—distinguishing XX from XY individuals," he said. "However, contamination is such a problem in the sensitive 'PCR test' that even in the best of hands some normal females will be 'typed' as males."[68] Simpson also argued that possession or absence of Y chromosomal material did not determine one's sex/gender. Correspondingly, Genel questioned the wisdom of replacing one disputed genetic test with another. "We should not end up simply substituting a dazzling but unproven technology for the outdated and discredited use of the buccal smear," he contended.[69] As Carlson pointedly explained, "Substituting one chromosome measure for another *misses the point.*"[70] Such concerns inundated the 1992 Winter and Summer Games. Although the IAAF and the IOC disagreed on methods—pitting physical exams against PCR testing—both organizations conceded that requiring a system of control remained imperative.

Protest over PCR: The 1992 Albertville Winter Olympics

Seeking to host the 1992 Winter Olympics, a record-setting seven locales outlined bids, a sharp contrast to the 1980 Winter Games, for which only Lake Placid showed interest. The realization that holding the Olympics could amass a tremendous profit—as first achieved in the 1984 Los Angeles Games through private-sector sponsorships—encouraged several cities to place bids. The organizing committee of Albertville therefore highlighted the area's accommodations, climate, economic stability, and telecommunications in an effort to impress the IOC's delegates. To further entice support, former Olympic skier Jean-Claude Killy spoke on behalf of the city; Killy had earned three gold medals in the 1968 Grenoble Winter Games, the last held in France. While the triple gold medalist impressed some, the Parisian loss for the 1992 Summer Olympics likely bolstered the Albertville victory. After five days of frenzied lobbying and six rounds of voting, Albertville emerged as the winner.[71]

As French citizens celebrated the triumph, an array of French authorities debated the appropriateness of permitting PCR testing to occur in France. Prior to the games, twenty-two French scientists, two of whom held Nobel Prizes, signed a petition denouncing PCR use on both medical and ethical grounds.[72] French ministers also wrote to Samaranch and called for him to terminate the control. Perhaps most coercively, the French Medical Association's ethics commission, the Conseil de l'Ordre des Médecins, threatened disciplinary action for any French doctor who participated in PCR verification during the Albertville Olympics. According to association president Louis Rene, the method was not only inaccurate but also a violation of privacy. "Such mistaken and uncontrolled use of a genetic test in sports goes against precautions taken against abuses," he explained.[73]

Others agreed. For example, US gynecologist John S. Fox criticized the medical commission's discriminatory gender stance. In addition, he reproached Olympic authorities for refusing to heed the advice of medical and scientific experts. "Despite the considerable amount of genetic, gynecological and psychological evidence that can be mustered in opposition to the process of gender verification," he argued, "the dinosaurs of the International Olympic Committee and its Medical Commission seem determined to pursue their current policy."[74] Six Italian pediatricians, employed by the University of Rome and involved in granting "sex passports" for over twenty years, also publicly denounced the technique. These officials depicted the new method as a form of physical abuse and urged "that this unpleasant and counterproductive practice be abolished" immediately.[75] The combination of inappropriate genetic techniques, prejudice of the IOC's "female only" test, failure to consider naturally produced biological differences, and the consequential stigmatization caused by a positive result created opposition from a variety of medical officials.[76] Yet such challenges did little to deter the medical commission in Albertville or Barcelona.

The Gender Control in Albertville

The IOC Medical Commission implemented PCR testing in the 1992 Albertville Winter Games. Dingeon, the French medical doctor largely responsible for the novel verification method, publicly dismissed the protests and called those behind it "spoilsports." He also claimed that the intervention of the French scientists was "more polemical than scientific" and argued that they did not possess "real knowledge" of the sporting world.[77] In other words, only Dingeon and the medical commission comprehended the gendered realities of Olympic competition. Somewhat inconceivably, then, the fundamental purpose of gender verification still remained unclear. For example, Dingeon reasoned that the new procedure differed from the chromosomal analysis in that "the old test sought to establish that a woman was female. We set out to prove she is not a man."[78] IOC spokesperson Michele Verdier noted, "It is not for the IOC to decide who is a man and who is a woman. We just want to make sure that athletes compete under fair conditions."[79] Dingeon and the IOC seemed to maintain dissimilar ideologies regarding the goal of gender verification. Nevertheless, both espoused rhetoric that embraced the discourses of fair play and protection. Dingeon later explained, "Only athletes competing in women's events are screened for fraud, as a woman winning in a male event is unheard of."[80] Such comments reinforced the notion of female athletic inferiority in sport.

Dingeon found a proponent of PCR testing in medical commission member Patrick Schamasch. Schamasch, a French orthopedic surgeon, served as the chief medical officer of the Albertville Olympics Organizing Committee. In this position he oversaw four types of services: health examinations, anti-doping checks, water quality tests, and gender verification. To ensure appropriate sex/gender, the medical team collected DNA samples from 557 female athletes in the Olympic Village and then sent them to Dingeon's hospital, the Hospitalier de Chambéry, for analysis.[81] Dingeon found that the procedure was "very easy to take, quick [and] painless." He did admit that only women conducted the actual analysis, so as to avoid contamination with the presence of male DNA.[82]

Regardless of the increased possibilities for false positives, both Dingeon and Schamasch concluded that PCR verification was successful. They cited four specific justifications for its continuation in Olympic competition. First, the doctors echoed the IOC's insistence regarding the necessity of sex/gender control and argued that PCR testing "excludes athletes who do not satisfy the requisite criteria to compete in a women's event." The two did not offer suggestions as to what comprised the "requisite criteria." Second, Dingeon and Schamasch highlighted the reliability of the method, claiming to have achieved better than a 99 percent success rate in Albertville. As a third point, they found the test necessary for the identification and removal of "transsexuals," a growing concern among the governing bodies of sport. Finally, the doctors pointed out that female athletes disliked undergoing gynecological examinations. According to Dingeon, the doodles female athletes left on the walls of the Albertville Gender Verification Centre signified their approval of the PCR test. The "signatures accompanied by kind words or little drawings showed that the athletes were in agreement with this control and appreciated the modalities of it," he explained. Some even "came out smiling."[83]

For demonstrating such prowess in Albertville, Schamasch was named the IOC's medical and scientific director a year later. He would later play a significant role in the creation of an Olympic transgender policy in 2003. Convinced by Dingeon's report, the medical commission opted to continue the use of the PCR test to verify sex/gender. Dingeon and Schamasch ensured that only women with the "requisite criteria" competed in the 1992 Barcelona Summer Olympics.

Protest over PCR: The 1992 Barcelona Summer Olympics

Paralleling the large number of bids put forward to host the 1992 Winter Games, six cities expressed interest in the 1992 Summer Games. Enticed by the possibility for both economic and symbolic profit, the organizing committees devoted millions of dollars to campaigns and also bartered with other locations for votes. Barcelona, Spain's second most populated city, outspent its competitors with the equivalent of a $10 million investment in promotions. The Spanish coordinators also allegedly received assistance from Horst Dassler, German president of Adidas and creator of International Sport and Leisure, a marketing firm that maintained a lucrative contract with the IOC. Allegedly, Dassler acquired the necessary votes for Barcelona, and Samaranch's position within the IOC further encouraged a victory for his hometown.[84] Although Dassler claimed he remained uninvolved during the voting process, Samaranch's influence seemingly wielded results. On October 17, 1986, he officially declared his home city the winning candidature.

The Barcelona Olympics embodied new international and economic philosophies. Coined the "New World Olympics," "Neo Olympics," and the "New-Order Olympics" by the *New York Times*, the 1992 Games marked the rise of newfangled global relations and the termination of the amateurism ideal. With the fall of the Berlin Wall and the collapse of the Iron Curtain, an unprecedented 175 countries competed in Barcelona. The dissolution of the Soviet Union allowed for the independent participation of Estonia, Latvia, and Lithuania, and for the first time since 1960, South Africa was allowed to attend. Moreover, athletes from East and West Germany competed under a single German flag. The 1992 Summer Games was the first not tarnished by a boycott since 1972.

In addition to showcasing this new world order, the Barcelona Games also included full-fledged professional athletes for the first time in Olympic history.[85] The Samaranch-headed IOC completely abandoned Coubertin's conviction in amateurism and continued to commercialize the Olympic movement. As journalist Michael Janofsky noted, "Sport has become engulfed in an unabashed chase of dollars, pounds, lira, francs, marks and yen." He further pointed out that in this money-driven era, "the quaint philosophies that once defined the Games" no longer held importance.[86] The IOC may have softened Coubertin's stance on amateurism, yet it maintained the founder's view on womanhood.

The Gender Test in Barcelona

Similar to the French scientists who denounced PCR testing, Spanish medical authorities also condemned the practice. Renowned Barcelonan geneticist Xavier Estivill refused to provide assistance when asked to do so by the Barcelona Olympics Organizing Committee (COOB'92). He rejected the COOB'92's offer because he feared that the relative ease with which PCR could be conducted would allow for the procedure to become commonplace, despite the expanding debate regarding the constitution of sex/gender. Furthermore, Estivill questioned the IOC Medical Commission's proficiency in explaining to an athlete what it means to produce a positive sample.[87] Without his assistance, the COOB'92 employed molecular science professor Angels Serrat and biochemistry professor Antonio García de Herreros to organize the sex/gender control. According to Serrat and de Herreros, female nurses successfully screened 2,406 Olympians.[88]

Of the 2,406 Olympians verified, 12 produced irregular results. Upon further testing, 1 sample proved to be a false positive—which further alarmed those who opposed the PCR method—6 passed upon closer inspection, and 5 showed genetic "abnormalities."[89] The medical commission requested that the 5 athletes who showcased the deviations undergo a gynecological inspection for admittance. Four were permitted as XY chromosomal females.[90] Bolivian athlete Sandra Cortez opted to forgo competition rather than proceed with further examination. With her withdrawal, the IOC immediately assumed Cortez was guilty of gender fraud. According to Hay, the Bolivian track and field athlete was "a genuine case of a normal male masquerading as a female." The IOC further applauded the PCR test for accurately detecting and deterring an "anatomical male."[91] However, many disregarded these conclusions because of anecdotes suggesting Cortez was a biological mother of three children. Many medical professionals feared that rather than an instance of gender fraudulence, Cortez's removal resulted from media harassment.[92]

* * *

Cortez encountered the same suspicions that Wengler and Patiño had experienced seven years earlier at the World University Games. Her name was thus added to the list of female athletes questioned on the basis of her sex/gender. When Wengler and Patiño "failed" the chromatin test in 1985, each woman received support from individuals with medical backgrounds—Wengler from her parents and Patiño from de la Chapelle. Cortez did not. Nonetheless, their plights convinced many that the method used in gender verification was discriminatory, inaccurate, and unethical. Protests thereby heightened in the 1988 Calgary Winter Games and Seoul Summer Games.

The increasingly vocal opposition eventually persuaded the IOC Medical Commission to discuss the matter with medical practitioners. Following the Calgary Olympics, de Mérode organized the Working Group on Gender Verification, which debated the purpose, practicalities, and ethics of gender testing. Despite the productive conversations shared between commission members and expert geneticists, the group achieved only minimal results. Therefore, when de Mérode did not reconvene the committee, Ljungqvist organized the Workshop on Femininity on behalf of the IAAF. This group outlined several recommendations, which the track and field federation immediately implemented. The IAAF consequently introduced a "health check" for all athletes in 1990. However, confusion over protocol, expenses required, and complaints about the unnecessary inclusion of male athletes in the testing compelled the IAAF to drop all forms of gender verification. Although the organization abandoned sex/gender control in 1992, it maintained the right to check any "suspicious" competitor, again linking biological sex to gender appearances. The IAAF also deemed verification redundant as the doping check unearthed any "abnormalities" through its requirement of visual inspection of urination. In homage to the 1960s "nude parades," the IAAF decided that if the purpose of the test was to prohibit men from participation, a simple anatomical check would suffice.

With the IAAF's change in protocol, the IOC also implemented a new technique. It replaced the chromatin exam with PCR testing for the 1992 Albertville Winter and Barcelona Summer Olympics. Because many people believed that substituting one scientific method with another did not solve the practical nor ethical problems of verification, those who were opposed to laboratory testing continued to fight for the IOC to terminate the practice. While de Mérode, Hay, and other Olympic officials disregarded the concerns voiced in France and Spain, the Norwegian government's stance eventually forced the IOC's hand.

7 "Gender Testing *Per Se* Is No Longer Necessary"

The IAAF's and the IOC's Continued Control

AS PROTEST OVER GENDER VERIFICATION increased, Bernard Dingeon, the French doctor responsible for overseeing the tests in Albertville, publicly supported the IOC's campaign. Writing in *JAMA*, he acknowledged the inadequacies of the formerly used chromatin check. However, Dingeon remained "convinced of its essential soundness," referring to the necessity of a control mechanism to ensure fair play in women's competition. He also criticized the meddlesome concerns raised by medical practitioners and the IAAF. In his view the introduction of the PCR test in Albertville should have quieted the opposition, for "PCR is perfectly suited to, and economically compatible with, the constraints of the Olympic Games."[1]

Not everyone agreed. Refuting Dingeon in the same *JAMA* issue, Albert de la Chapelle, Alison Carlson, Anke A. Ehrhardt, Malcolm Andrew Ferguson-Smith, Elizabeth Ferris, Myron Genel, Arne Ljungqvist, and Joe Leigh Simpson called for the abolishment of Olympic gender controls. Again the protesters questioned the fundamental purpose of verification, a nebulous subject since its introduction. It seemed that the IOC's main intent still remained unclear. At different times the medical commission rationalized the procedure as a defense against male masqueraders, a deterrent for female doping, and a system to curb biological advantage. The eight authors pressed the commission and Dingeon to recognize "the inadvertent damage done by laboratory-based testing" and to adopt the physical examination recently embraced by the IAAF. "Gender testing *per se* is no longer necessary," they reasoned.[2] Although the leading protesters disagreed with the method, they did not refute the underlying belief that some type of check remained necessary.

On the surface the IAAF and IOC appeared to embrace oppositional perspectives. This gulf seemed to widen in 1992 when the track and field federation abandoned its "health check." The IAAF thereby terminated all mandatory gender controls while the IOC Medical Commission remained loyal to PCR testing, maintaining the procedure for the 1994 Lillehammer Olympics, 1996 Atlanta Olympics, and 1998 Nagano Olympics. As a result, the IOC experienced opposition throughout the 1990s from concerned physicians, national governments, and medically trained athletes. The medical community continued to press the IOC to drop the controversial check, citing the impossibility of determining sex in a laboratory. Noting similar ethical concerns, the Norwegian government outlawed verification and Norwegian scientists refused assistance in Lillehammer. Finally, the newly formed IOC Athletes' Commission recommended that the IOC end the practice. Based on these three challenges, the IOC Executive Board voted in 1999 to stop testing. However, the medical commission did not relinquish complete control. Through suspicion-based checks, anti-doping techniques, and the Stockholm Consensus, Olympic authorities continued to uphold a binary notion of sex/gender and to promote Western norms of femininity. Thus even though the IAAF and the IOC may have disagreed on the correct method, both organizations still believed that sex/gender control was crucial in elite sport.

Confusion in International Sport

Following the 1991 Tokyo World Championships and the 1992 Barcelona Olympics, sport federations questioned the methods to be used for—and the legality of—gender verification. With the IAAF's abandonment of the chromatin check and the IOC's reiteration of genetic testing, the organizations charged with running multisport events were unsure of the correct sex/gender protocol. Their puzzlement increased as the IAAF-IOC debate intensified. In the two years before the 1994 Lillehammer Olympics, different athletic forums implemented a range of control measures, highlighting the tenuous nature of gender verification in sport.

In 1993 Buffalo, New York, hosted the World University Games. Although previous games had mandated sex/gender checks, the Buffalo coordinators questioned the appropriate methods to implement. Medical services director Virginia Scahill initially supported the IOC's efforts. To follow the medical commission's decree, she arranged for Roche Diagnostics, a clinical laboratory, to conduct the PCR test. When de la Chapelle asked Scahill to instead follow the example set by the IAAF and stop gender verification, she did not believe his claim that the international federation had eliminated the policy.

After receiving several imploring contacts from the Finnish geneticist, she refused to answer his calls. As de la Chapelle explained, "All I can say is that history seems to be repeating itself with stunning precision: we fail again." He further noted, "The only new thing this time is that I have been dealing with a female organizer rather than a male one."[3] However, when Genel, Ljungqvist, and IAAF president Primo Nebiolo all contacted Scahill, she agreed to halt the check in Buffalo.[4] She also reversed her previous position and publicly advocated for the complete termination of gender verification in sport, suggesting such tests were "unfair and unnecessary."[5] Therefore, under the advisement of de la Chapelle, Genel, Ljungqvist, and Nebiolo, organizers suspended blanket screening in the Buffalo World University Games. In parallel fashion, the Vancouver promoters of the 1994 Commonwealth Games also decided to discontinue the practice.[6]

The abrupt suspension of gender verification in Buffalo and Vancouver appears to have raised little concern. The nonresponse may have stemmed from the fact that at the time just four international federations conducted on-site screening during world championships, those that oversaw basketball, skiing, volleyball, and weight lifting.[7] The other international federations followed Olympic protocol only during the Olympic Games.

Along with the growing confusion regarding the logistics of sex/gender testing, women's rights groups became more vocal in their objections. In 1994 the British Sports Council organized the first World Conference on Women and Sport in Brighton, England. The 280 delegates from eighty-two countries congregated to formulate a plan that would encourage the full involvement of women in all aspects of sport. Two years later, recognizing the importance of diverse opinions and the need for gender equality in sport, the IOC followed suit and organized its own forum. In 1996, 220 delegates from ninety-six countries attended the IOC World Conference on Women and Sport, held at the Olympic Museum in Lausanne, Switzerland.[8] The first draft of the program did not mention gender verification; Ljungqvist later added it as a topic of discussion and the 220 delegates debated the IOC's sex/gender practices. As a result, the conference passed a resolution suggesting that the IOC "discontinue the current process of gender verification."[9] A range of internationally significant women supported this initiative, including former prime minister of Pakistan Benazir Bhutto; former prime minister of Norway Gro Harlem Brundtland; Hillary Rodham Clinton, first lady of the United States; Queen Noor of Jordan; and Mary Robinson, president of the Republic of Ireland.

Nevertheless, the IOC Medical Commission maintained the necessity of Olympic genetic testing. Although the dispute fostered confusion in competition and encouraged calls for change, opposition remained relatively limited to medical practitioners and women's groups. However, Norwegian gender politics added governmental involvement to the debate.

The 1994 Lillehammer Winter Olympics

Prior to the 1994 Winter Olympics, Lillehammer citizens joked that the city's greatest accomplishment was that it served as the birthplace of Thor Bjøerk-land, the man who invented the cheese slicer. Perhaps disenchanted with the area's dairy-related fame, in 1981 a handful of "dreamy locals" conspired to swing the international spotlight to the small Norwegian city.[10] Although the IOC initially considered Lillehammer for the 1992 Winter Games, the executive board eventually voted for Albertville, France. Determined to re-turn the Olympics to Norway, the local hopefuls reintroduced the bid two years later. In the 94th Session of the IOC in Seoul, Lillehammer earned the right to host the 1994 Winter Games, the first Olympics held outside of the traditional four-year cycle.[11]

The IOC selected Lillehammer for the city's conception of holding "com-pact games." Concerned with the ever-growing "gigantism" of the Olym-pics, the IOC welcomed the Lillehammer Olympics Organizing Committee's (LOOC) intent to keep all events close to the city. Although Lillehammer won the bid on the basis of this objective, the reality of hosting the Winter Olympics forced the LOOC to move certain events to distant locations. For example, Alpine skiing occurred in Øyer and Ringebu, ice hockey in Gjøvik, and skating in Hamar, distances of approximately twelve, thirty, and forty miles from Lillehammer, respectively. Furthermore, many credit the Lille-hammer Olympics as serving as the foundation for future "green games." This aspiration did not appear in the original bid; however, the LOOC worked to curb pollution and encourage environmental sustainability. The IOC used the idea for later games.[12] While Olympic authorities applauded the LOOC's progressivism with regard to location and environment, the medical com-mission would come to dislike the country's stance on sex/gender.

Women's Rights in Norway

Perhaps more than any other nation in the West, Norway has historically been lauded as a pioneer of gender equality. Starting in the nineteenth century, the country granted women unprecedented rights, far ahead of its European counterparts. For example, in the mid-1800s, Norwegian women gained ac-cess to craft and commerce and earned both property rights and the equal right of inheritance.[13] The government granted female suffrage in 1913, the first sovereign state in Europe to extend political citizenship to women. Although feminist thought wavered throughout the early part of the twentieth century—epitomized by the mid-century Norwegian Labour Party's conservative stance toward women—the 1960s marked a significant turning point as a new generation of women embraced critical stands toward gender politics. Individuals involved in the "second wave" of feminism fought to alter the fundamental nature of the state and concurrently demanded the same rights as men. The 1970s was thus a moment of a strong and visible women's movement in Norway. With forceful encouragement from Norwegian feminists, the government accepted responsibility for requiring gender equality and passed the Equal Status Act of 1978, which prohibited all discrimination on the basis of gender. According to historian Gro Hagemann, this piece of legislation "has been the key pillar of Norwegian equal status policy in the last decades of the twentieth century."[14]

Norway also ratified all United Nation (UN) agreements on human rights, including the Universal Declaration of Human Rights and the Convention on the Elimination of All Forms of Discrimination against Women (CEDAW). The Universal Declaration of Human Rights—adopted by the UN General Assembly in 1948 and signed by Norway in the same year—served as the first international expression of the rights to which all humanity is entitled. Some who questioned the IOC Medical Commission's gender policies hinted that sex testing breached this doctrine. In particular, Article 2 prohibits discrimination on the basis of "race, colour, sex, language, religion, political or other opinion, national or social origin, property, birth, or other status," and Article 3 guarantees "life, liberty and security of person." Taken in conjunction with Article 12, which states that "no one shall be subjected to arbitrary interference with his privacy . . . nor to attacks upon his honour and reputation," Olympic sex testing could be viewed as both a discriminatory violation and as a harmful invasion of an individual's privacy.[15]

The CEDAW further bolstered gender equality worldwide. Colloquially described as the "international bill of rights for women," the document originated from a 1979 UN General Assembly convention. The CEDAW defines what constitutes discrimination against women and outlines an agenda to terminate such practices. Importantly, countries that accepted the doctrine were required to "ensure the elimination of all acts of discrimination against women by persons, organizations or enterprises."[16] Norway ratified the CEDAW on May 21, 1981. Since then, the country has touted gender equality and placed women in substantial leading roles. As one emblematic example, in 1985 Prime Minister Brundtland's ministerial appointments were

44 percent women.[17] Not surprisingly, the substantial changes in political and economic gender relations paved the way for significant advancements in women's sport.

Women's Sport in Norway

In the decades before the opening of women's athletic opportunities in Norway, Norwegian sport mostly resembled the sporting norms of England. Comparably to the command English medical officials held in the United Kingdom, Norwegian male doctors similarly legitimized women's strength and stature as inferior to men's. These authorities posited that strenuous exercise and exertion fostered female demise and ruin, which thereby cemented sport as male endeavor.[18] Although this conception remained rooted in Norwegian sport, alternative ideologies occasionally permeated the hegemonic ideal. Prior to World War I, the Workers Sports Confederation (AIF), one of the two large sport federations in Norway, articulated a political goal of promoting equality between men and women. During the interwar period, the AIF notably appointed a Women's Committee and outlined the first sport-specific policy for women. In 1946, when the AIF merged with the Norwegian Confederation of Sport (NCS), the women's group remained intact; however, in 1953 the committee was abolished. Although the NCS Committee for Instruction and Information was expected to incorporate policies specifically for female athletes, few were passed.

Faced with limited sporting prospects, Norwegian women mobilized in the 1980s. On the coattails of the larger women's movement, female athletes demanded increased access to sport. The Norwegian Equal Status Council therefore arranged a hearing to assess women's participation in physical activities in 1984, which led to the reinstitution of a Women's Committee within the NCS. This newly formulated women's organization sought to appraise the current situation and draft solutions to boost female involvement. Within the same year, the NCS further adopted a specific plan of action and outlined three main goals: to legalize working with women's rights in the organization, to establish a formal network for women, and to coordinate activities for females.[19] Additionally, the NCS passed the first gender quota for sport organizations in 1987. The legally delegated quota system required that each gender be represented on elected boards and committees. Although the quota system was celebrated for elevating female representation in various federations, the more powerful positions remained occupied by men.[20] Nevertheless, the country's unique combination of embracing human rights, encouraging female athleticism, and requiring legal equality coalesced in the

1990s, allowing Norway to stand as the first country to directly challenge Olympic gender verification practices.

Gender Testing in Lillehammer

The Lillehammer Olympics was a turning point in the history of Olympic sex/gender testing. In 1994 the Norwegian government declared gender verification "illegal and unethical" and Norwegian scientists denied the IOC assistance.[21] Without the support of the government or the expertise of the country's medical authorities, the IOC Medical Commission scrambled to find replacements to conduct the examinations. The group experienced substantial difficulty locating willing European specialists due to the growing concern regarding the ethics and legality of PCR testing. Finally, Dingeon, the individual responsible for gender verification in Albertville, agreed to assume control.[22]

The commission eventually found alternate geneticists to complete the examinations. However, the Norwegian government's overt refusal to support gender verification, which followed closely on the heels of the protests in Barcelona and Albertville, clearly irked some Olympic officials. To mitigate these concerns, the IOC employed the Norwegian Sports University to determine the sentiments of female Olympians in Lillehammer. Headed by Professor Berit Skirstad, the research posed eleven questions regarding personal perception of gender verification to 115 athletes. Skirstad found that the less information about the procedure the Olympian had, the more supportive she was about its necessity.[23] "The athletes in general have not known enough about the complications attached to the test to question them," she concluded. "They tend to think that the test protects against male intruders in female competitions." After completing the research, Skirstad joined the growing list of those opposed to gender verification.[24]

The approval of gender verification by female Olympians is not surprising. Women largely supported sex/gender testing for a variety of reasons, all primarily rooted in cultural norms and social anxieties. First, many competitors accepted the IOC's suggestion that female athletes needed protection from gender transgressive individuals. For example, in Lillehammer 87 percent of the female athletes questioned found it "reassuring" that other competitors had gender certificates and believed "the test was necessary." Approximately 13 percent thought they had previously competed against a disguised male athlete.[25] Second, several female athletes believed that passing the sex test proved their womanhood. Because social biases suggested strong women breached femininity and heterosexuality, earning a femininity certificate substantiated one's sex/gender. "I looked forward to the opportunity to show that I was not cheating," explains US swimmer Nancy Hogshead-Makar. "I faced all these questions about being so strong. . . . In that context, I wanted to show I was not cheating."[26] Finally, a majority of the Olympians failed to recognize the flawed nature of the control methods. According to gynecologist John S. Fox, "Most female athletes are ignorant of the limitations of the test . . . and of the disastrous emotional and social consequences for the individual who has the misfortune to fail."[27] The acceptance demonstrated by a majority of female Olympians is one reason why the IOC continued to test.

Following the 1994 Winter Olympics, the Norwegian government passed several laws to clearly and unequivocally prohibit sex testing in the future. First, six months after the close of the Lillehammer Games, the Parliament passed the Act on Medical Use of Biotechnology (Act no. 56 of August 5, 1994).[28] This piece of legislation required informed consent on any medical use of biotechnology.[29] In addition, when the 1995 Junior World Championships in alpine skiing occurred in Voss, Norway, the organizers successfully argued that gender verification practices violated Norwegian law, derailing any efforts to implement the exam.[30] The Norwegian Biotechnology Advisory Board, an independent body appointed by the government, bolstered the national position by evaluating the test in 1996 and declaring it illegal. When the board relayed its findings to the NCS, sex testing was prohibited in the 1997 Nordic Skiing Championships in Trondheim, Norway.[31] Finally, in January 1997 the Parliament proposed an additional amendment to further deem gender verification illegal in Norway.[32] The amendment passed in April 1997, officially outlawing sex tests conducted for nonmedical reasons. Frustrated with the ceaseless opposition, Alexandre de Mérode suggested, "If they have a rule in Norway . . . then let them make men and women equal in competitions and see what the reaction is."[33] Norway joined with the IAAF and refused to support testing; however, others still voiced support, similar to de Mérode's, and found control imperative.

The New Racial "Other" in Olympic Competition

In the midst of the IOC and the IAAF's battle over gender verification, Chinese athletes started to shine in international sport. Similar to the Soviet Union's rejoinder in 1952, the People's Republic of China returned to the Olympics in 1984 after a twenty-four-year boycott. The country immediately showcased tremendous athletic capabilities. For example, after earning 28 medals in the 1988 Seoul Olympics (compared to the USSR's 132 and US's 102), Chinese athletes secured 50 in the 1996 Atlanta Games, finishing fourth in the medal count. This upward trend continued.

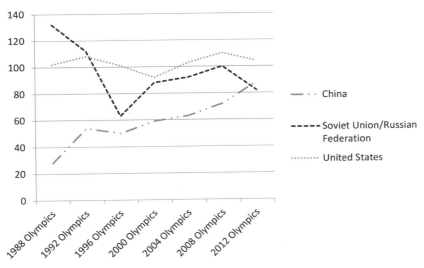

Medals won in the Summer Olympics, 1988–2012. (International Olympic Committee, "Olympic.org," *Official Website of the Olympic Movement.*)

Even more noticeably, women from the People's Republic of China dominated international track and field. For example, in the 1993 World Championships, Chinese competitors earned six of the possible nine medals in the women's long-distance races. The previously undecorated athletes also set several world records a few months later during the Chinese National Games, in the 1,500-meter, 3,000-meter, and 10,000-meter races. Yet, rather than celebrate these impressive triumphs, many in the West doubted the legitimacy of the achievements. Chinese female competitors in many sports faced criticisms; however, because the IAAF had terminated gender control, it was in track and field where the questions regarding gender authenticity appeared. "I would love to jump up and down and say 'Fabulous!'" said US athlete PattiSue Plumer, "but to smash those records by that much, it needs investigation." Similarly, US teammate Mary Decker Slaney, argued, "If they ratify these records, it will set women's middle distance and distance running back 25 years. . . . It will ruin the sport.[34]

Such sentiments surfaced in the West, thus denying female athleticism and "othering" the Chinese women. According to sport sociologist Darcy C. Plymire, an assessment of the Western coverage in 1993 demonstrates its tendency to construct the victorious Chinese athletes as fraudulent and unnatural.[35] As illustrated in the reports, female success was cause for suspicion, not celebration. Although no Chinese woman failed the compulsory drug test, journalists voiced suspicions of steroid abuse as a tactic to protect the rightful claimants to athletic victories—white, hetero-feminine, Western women. In addition, the doping accusations allowed many to liken the Chinese athletes to those of the Eastern bloc who had raised gender anxieties in the early stages of the Cold War. For example, after Wang Junxia broke her own 3,000-meter world record by six seconds, British Olympic Athletics team manager Joan Allison commented, "I walked away from the sport once because I was so disillusioned about the drugs being taken by the Eastern bloc competitors. I just throw my hands up and say: 'Here we go again.'"[36] The West depicted the Chinese athletes as guilty due to their governmental correlation to the Soviet Union. As Plymire notes, "In the eyes of some, the Chinese are the inevitable heirs to the legacy of the 'Big Red Machine' simply because they are a communist nation."[37]

With the animosities between the two superpowers largely dissolved, the West transferred its Cold War anxieties onto the geographic East, specifically onto China—the newest threat in the global establishment. Approximately one year after the Soviet Union collapsed, China's power status emerged. Notably, in 1992 China's economy grew at 12.8 percent, and just three years later the country's gross domestic product was 56 percent that of the United States.[38] The new economic competition, combined with China's increasing international political influence, concerned many in the West.

Consequently, Chinese women were increasingly established as the racial and gendered "other" in the realm of sport. The sentiments launched against the Asian nation in the 1990s paralleled the criticisms voiced about the Eastern bloc women in the height of the Cold War. Furthermore, the concerns sparked by the Chinese runners' rapid ascendancy increased when additional Eastern athletes faced sex/gender scrutiny. In the 1990 Asian Games in Beijing, organizers reportedly expelled an Indian female hockey player after she failed the requisite gender verification test.[39] Three years later, during the Southeast Asian Games, four women experienced similar expulsion. Kong Chuan, head of the games' medical committee, reported not only that the discoveries resulted in the immediate removal of the athletes but also that two women "did not know they were not females until they were told." Although Kong refused to identify the athletes or name the nationalities of the disqualified, the media highlighted the possibility of gender fraudulence in the East.[40]

Prompted by these speculations of ambiguously sexed/gendered Chinese female athletes, several Western running authorities publicly lamented the IAAF's decision to abolish gender verification. Editor of *Keeping Track: International Track & Field Newsletter*, Janet Heinonen, led the charge. She explained that as the "new world order" permeated athletics, China—like East

Germany in the 1970s—built "its own version of the state-supported, behind-closed-doors sports system." From her point of view, the legitimacy of the country's sudden achievements was doubtful. In particular, Heinonen argued that the dramatic successes of the Chinese female runners highlighted "the holes" in the IAAF's abandonment of gender verification. Accordingly, after "it became obvious that world records in track and field could be set without any requirement of gender verification," male masqueraders returned to the sport. As a result, some people "wanted the reassurance that drugs or no, all those new marks on the all-time world lists were being set by women, not men."[41] Heinonen not only drew parallels between the German Democratic Republic and China but also suggested that Western female athletes needed protection from male interlopers.

She additionally reaffirmed a belief in dimorphic sex and polarized gender.[42] Heinonen repeatedly declared that no biological overlap existed between men and women, a conviction she derived from conversations with steroid expert Don Catlin. Catlin, founder of the UCLA Olympic Analytical Lab, prioritized testosterone levels in the determination of sex/gender. With this information gleaned from Catlin, Heinonen suggested that the IAAF should return to a gynecological exam for all women competitors, supplemented with blood testing in cases of questionable results.[43]

On February 24, 1994, sixteen female runners followed Heinonen's lead and formally petitioned the IAAF to reinstitute gender verification for all "high stakes" women's events. Dubbed the "Heinonen Sixteen," the group consisted of several famous world-class athletes, most of whom competed for the United States. South African Colleen de Reuck was the only non-US runner to sign the appeal; however, she gained US citizenship six years later.[44] Galvanized by fears of female dopers, gender fraud, and Chinese victories, the Heinonen Sixteen articulated five major demands to the IAAF. First, the athletes requested the return of gender verification in any event that awarded medals or prize money. Accordingly, the group's proposed protocol served to deter three types of competitors: male imposters, transsexuals, and athletes who fell into the "gray area" of sex.[45] Second, the group asked that all women who desired to participate in such competitions be forced to agree to sex/gender control if victorious. Third, the Heinonen Sixteen suggested that the check—a chromosomal analysis as well as a pelvic examination—be completed within forty-eight hours of the race and occur in a clinical setting, under the supervision of the IAAF. If any question surfaced, the runners desired that both blood and hormonal testing occur. Fourth, the group requested a continuation of the femininity certification process. Finally, the Heinonen Sixteen demanded gender verification start immediately. "We are willing to undergo testing," they declared, "to ensure that women are competing for women's awards."[46]

The Heinonen Sixteen's demands quickly gained credence. For example, in October a conference was held alongside the 1994 Asian Games in Hiroshima, Japan, to answer questions about gender verification. According to reporter Phyllis Fang, the impetus for this symposium stemmed from newfangled global anxieties. "The conference was held against a background of accusations by some western coaches that there was something suspicious about the sudden emergence of China's recent women world record swimmers and middle-distance runners," she said.[47] Such speculations bolstered the IOC's decision to maintain gender verification.

The opposition voiced by the Heinonen Sixteen and other track and field competitors did not surprise the original members of the IAAF Workshop on Femininity. According to Ferguson-Smith, people's lack of insight into human biology ensured misunderstanding. The IOC's steadfast reliance on scientific technologies to uphold sex/gender difference also led to confusion. He therefore suggested that the protests be utilized as an opportunity to both reemphasize the underlying discrimination of the IOC's policy and provide sweeping education for athletes. Carlson agreed. In her view the Heinonen Sixteen "need to know that they are asking doctors to play god and make subjective assessments of advantage and womanhood."[48] Ferguson-Smith's and Carlson's advisement of education would eventually prove significant for the eventual termination of the IOC's gender verification requirement. However, until Olympians expressed aversion, the IOC continued to rely on PCR testing.

The 1996 Olympic bid went to Atlanta, United States. Although the country did not have federal requirements prohibiting gender verification, many people hoped that the recurrent criticisms and increased opposition would force the IOC to end gender verification. "We don't know what will happen in Atlanta in 1996," said a hopeful Ljungqvist. "It could be a turning point, if they don't allow this sort of testing to occur."[49] His optimism would prove to be misplaced.

The 1996 Atlanta Summer Olympics

To gain international attention and foster a reputation as a center of racial justice and economic prosperity, Atlanta vied for the 1996 Summer Olympic bid. Led by William "Billy" Porter Payne, and with the support of Mayor Andrew Young, Atlanta put forward a bid to the IOC. Although US president George H. W. Bush also endorsed the ambition, the Atlanta proposition was considered largely implausible as the United States had hosted the Olympics twelve years earlier in Los Angeles. Furthermore, with centennial implications, many assumed Athens was the obvious choice. However, after IOC delegates examined the candidatures' hotel accommodations and flight connections, as well as their proposed conditions for athletes, economic stability, facilities, police presence, and security measures, Atlanta edged out Athens, 51–35. In the 96th Session of the IOC, Juan Antonio Samaranch awarded the US city the Centennial Games.

The Olympics of the Woman?

With the victory, Atlanta hoped to highlight certain achievements to a global audience. In particular, the Atlanta Committee for the Olympic Games (ACOG) recognized the unprecedented increase in sporting opportunities for women in the United States and sought to promote this phenomenon. The National Broadcasting Company (NBC), the US commercial network entrusted with televising the 1996 Olympics, promoted the Atlanta Games as the "Olympics of the Woman." In NBC's line of reasoning, the Centennial Olympics served as the culmination of feminism and Title IX, a significant piece of legislation in the United States that required sex equitability in federally funded sport. Although the US media proclaimed the Atlanta Games as the "Olympics of the Woman," the validity of the assertion was questionable. Certain gender biases remained intact. For example, media coverage continued to favor male athletes, in both amount and description, despite the network's declaration that increased female exposure was an important goal. Furthermore, although US women accounted for a greater proportional share of medals than the men in 1996, NBC dedicated more airtime to male figures, including athletes, coaches, fans, and commentators. Finally, reinforcing femininity in women's sport, NBC awarded twice as much time to women in individual events as compared to women in team sports.[50] While NBC claimed to shine a new light on female Olympians, the coverage actually highlighted the ubiquitous nature of Western concerns with femininity.[51]

Gender Verification in Atlanta

By 1996 virtually all major medical societies had called for the IOC to terminate gender verification. Within the United States, the American Academy of Pediatrics, American College of Obstetricians and Gynecologists, American College of Physicians, American Medical Association, American Society of Human Genetics, and the Endocrine Society publicly opposed the practice.[52] The most oft-cited reasons were the inherent flaw in seeking biological sex distinction and the reliance on error-prone test methods. As Emory University geneticists Louis J. Elsas, Risa P. Hayes, and Kasinathan Muralidharan explained in the *Journal of the Medical Association of Georgia*, "The combination of non-valid screening tests, discriminatory aspects of 'female only' gender verification, failure to take into account problems of intersex and consequent stigmatization of positive screenes [*sic*] all created a backlash of resentment among medical professionals towards gender verification in sports."[53] Despite these objections, the IOC Medical Commission believed that gender verification was a necessity for women's competition. The group also articulated a new anxiety. With the expansion of sport globally, de Mérode and Eduardo Hay feared the purposeful use of sex/gender fraudulent women by third world countries.[54] Verification thus continued in Atlanta.

Learning from a past mistake—permitting Norway to challenge the IOC and refuse assistance in Lillehammer—the medical commission forced the ACOG to sign a contract. The document required on-site gender verification, legally binding the city to the procedure. To uphold the agreement, the ACOG medical commission requested support from Emory University's genetics department.[55] According to Elsas, an Emory professor, his colleagues largely disagreed with PCR testing; however, they conceded that, if required, medically trained specialists should conduct gender verification. Because the ACOG would otherwise turn to a commercial group, Emory's geneticists agreed to oversee the control.[56]

The physicians established two main priorities regarding the check. They sought to "prevent masquerading males from competing and do no harm to females with anticipated problems of intersex." For the actual DNA collection, only female technicians worked with the athletes, due to the sensitivity of the PCR test. The ACOG also had gynecologists, psychiatrists, urologists, and endocrinologists on standby, insinuating that the medical commission still struggled to determine exactly how to identify sex.[57]

Of the 3,387 participants checked, 8 demonstrated inconclusive results. According to the geneticists, 7 of the 8 exhibited androgen insensitivity syndrome. Had previous measures been in place, the 8 likely would have been quickly and quietly disqualified. However, with the consultation of a plethora of medical experts, the ACOG medical commission determined that "no men masquerading as women were encountered, and all participants were cleared for competition."[58]

Similar to the research conducted in Lillehammer, the genetics department interviewed female participants to determine their perspective on sex control. Through exit interviews, 94 percent of the respondents noted that they did not feel "anxious" regarding the screening, and 82 percent believed that the test should continue to be required for future competitions. Furthermore, seventy-nine women opted to write comments, from which a handful of recurrent themes surfaced. First, some women supported the notion of male biological superiority and bought into the scare of male masqueraders. One simply commented, "I do not want to race men." In the same vein, several women raised the notion of fairness. One commentator suggested that the IOC "should test all athletes who win," and another surmised that gender verification is "necessary for fairness." Finally, some recognized the obtrusiveness of the process. One posited, "I don't think we should take the test more than once," and another that it was an "expensive and labor intensive procedure."[59] Comparable to the results unearthed in Lillehammer, gender anxieties and concerns of fairness led most female Olympians to view gender verification as a necessity.

The 1998 Nagano Olympics

In 1991 the IOC selected Nagano as the second Asian city to host the Winter Olympics. During the 97th Session of the IOC, the Japanese mountain metropolis and Salt Lake City emerged as the top two contenders. The other three candidatures, Aosta, Italy; Jaca, Spain; and Östersund, Sweden, were considered too "small fry" to host the Winter Games.[60] Initially the IOC favored Salt Lake City, due to its geographic location, as well as the area's airport, athletic facilities, housing, and transportation. However, Atlanta's successful bid for the 1996 Centennial Games bolstered Nagano's position. The IOC was reluctant to award the Olympics to the same country consecutively. Therefore, in the fifth round of voting, Nagano, the "Roof of Japan," trumped Salt Lake City by a mere four votes.[61]

Despite the incongruities reported in Atlanta, and the continued criticism of the practice, the IOC continued gender verification in the Nagano Winter Games. To fulfill the medical commission's regulations, the Organising Committee for the Olympic Winter Games in Nagano created its own Medical Services Commission, comprised of nineteen experts from various medical and governmental organizations. Headed by Professor Yoshio Kuroda, the NAOC's Medical Services Commission provided general health-related care, oversaw sanitation, supervised anti-doping checks, and conducted PCR testing. For the sex/gender control, 679 of the 815 winter Olympians did not possess valid femininity certificates issued by the IOC. As a result, the commission collected both chromosomal and DNA samples from the participants and sent the screens to the Nagano Municipal Hospital for analysis.[62] Director Kuroda did not publicly report any failures. Although the PCR testing in Nagano may have proceeded more smoothly than in Lillehammer and Atlanta, Olympians increasingly resented the process. Through the IOC Athletes' Commission, competitors themselves altered the course of gender verification.

The Athletes' Commission

During the 1996 Atlanta and 1998 Nagano Games, Olympians voted for fellow competitors to serve as representatives on the IOC Athletes' Commission. The IOC founded the commission in 1981 to act as the liaison between the participants and the governing body. After the 1980 US-led boycott, many competitors felt powerless in the Olympic movement and expressed their frustrations the following year at the Olympic Congress in Baden-Baden. They argued that the IOC did not listen to athletes and had too few former Olympians as members and that those who were former Olympians were too far removed from competition to fully understand the contemporary issues in sport. Based on these complaints, Samaranch created the athletes' commission and appointed Finnish yachtsman Peter Tallberg as its first chair.[63]

The IOC initially selected the membership of the athletes' commission; however, for the Atlanta and Nagano Games it allowed competitors to choose their own representatives. In 1996, 54 percent of Olympians cast votes and elected rower Roland Baar (Germany), track and field athlete Hassiba Boulmerka (Algeria), track and field athlete Sergey Bubka (Ukraine), volleyball player Charmaine Crooks (Canada), swimmer Alexander Popov (Russia), and track and field athlete Jan Železný (Czech Republic).[64] Following comparable elections in 1998, in which 58 percent of participants voted, cross-country skier Manuela di Centa (Italy), speed skater Johann Olav Koss (Norway), and cross-country skier Vladimir Smirnov (Kazakhstan) joined the seven summer members.[65] The IOC also included nine additional individuals to ensure gender, geographic, and sport balance.

Three years after the initial 1996 vote, the athletes' commission became embroiled in the gender verification protests. Influenced by the Norwegian opposition, Tallberg suggested Olympians discuss the IOC Medical Commission's procedure. In 1998 he invited Ljungqvist and IOC vice president Anita DeFrantz to a meeting to debate the advantages and disadvantages of the policy. Ljungqvist outlined his concerns and DeFrantz underlined the necessity of fairness in elite competition. After listening to both assessments, Tallberg enlisted Norwegian speed skater Koss to further study the issue on behalf of the athletes' commission.[66] Koss, who had earned three gold medals in the 1994 Lillehammer Games, was also trained as a physician. After he reported to the group in 1999, the commission recommended that the IOC discontinue gender verification immediately.[67]

The End of Olympic Gender Verification?

While the athletes' commission advocated for an end to compulsory gender verification, the group also suggested that the IOC maintain the right to suspicion-based checks. The recommendation would allow for the "intervention and evaluation of individual athletes . . . if there is any question regarding gender identity."[68] It would seem that many people still associated outward appearances with sex/gender. With a proposal from the athletes' commission, Samaranch announced the termination of Olympic gender verification in 1999. The executive board voted to strengthen anti-doping checks and terminate sex/gender testing, "on an experimental basis," for the 2000 Sydney Summer Olympics.[69]

At first glance this decision seemed to indicate that the IOC had capitulated. Many people welcomed the change and applauded the Olympic authorities. However, upon closer examination it became clear that the medical commission maintained jurisdiction in the determination of sex/gender. The group merely fulfilled its intentions elsewhere. As Genel and Ljungqvist argued, Samaranch's announcement was largely misinterpreted. They warned that "gender verification has not, as some believe, been completely abandoned."[70] The IOC continued to dictate womanhood in three ways, again casting doubt on athletes who did not demonstrate normative notions of Western femininity.

First, the IOC increased the authority granted to anti-doping exams. The medical commission repeatedly conflated the purposes of the anti-doping checks and sex test/gender verification measures. While this association waxed and waned for three decades, the two were conjoined again in 1999 when the IOC terminated chromatin and DNA assessments. Rather than completely abandon control, the commission simply couched gender verification in doping methods. Most notably, the urination component of the doping test required visual inspection by an Olympic official, which permitted authorities to scrutinize an athlete's genitalia. As chief medical officer for the 1988 US Olympic team James C. Puffer explained, the possibility for the inclusion of a male masquerader was "laughable" due to the "direct observation of athletes providing urine specimens from their urethras." Similarly, Genel, Barry Dickinson, Carolyn B. Robinowitz, Patricia L. Turner, and Gary L. Woods posited that the urination examination "would seem to obviate the possibility of male imposters successfully competing."[71]

Still concerned with fraudulent competitors, the IOC's hidden agenda was problematic. Cloaking the control in anti-doping techniques again tied a woman's sex/gender to her reproductive organs. In doing so the IOC replicated the "nude parades" implemented during the early stages of the Cold War. Moreover, the inclusion of gender determination in anti-doping measurements permitted the IOC to further naturalize the body. In particular, the subtle focus on hormone levels created an arbitrary division between "normal" and "masculine" women. This subjective demarcation helped exclude athletes whose bodies fell outside conventional sex/gender norms.[72]

Second, for the 2000 Sydney Summer Olympics onward, the IOC Medical Commission embraced suspicion-based checks. Mirroring the IAAF's gender stipulations, the IOC upheld its right to verify any woman participant if a challenge should arise. In other words, Olympic authorities could require a female athlete who appeared too "suspicious" (non-feminine/non-Western) to undergo the PCR test.[73] The medical commission again suggested that overt performances of hetero-femininity demonstrated womanhood. Officials required three powerful Olympians to undergo testing in Sydney, basing their selections on the athletes' appearances.[74] Suspicion-based exams overtly criminalized strong-looking women and established athleticism and femininity as polar characteristics.

Finally, in 2003 the IOC cemented a dichotomy in Olympic competition through its guidelines for transgender athletic inclusion. The medical commission's policy known as "The Stockholm Consensus" outlined very specific rules to stipulate transgender performances in the Olympics.[75] First, the guidelines stated that in order to compete in Olympic events, a transgender individual must undergo sex-reassignment surgery and alter external genitalia. The second requirement varied upon country of residence; however, the rules required all competitors to receive legal recognition by "appropriate official authorities." Third, the IOC mandated transgender athletes administer hormone therapy "appropriate for the assigned sex" in order to minimize "gender-related advantages."[76]

With the Stockholm Consensus the medical commission again demonstrated a geographic Western bias. The policy notably discriminated against individuals from less-industrialized nations, but it also allowed the IOC to maintain a grasp on the determination of sex/gender.[77] For example, the concept of hormone levels "appropriate for the assigned sex" remains disputable, as no one standard exists. The use of conservative medical criteria not only diminished accessibility for many transgender athletes but also suggested that hormone levels exist in humans in a binary rather than in a spectrum. Furthermore, by embracing discourses of fairness, the IOC reified assumptions of male biological superiority. The claim that the Stockholm Consensus guaranteed a level playing field stemmed from fears of male-to-female transgender inclusion, comparable to the anxieties sparked by muscular women. Such fears of sex/gender-transgressive women had plagued the IOC from the onset of Olympic competition.

* * *

When the track and field federation abandoned gender verification, it seemed to put the IAAF at odds with the IOC. The medical commission reacted by arguing that some type of laboratory technique remained necessary to maintain fairness in Olympic competition. Responding to protests about the buccal smear test, the group replaced the chromatin check with PCR verification in 1992. Thus for the 1994 Lillehammer Games, 1996 Atlanta Games, and 1998 Nagano Games all female Olympians continued to undergo PCR control. Opposition subsequently increased. The objections voiced by the medical community, Norway, and the athletes eventually convinced the IOC to abandon the protocol in 1999, at least on the surface. Also in this time of transition, Alexandre de Mérode, longtime leader of the medical commission, died on November 19, 2002, at the age of sixty-eight. For more than three decades he had overseen the IOC's medical operations, including the introduction, continuation, and supposed abolishment of sex/gender testing. Moreover, throughout his Olympic tenure de Mérode had remained unwavering in his belief that some type of control mechanism for female athletes was essential for the sake of fair play in sport. When medical commission vice president Ljungqvist succeeded de Mérode in 2003, he embraced stricter doping tenets yet momentarily eased gender regulations.

The IOC Medical Commission seemingly terminated gender verification in 1999. However, the group actually continued to control female Olympians' sex/gender. The commission extended anatomical surveillance into doping checks, again placing sex/gender determination on Olympians' anatomy. Additionally, the group had the right to check any competitor it found "suspicious." In other words, it could investigate those it deemed non-feminine. Finally, the Stockholm Consensus established strict guidelines for the inclusion of transgender athletes in the Olympics. The policy was Western in orientation and premised upon the idea of sex/gender difference.

After three decades of protest the IOC followed the example set by the IAAF and abandoned mandatory gender verification. "It took a long battle to put an end to gender testing," Ljungqvist recalls. "This was a decades-long example of sexual harassment within sport. Gender testing was a flagrant abuse, nothing else."[78] Unfortunately, the IOC's "flagrant abuse" did not end in 1999.

Epilogue

The Reintroduction of Gender Verification

IN 1999 LJUNGQVIST ANNOUNCED, "Victory is finally ours—the genetic based test for screening for female gender at the Olympic Games has gone into the history books!"[1] His jubilant declaration proved premature. Seven years after the IOC abandoned PCR screening, sex and gender anxieties again plagued international sport. In the 2006 Asian Games twenty-five-year-old Indian middle-distance runner Santhi Soundarajan finished second in the women's 800-meter final. After the closely contested race, the Tamil Nadu native stood victoriously on the podium and happily showcased her medal. Her triumph would be short-lived. The day after she earned silver, Soundarajan, a world-class athlete who had previously garnered several first- and second-place finishes in international events, was asked to submit to a gender verification test.[2] Although the IAAF and the IOC had abolished compulsory screening in the 1990s, sport authorities still maintained the right to require its competitors to undergo an exam at any time. Therefore, four IAAF doctors, none of whom spoke Tamil, Soundarajan's native language, extracted blood and scrutinized her body. The silver medalist was told neither the purpose nor the outcome of the thirty-minute examination. It was days later, back in India, that Soundarajan learned from the evening news that she had "failed" the test. "That was the end of my sports life," she recalled. The IAAF immediately stripped Soundarajan of her medal and barred her from future competitions.[3] Traumatized and publically humiliated, she fell into depression.[4]

Three years later eighteen-year-old South African athlete Caster Semenya gained similar worldwide recognition during the 2009 World Track and Field Championships. In the 800-meter race the middle-distance runner over-

2006 Asian Games medalists. From left to right: silver medalist Santhi
Soundarajan of India, gold medalist Maryam Yusuf Jamal of Bahrain,
and bronze medalist Viktoriya Yalovtseva.

whelmed her competitors by a margin of more than two seconds, considered
a tremendous gap in the event. Semenya's noteworthy victory, which was
three seconds slower than the world record, was quickly overshadowed by the
hostile criticisms voiced by those she defeated.[5] "Just look at her," said Mariya
Savinova of Russia, presumably referring to Semenya's muscular stature.[6]
Italian middle-distance runner Elisa Cusma scoffed, "These kinds of people
should not run with us. For me, she's not a woman. She's a man."[7] Such vicious
comments stemmed from Semenya's notable improvement, powerfully built
body, and deep voice.[8] According to IAAF spokesperson Nick Davies, "There
were some doubts, really, about her gender."[9] Thus equally skeptical, the IAAF
required that her sex be scientifically verified. As sport scholar Jaime Schultz
notes, the public scrutiny of Semenya, particularly the focus on her genitals,
"smacked of the same insidious European exhibition and enfreakment of
Saartjie Baartman."[10] Or as historian Carina Ray succinctly surmises, "Fast
forward nearly two hundred years and the genitals of another young South
African woman, runner Caster Semenya, have once again become the target
of western scientists' prodding and poking."[11] Although two centuries apart,
the treatment of Baartman, Soundarajan, and Semenya illustrates Western
society's mistreatment of non-feminine, non-Western, non-white women.
    Influenced by Soundarajan's and Semenya's physiques, appearances, and
international plights, the IAAF and the IOC reconsidered the value of gender

South Africa's Caster Semenya celebrates after winning the women's 800-meter final of the 2009 IAAF Athletics World Championships in Berlin, Germany, August 19, 2009. Courtesy of Corbis.

verification.[12] Collectively the organizations sponsored six workshops to discuss the various techniques that could uphold sex/gender segregation in elite sport.[13] The most influential meeting occurred in January 2010, immediately following the Second World Conference on the Hormonal and Genetic Basis of Sexual Differentiation Disorders. In a two-day closed-door gathering, the IOC invited fifteen scientists, medical experts, and sport physicians—many with previous gender verification experience—to "draw up guidelines for dealing with 'ambiguous' gender cases."[14] The group's conclusions laid the foundation for the IOC's final 2011 policy, the "IOC Regulations on Female Hyperandrogenism."

Hyperandrogenism and Elite Sport

Once again the official Olympic policy targeted "deviant" female athletes. This time the IOC targeted women with higher than average levels of androgens.[15] Androgenic hormones control muscular development, and women with hyperandrogenism typically create a greater amount of naturally produced testosterone. Richard Budgett, sports physician and the current IOC medical and scientific director, argued that the group believed that testosterone was the deciding factor between male and female athletes. "It's the hormone that makes the difference," he explained. "If the thing that actually makes the difference in anybody . . . men or women, is testosterone, then it makes sense to look at that."[16] Therefore, the IOC required all NOCs to "actively investigate any perceived deviations in sex characteristics."[17] According to Stéphane Bermon, a coordinator of the working group on Hyperandrogenism and Sex Reassignment in Female Athletics, women with this condition have an "unfair advantage," because it produces "more muscle mass, easier recovery and a higher level of blood cells."[18] Echoing these anxieties, the IAAF adopted a similar policy.

The track and field federation outlined the "IAAF Regulations Governing Eligibility of Females with Hyperandrogenism to Compete in Women's Competition." In line with the IOC's protocol, the IAAF identified several underlying rationalizations. Of note, the organization justified the new policy out of "a respect for the fundamental notion of fairness of competition in female Athletics."[19] The IAAF later clarified its responsibility in its "Hyperandrogenism Regulations: Explanatory Notes." According to this document, the federation's role "is first and foremost to guarantee the fairness and integrity of the competitions." For the sake of equality, a woman would be prohibited if "she has functional androgen levels that are in the male range."[20]

To maintain biological fairness, the IOC and IAAF also prescribed remedies for athletes who wished to continue competing. Those suspected of having the "disorder" needed to be examined and diagnosed at preselected reference centers, which were located in Australia, Brazil, France, Japan, Sweden, and the United States. No approved resource centers existed in Africa or India.[21] Once diagnosed, the athlete had to undergo "treatment" to "normalize" her androgen levels, at her own expense.[22] Neither the IOC nor the IAAF identified what such a procedure entailed or cost.[23]

The IOC implemented the policy for the 2012 London Olympics and problems immediately surfaced. Four female athletes, ages twenty-one and younger, were identified as having hyperandrogenism. The appearance of one competitor's genitals raised suspicions during an anti-doping urine screening. Hormonal changes noted on the Athlete Biological Passport raised suspicion of two athletes. The Athlete Biological Passport, introduced by the World Anti-Doping Agency in 2002, monitored biological variables over time to determine if an athlete had manipulated his or her physiology. The fourth woman was referred to the international federation by a national federation doctor. After the IOC barred all four Olympic hopefuls, they were "whisked away" to Nice and Montpellier, France, for treatment.[24] Those responsible for the medical intervention described the women as tall, slim, and muscular and noted that they hailed from "rural or mountainous regions of developing countries."[25] The doctors recommended that the athletes undergo a corrective measure to ensure their future participation in sport. As stated in the report, forgoing the surgery "carries no health risks," while undergoing the surgery "would most likely decrease their performance." Still, the procedure would "allow them to continue elite sport in the female category." The specialists also performed "feminizing vaginoplasty," an aesthetic (re)construction of the vagina.[26] Put simply, the doctors completed an unnecessary operation that did not alleviate a health issue and then executed plastic surgery to ensure that the women's genitals aligned with accepted anatomical compositions.

Protests ensued and issues continued. In advance of the 2014 Glasgow Commonwealth Games, officials from the Sports Authority of India (SAI), the central sporting body of the country, took Indian sprinter Dutee Chand aside for medical tests. The SAI did so at the behest of the Athletics Federation of India, the country's track and field federation. Chand, a bronze medal winner in the Asian Athletics Championships, was told neither the reason for nor the purpose of the exam. Days before the competition the SAI deemed her ineligible. "I cried for three straight days," Chand explained through an interpreter. "They were saying, 'Dutee: Boy or girl?' and I thought, how can you say those things. I have always been a girl."[27] The SAI initially offered to assist Chand with the required treatment. "I was told I must undergo surgery or take hormonal treatment if I wanted to salvage my career," she said. "It's so cruel. . . . I don't want to change anything and I also don't want to give up sports."[28] When Chand refused the medical intervention, the SAI agreed to help her protest the IAAF's policy. With the support, she filed an appeal in the Court of Arbitration (CAS), an independent organization outside the dominion of the IAAF and the IOC that settles sports-related disputes.

On July 24, 2015, CAS permitted Chand's return to competition. The court concluded that the IAAF had failed to scientifically verify the athletic benefits of possessing higher-than-average testosterone levels. "There is presently insufficient evidence about the *degree* of the advantage that androgen-sensitive hyperandrogenic females enjoy over non-hyperandrogenic females," the CAS noted.[29] Therefore the court suspended hyperandrogenism regulations for two years, during which time the IAAF must submit new scientific evidence. If the international federation is unable to conclusively demonstrate advantage, the policy will be completely voided. Although it had been more than forty years after the IAAF and IOC first introduced gender testing, the hyperandrogenism policies, practices, and exclusionary tendencies illustrate the same gendered and racialized anxieties that surfaced in the 1960s, as well as the continued medico-scientific interpretation of womanhood.

Sex Testing, Gender Verification, and Regulations on Female Hyperandrogenism

Protests of the hyperandrogenism policies likened the new control to the Olympic sex/gender test unveiled in 1968. In the 1968 Mexico City Summer Games, the IOC implemented compulsory screening for female athletes, a policy that dictated Olympic womanhood until 1999. For over three decades, sport officials policed sex/gender through a variety of methods, including physical inspections, chromosomal analyses, and DNA assessments. The inclusion of hormone testing thus merely added a different technique to this list. Throughout the history of sex testing/gender verification, sport officials repeatedly extolled the necessity of fairness, raised suspicions based on women's appearances, failed to locate a clear division between men and women, and undermined the progress of female athletes in sport.

The IAAF and IOC frequently argued that testing ensured fair play. Influenced by a belief in biological advantage, both organizations suggested that feminine women needed a safeguard against masculine interlopers. This line of reasoning insinuated that sex testing/gender verification maintained equality by allowing only those who were scrutinized, poked, probed, and prodded into competition. Such claims fell short for two reasons. First, the IOC never considered incorporating a reciprocal exam to safeguard fairness in men's events. Only women needed a defense against competitors with an advantageous biological makeup; men could participate unhindered. When the IAAF did introduce a "health check" for all athletes in 1990, critics immediately condemned the decision. Verifying male athletes was unnecessary and irrational, they argued. The hyperandrogenism protocols outlined in

2011 and enacted in 2012 similarly did not bar men with abnormal levels of naturally produced androgens, either higher or lower. If fairness was truly the driving factor, why did the IOC and IAAF not impose a parallel ceiling on men? The hyperandrogenism policies thereby continued "the legacy of double-standard policies," singling out female athletes and "casting doubt on [their] sex, gender, and sexuality."[30] The fact that only women faced derision, suspicion, and testing highlights the parameters of gender acceptability in sport: femininity and athleticism are oxymoronic and inappropriate, whereas masculinity and athleticism are natural and correct.

Second, fairness is an abstract concept that does not exist in elite sport. As Claire F. Sullivan has surmised, "The fact is the playing field has never been level."[31] Various genetic predispositions and social advantages guarantee that inequalities abound in competition. For example, both height and wealth improve an athlete's chances for success. Sex/gender controls targeted women's abilities while all other beneficial dispositions remained unmonitored. "Why are we bent on reducing or eliminating an inherent advantage that a woman is born with?" asks SAI director Jiji Thomson. "Just because Usain Bolt's height is to his advantage will the international authorities want his legs chopped off to ensure a level-playing field?"[32]

Rather than bolster fairness, drawing an arbitrary line between men and women actually promoted discrimination. For over half a century, female athletes deemed medically different by sport organizations faced unjust exclusion. In the words of the Canadian Centre for Ethics in Sport, "While the threat to fair competition turns out to be virtually non-existent, the actual harm experienced by athletes from such testing have been acute, and in a few instances, catastrophic."[33] Female Olympians with different anatomical and chromosomal compositions were initially excluded; in 2012 female Olympians with different androgen levels faced prohibition.

Furthermore, the IAAF's and IOC's repeated insistence on the need for sex/gender verification illustrates the anxieties sparked by non-feminine, non-Western, non-white women. The organizations may have claimed that fairness was at stake; however, concerns about athletes' appearances actually led the campaign. Public accounts vilified women as sport officials questioned their sex/gender. With the rise of women's track and field in the early twentieth century, many lamented the loss of femininity as female athletes excelled in physical activities previously reserved for men. Next, Cold War politics, combined with Eastern European women's successes, increased the IAAF's and the IOC's worries. As Amanda Nicole Schweinbenz and Alexandria Cronk explaines, these concerns "prompted physicians and sport administrators to re-examine the biological and social definitions of femininity."[34]

The ensuing eligibility requirements suggested that sex/gender-normative women needed protection from sex/gender-transgressive women—those with anatomical ambiguity, chromosomal anomalies, and hyperandrogenism. In other words, the IOC and IAAF wanted to protect "real" female competitors from those with suspected biological differences.

The efforts to protect "real" women vilified non-Western female athletes. During the Cold War, competitors from Eastern Europe were viewed with suspicion and contempt. In the 1990s Chinese runners evolved into the scapegoats for gender transgression. And the hyperandrogenism guidelines of 2012 disproportionately impacted women of color from countries that were less developed. The proposed remedies were founded upon Western medico-scientific thought, and approved resource centers were geographically limited. Athletes who did not conform to Western standards of white femininity consistently faced the greatest scrutiny, experienced the cruelest hostility, and underwent the most testing.

Finally, the history of sex testing/gender verification not only indicates female Olympians' inferior position in the Olympic movement but also demonstrates women's secondary status in sport. Olympic authorities prioritized gender and investigated sex, allowing other athletes, experts, nonexperts, organizations, and structures to similarly question the appropriateness of women in physical activities. The various iterations of sex/gender testing all suggested that athleticism and femaleness were antithetical. As Canadian sports policy advisor Bruce Kidd argues, "It's still the old patriarchal fear, or doubt, that women can do outstanding athletic performances. If they do, they can't be real women."[35] The notion that "real" women cannot succeed in physical contests reserves sport as a male endeavor. Because of the IOC's influence internationally, this message was extended far beyond the Olympic Games.

The motivations of the 2012 control clearly echoed those articulated for the antecedent exam of the 1960s. Once again the IAAF and the IOC sought to control women's bodies and bar certain types of female athletes from competition. And once again the sex/gender verification measures stemmed more from social ideologies about women's role in sport than scientific factors about sex determination. The historical elusiveness of identifying sex and the harm that sex/gender testing has caused women illustrate the need to dismantle the "structures of suspicion."[36] Testing in all forms, whether based on anatomy, chromosomes, or testosterone, unethically criminalized women who did not subscribe to conventional, white, hetero-femininity.

Notes

Introduction

1. Associated Press, "Soviet Girls Set Track Records," *Los Angeles Times*, April 3, 1964, B5.

2. Arthur Daley, "Sports of the Times: The Red-Faced Reds," *New York Times*, October 23, 1964, 47.

3. Sid Ziff, "On Babka and Girls," *Los Angeles Times*, July 1, 1966, B3.

4. Braven Dyer, "Sex Rears Its Ugly Head and Sports Columnist Finds Himself in Trouble," *Los Angeles Times*, August 8, 1936, 13.

5. Charles Maher, "On Fast Women," *Los Angeles Times*, July 2, 1970, E2.

6. According to Susan Birrell, in the 1980s sport scholars recognized the role of language in creating and reproducing notions of women, femininity, physicality, sexuality, and the body. Birrell, "Discourses on the Gender/Sport Relationship: From Women in Sport to Gender Relations."

7. After a review of the literature that discussed aspects of gender variance in sport, Kevin B. Wamsley found that "sex" typically connoted visible anatomy, and "gender" described social perceptions of identification. Wamsley, "Social Science Literature on Sport and Transitioning/Transitioned Athletes." Yet Anne Fausto-Sterling recognized that by ceding this division, feminists opened themselves up to attacks of biological difference. According to Fausto-Sterling, the body is too complex to provide clear-cut answers about sexual difference. Fausto-Sterling, *Sexing the Body: Gender Politics and the Construction of Sexuality*, 4–5.

8. See Rachel M. McBride and Jehannine Austin, "Sex Testing or Gender Verification: Is There a Difference and Does It Matter?" and April Vannini and Barbara Fornssler, "Girl, Interrupted: Interpreting Semenya's Body, Gender Verification Testing, and Public Discourse."

9. Annemarie Jutel, "Sociology of Diagnosis: A Preliminary Review."

10. Elizabeth Reis, *Bodies in Doubt: An American History of Intersex*, x.

11. David Epstein, *The Sports Gene: Inside the Science of Extraordinary Athletic Performance*, 58.

12. The Centre for Genetics Education, "Genes and Chromosomes: The Genome," *Genetics.edu*, September 8, 2015, http://www.genetics.edu.au/Publications-and -Resources/Genetics-Fact-Sheets/FS1.

13. Zine Magubane, "Spectacles and Scholarship: Caster Semenya, Intersex Studies, and the Problem of Race in Feminist Theory," 768–771.

14. Reis, *Bodies in Doubt*, xii.

15. Anne Fausto-Sterling, "Gender, Race, and Nation: The Comparative Anatomy of 'Hottentot' Women in Europe, 1815–1817."

16. Susan K. Cahn, *Coming on Strong: Gender and Sexuality in Twentieth-Century Women's Sport*, 132–33.

17. Patricia Hill Collins, *Black Sexual Politics: African Americans, Gender, and the New Racism*, 44.

18. Ronald Grigor Suny, *The Revenge of the Past: Nationalism, Revolution, and the Collapse of the Soviet Union*.

19. Eduardo Hay, "Femininity Tests at the Olympic Games," 120; emphasis added.

20. Seoul Olympic Organizing Committee, *Official Report*, vol. 1, part 3, 182; emphasis added. (All Olympic reports have been digitized and can be found online.)

21. For the scientific perspective, see John S. Fox, "Gender Verification: What Purpose? What Price?"; Helen Pearson, "Physiology: Freaks of Nature?"; and J. C. Reeser, "Gender Identity and Sport: Is the Playing Field Level?" For the philosophical perspective, see Christian Munthe, "Selected Champions: Making Winners in the Age of Genetic Technology."

22. J. Michael Bostwick and Michael J. Joyner, "The Limits of Acceptable Biological Variation in Elite Athletes: Should Sex Ambiguity Be Treated Differently from Other Advantageous Genetic Traits?"

23. Vicki Michaelis, "Built to Swim, Phelps Found a Focus and Refuge in Water," *USA Today*, August 8, 2008, 01A; Adam Hadhazy, "What Makes Michael Phelps So Good?" *Scientific American*, August 18, 2008, http://www.scientificamerican.com /article.cfm?id=what-makes-michael-phelps-so-good.

24. Richard Demak, "Marfan Syndrome: A Silent Killer," *Sports Illustrated*, February 17, 1986, 30.

25. Jaime Schultz, "Caster Semenya and the 'Question of Too': Sex Testing in Elite Women's Sport and the Issue of Advantage," 233.

26. "Report on the Medical Organization at the Grenoble Games," July 14–17, 1968, Box 89, IOC Meetings, Medical Commission Report Folder, Avery Brundage Collection, University of Illinois Archives (hereafter Brundage Collection).

27. According to John W. Loy and his colleagues, Eleanor Metheny's principles provide sociological explanation for the controlled development of women's Olympic inclusion. Loy et al., "Connotations of Female Movement and Meaning."

28. A majority of the sex/gender testing scholarship focuses on the Cold War con-

text of the control's first iteration. These publications cite Cold War fears of powerful Eastern European women as the primary reason behind the introduction of the sex/ gender checks. For examples, see Rob Beamish and Ian Ritchie, *Fastest, Highest, Strongest: A Critique of High-Performance Sport*, 31–45; Ian Ritchie, "Sex Tested, Gender Verified: Controlling Female Sexuality in the Age of Containment"; Claire Sullivan, "Gender Verification and Gender Policies in Elite Sport: Eligibility and 'Fair Play'"; and Stefan Wiederkehr, "'We Shall Never Know the Exact Number of Men Who Have Competed in the Olympics Posing as Women': Sport, Gender Verification, and the Cold War." Other works provide a feminist interpretation of sex/gender classification to challenge the dichotomization of the body and unsettle a binary notion of sex. For examples, see Sylvain Ferez, "From Women's Exclusion to Gender Institution: A Brief History of the Sexual Categorisation Process within Sport"; Amanda Nicole Schweinbenz and Alexandria Cronk, "Femininity Control at the Olympic Games"; and Laura A. Wackwitz, "Verifying the Myth: Olympic Sex Testing and the Category of 'Woman.'" Finally, several scholars used the plight of South African runner Caster Semenya, who was internationally scrutinized after triumphing in the 2009 World Championships, as a case study to revisit society's dependence on a binary system of sex/gender. For examples, see Susan K. Cahn, "Testing Sex, Attributing Gender: What Caster Semenya Means to Women's Sports"; Silvia Camporesi and Paolo Maugeri, "Caster Semenya: Sport, Categories, and the Creative Role of Ethics"; Tavia Nyong'o, "The Unforgiveable Transgression of Being Caster Semenya"; Schultz, "Caster Semenya"; and Vannini and Fornssler, "Girl, Interrupted."

Chapter 1. Sex/Gender Anxieties in Track and Field

1. Bill Henry, "Marks Set by Yanks in Games," *Los Angeles Times*, August 4, 1936, 1.

2. In the 1935 National Amateur Athletic Union Championships, the unknown Stephens defeated the internationally lauded Walsh in the 50-meter sprint. After the race a *St. Louis Post-Dispatch* reporter asked Stephens if she realized that she "outran Stella Walasiewicz." Either attempting to be humorous or unfamiliar with Walsh's Polish name, Stephens famously responded, "Stella who?" Regardless of intent, the remark allowed the press to craft a supposed feud between the two runners. Sharon Kinney Hanson, *The Life of Helen Stephens: The Fulton Flash*, 25–27.

3. The IAAF did not ratify either of Stephens's world record times, refusing to recognize her 11.4-second finish in the qualifying round and 11.5-second finish in the final. The IAAF required the measurement of tailwinds, winds that blow in the direction of the athlete's trajectory, to eliminate the possibility of "wind assistance" in outdoor events. In 1952 Marjorie Jackson of Australia equaled Stephens's qualifying time and officially claimed the 100-meter world record; in 1955 Shirley Strickland of Australia set the world record with a time of 11.3 seconds, nineteen years after Stephens's Berlin performance. International Association of Athletics Federation, *Competition Rules, 2014–2015*, 259–260.

4. "Fulton, Mo., Ignores Primary for News of Girl Athletic Star," *New York Times*, August 5, 1936, 27.

5. Bob Ray, "The Sports X-Ray," *Los Angeles Times*, August 8, 1936, 15; Braven Dyer, "Sex Rears Its Ugly Head," *Los Angeles Times*, August 8, 1936, 13; "Helen Stephens a Man, Polish Writer Thinks," *Chicago Daily Tribune*, August 6, 1936, 20.

6. "Polish Writer Calls Helen Stephens a 'Man,'" *Los Angeles Times*, August 6, 1936, A9.

7. "German Officials Conduct Inquiry," *Los Angeles Times*, August 6, 1936, A14.

8. Donald G. Kyle, *Sport and Spectacle in the Ancient World*, 94–98; Thomas F. Scanlon, *Eros & Greek Athletics*, 9–11.

9. John Mouratidis, "Heracles at Olympia and the Exclusion of Women from the Ancient Olympic Games," 50–51.

10. Ibid., 53; Scanlon, *Eros & Greek Athletics*, 98–120. Not all scholars agree that the Heraean Games existed in this form. Kyle suggests that some scholars exaggerate the role of women in ancient athletics in an attempt to locate positive female examples. Kyle, *Sport and Spectacle*, 217–228.

11. Allen Guttmann, *The Olympics: A History of the Modern Games*, 7–20.

12. John Hoberman, *The Olympic Crisis: Sport, Politics, and the Moral Order*, 33–36.

13. Quoted in Mark Dyreson, *Making the American Team: Sport, Culture, and the Olympic Experience*, 34.

14. Alan Tomlinson, "Carrying the Torch for Whom?" 179.

15. Pierre de Coubertin, "The Women at the Olympic Games," 542–546.

16. Dikaia Chatziefstathiou, "Reading Baron Pierre de Coubertin: Issues of Race and Gender," 99–101.

17. From 1900 to 1912 women participated on a provisional basis. In 1912 the IOC granted female athletes official status, albeit only in archery, gymnastics, skating, and swimming events. Bruce Kidd, "'Another World is Possible': Recapturing Alternative Olympic Histories, Imagining Different Games," 149–150; and Sheila Mitchell, "Women's Participation in the Olympic Games, 1900–1926."

18. The International Olympic Committee was created in 1894. Fifteen members were originally selected, with Dr. Willibald Gebhardt of Germany added in 1895.

19. Guttmann, *Olympics*, 15.

20. Karl Lennartz, "Biographies of IOC-Members," 56–58.

21. Kay Schiller and Christopher Young, *The 1972 Munich Olympics and the Making of Modern Germany*, 14.

22. Jennifer Hargreaves, *Sporting Females: Critical Issues in the History and Sociology of Women's Sports*, 131–133.

23. Cahn, *Coming on Strong*, 114.

24. One woman also competed in sailing, which was not a sex-segregated sport. International Olympic Committee, "Factsheet: Women in the Olympic Movement," May 2014, *Olympic.org*, http://www.olympic.org/Documents/Reference_documents _Factsheets/Women_in_Olympic_Movement.pdf.

25. The FSFI added additional events for the 1926 Women's Olympics, including the

100-meter track walk, 250-meter race, and discus. For the 1930 Women's Games the FSFI incorporated the 80-meter hurdles, 100-meter race, 200-meter race, 800-meter race, 4 x 100-meter relay, and triathlon. For the final Women's Games, the pentathlon was added. Cahn, *Coming on Strong*, 57–59; Athletics Weekly, "FSFI Women's World Games," accessed September 22, 2015, *GBRAthletics*, http://www.gbrathletics.com/ic/fsfi.htm.

26. Florence Carpentier and Jean-Pierre Lefévre, "The Modern Olympic Movement, Women's Sport, and the Social Order during the Inter-War Period."

27. During the interwar era, separate men's and women's physical education departments became common but not universal. The separation ensured women's control over women's development. Martha H. Verbrugge, *Active Bodies: A History of Women's Physical Education in Twentieth-Century America*, 53.

28. Jaime Schultz, *Qualifying Times: Points of Change in U.S. Women's Sport*, 73.

29. Jennifer H. Lansbury, *A Spectacular Leap: Black Women Athletes in Twentieth-Century America*, 51.

30. Carpentier and Lefévre, "Modern Olympic Movement."

31. Kidd, "'Another World Is Possible,'" 147–150.

32. The nine runners in the final included Marie Dollinger (Germany), Inga Gentzel (Sweden), Gertruda Kilosówna (Poland), Hitomi Kinue (Japan), Florence McDonald (USA), Lina Radke (Germany), Fanny Rosenfeld (Canada), Jenny Thompson (Canada), and Elfreide Wewer (Germany).

33. Quoted in Allen Guttmann, *Women's Sports: A History*, 169.

34. Cahn, *Coming on Strong*, 115.

35. Guttmann, *Women's Sports*, 166–171.

36. "Women Athletes," *Washington Post*, August 3, 1932, 6.

37. Hitomi envisioned herself as a *moga*, a modern woman. In Japan, *mogas* drank alcohol, smoked cigarettes, flaunted singlehood and sexual independence, and embraced financial independence. Dennis Frost, *Seeing Stars: Sports Celebrity, Identity, and Body Culture in Modern Japan*, 142.

38. Ibid., 117.

39. Ibid., 144.

40. Robin Kietlinski, *Japanese Women and Sport: Beyond Baseball and Sumo*, 49–65.

41. Quoted in Frost, *Seeing Stars*, 143–144. According to Frost, Kōshin believed that all individuals were combinations of male and female components.

42. Grantland Rice, "Separate Olympics for Sexes in 1940 Planned," *Los Angeles Times*, August 12, 1936, A9.

43. Didrikson tied with Jean Shiley in the running high jump with a height of 5 feet 5¼ inches. But because she performed the "Western Roll," a headfirst approach not used in Olympic competition at the time, Didrikson was awarded second place. Symbolic of the controversy, she was given a half-gold and half-silver medal. Susan E. Cayleff, *Babe: The Life and Legend of Babe Didrikson Zaharias*, 68–71.

44. Lansbury, *Spectacular Leap*, 51.

45. Cahn, *Coming on Strong*, 110–117.

46. Paul Gallico, "The Little Babe from Texas Turned Out to Be One of the World's Greatest Athletes," 48.

47. Schultz, *Qualifying Times,* 79.

48. Betty Hardesty, "Do Sports Subtract Feminine Charm?" *Washington Post,* June 25, 1933, 49.

49. A. F. Carylon-Hendry, "Our Modern Amazons: New Problems for Scientists," *Times of India,* October 1, 1928, 10.

50. Bill Henry, "Bill Henry Says," *Los Angeles Times,* January 15, 1933, E1.

51. Alexandrine Gibb, "No Man's Land of Sport," *Toronto Daily Star,* May 30, 1936, 13.

52. Quoted in M. Ann Hall, "Alexandrine Gibb: In 'No Man's Land of Sport,'" 159–160.

53. Gibb, "No Man's Land," 13.

54. Arnd Krüger and William Murray, *The Nazi Olympics: Sport, Politics, and Appeasement in the 1930s;* Richard Mandell, *The Nazi Olympics.*

55. Hanson, *Life of Helen Stephens,* 15.

56. Ibid., 13–19.

57. "Helen Stephens a Man, Polish Writer Thinks," 20; "Polish Writer Calls Helen Stephens a 'Man,'" A9.

58. Hanson, *Life of Helen Stephens,* 95–96.

59. "German Officials Conduct Inquiry," A14.

60. Paul Gallico, *Farewell to Sport,* 234.

61. Meeting Minutes of the International Olympic Committee Session in Berlin, July 31, 1936, Archives of the International Olympic Committee, Olympic Studies Centre, Lausanne, Switzerland (hereafter cited as OSC Archives).

62. Matt Tullis, "Who Was Stella Walsh? The Story of the Intersex Olympian," *SB Nation,* June 27, 2003, http://www.sbnation.com/longform/2013/6/27/4466724 /stella-walsh-profile-intersex-olympian.

63. Neil Amdur, "Miss Walsh Remains a Heroine," *New York Times,* December 21, 1980, S9.

64. Tullis, "Who Was Stella Walsh?"

65. Ellen W. Gerber et al., *The American Woman in Sport,* 418–421; George Eisen, "The Voices of Sanity: American Diplomatic Reports from the 1936 Berlin Olympiad," 73.

66. Upon Ratjen's arrest and subsequent medical examination, the officers sent a radio message to Berlin seeking advice on how to proceed. The communication explained, "Women's European high-jumping champion Ratjen, first name Dora, is not a woman, but a man. Please notify the Reich Sports Ministry at once. Awaiting orders by radio." Quoted in Stefan Berg, "1936 Berlin Olympics: How Dora the Man Competed in the Women's High Jump."

67. Ibid.

68. Vanessa Heggie, "Testing Sex and Gender in Sports; Reinventing, Reimagining, and Reconstructing Histories," 157–158.

69. Quoted in Jennifer Hargreaves, "Olympic Women: A Struggle for Recognition," 11.

70. "Change of Sex," *Time*, August 24, 1936, 39–40.

71. Heather Sykes, "Transsexual and Transgender Policies in Sport."

72. Joanne Meyerowitz, *How Sex Changed: A History of Transsexuality in the United States*, 33–34.

73. Donald Furthman Wickets, "Can Sex in Humans Be Changed?" 16–17.

74. Ibid., 16–17; "Girl Changes into Man," *Your Body*, 309–311.

75. "Athlete, Once Girl, Comes to U.S. as a Man," *Chicago Daily Tribune*, August 13, 1936, 20.

76. Meyerowitz, *How Sex Changed*, 34–35.

77. Milton Bronner, "The Girl Who Became a Bridegroom," *Times Daily* (Florence, AL), August 20, 1936, 5.

78. "Change of Sex," 39–40; Wickets, "Can Sex in Humans Be Changed?" 16–17.

79. Bronner, "Girl Who Became a Bridegroom," 5.

80. Gibb, "No Man's Land," 13.

81. Avery Brundage, "Letter to Count Henri Baillet-Latour," June 23, 1936, published in entirety in Mary H. Leigh, "The Enigma of Avery Brundage," 11–21.

82. "Change of Sex," 39–40.

83. "Brundage Urges Sex Examinations," *Los Angeles Times*, August 1, 1936, 13.

84. Leon Caurla publicly confirmed the results of his sex-reassignment surgery in 1952, eighteen months after the procedure. "Girl Changed to Boy," *Barrier Miner* (Broken Hill), March 4, 1952, Z; "Athlete, 25, Changes Sex," *Sydney Morning Herald*, March 5, 1952, 3.

85. "Are Girl Athletes Really Girls?" 63–66.

86. "Helga, Great 'Girl' Athlete, Becomes Boy," *Chicago Daily Tribune*, December 14, 1952, 1.

87. Heggie, "Testing Sex and Gender," 157–163.

88. M. A. Ferguson-Smith and Elizabeth A. Ferris, "Gender Verification in Sport: The Need for Change?" 17.

89. Neena A. Xavier and Janet B. McGill, "Hyperandrogenism and Intersex Controversies in Women's Olympics," 3904. Janice Lee Romary, member of the US Olympic teams from 1948 to 1968, detailed the IOC's request. According to a *Chicago Tribune* article, athletes could have any doctor sign the form, opening the possibility for bribery. Romary explained that she carried the "oft-folded and yellowed piece of paper for use as a good cocktail party gag." "Sex Tests No Turnoff Now," *Chicago Tribune*, July 14, 1976, C4.

90. Ballantyne et al., "Sex and Gender Issues in Competitive Sports."

91. Max Dohle, "Biography of Foekje Dillema: English Summary," 2012, http://www.foekjedillema.nl/index_fd_eng.html.

92. Ballantyne et al., "Sex and Gender Issues."

93. "Charges against Sex of Woman Athlete 'A Slur,'" *Times of India*, August 22, 1960, 8.

94. "Olympic Women 'Have Medical Certificates,'" *Times* (London), August 22, 1960, 4.

Chapter 2. Cold War Gender Norms and International Sport

1. William Barry Furlong, "Venus Wasn't a Shot-Putter," *New York Times*, August 28, 1960, SM14.

2. Shirley Povich, "This Morning," *Washington Post*, April 5, 1956, 53.

3. Frank True, "Red 'Wolves' in Skirts?" *Sarasota Herald Tribune*, September 13, 1966, 17.

4. John Lewis Gaddis, *The Cold War: A New History*, 6.

5. David J. Romagnolo, "Speech Delivered by J. V. Stalin at a Meeting of Voters of the Stalin Electorate District, Moscow," *From Marx to Mao*, July 2000, http://www .marx2mao.com/Stalin/SS46.html.

6. Gaddis, *Cold War*, 26.

7. Efstathios T. Fakiolas, "Kennan's Long Telegram and NSC-68: A Comparative Theoretical Analysis," 418.

8. George Kennan, "The Long Telegram," *George Washington University*, September 27, 1998, http://www.gwu.edu/~nsarchiv/coldwar/documents/episode-1/kennan.htm.

9. Kennan originally published "The Sources of Soviet Conduct" anonymously in *Foreign Affairs* in July 1947. For a reprint, see "X" (George Kennan), "The Sources of Soviet Conduct," 852–68. Available at https://www.foreignaffairs.com/articles /russian-federation/1947-07-01/sources-soviet-conduct.

10. Gaddis, *Cold War*, 62–70.

11. Drew Middleton, "Khrushchev Says Soviet Will Make H-Bomb Missile: Warns Briton," *New York Times*, April 24, 1956, 1; James Feron, "Britain Is Atomic-War Target, Khrushchev Warns Laborites," *New York Times*, October 31, 1961, 14.

12. "Khrushchev Invites U.S. to Missile Shooting Match," *New York Times*, November 16, 1957, 1.

13. Direct altercation proved avoidable; however, the two countries clashed in decolonizing other countries, notably engaging in conflicts in Korea and Vietnam. The United States and the Soviet Union engaged in warfare in Korea but tacitly agreed to cover up the fighting. Gaddis, *Cold War*, 59–79; emphasis in original.

14. "The Kitchen Debate—Transcript," *Central Intelligence Agency*, July 24, 1959, http://www.foia.cia.gov/sites/default/files/document_conversions/16/1959-07-24.pdf.

15. Emily S. Rosenberg, "Consuming Women: Images of Americanization in the American Century," 487.

16. Nancy Cott, *No Small Courage: A History of Women in the United States*, 491.

17. Elaine Tyler May, *Homeward Bound: American Families in the Cold War*, 13–14.

18. Marital literature and medicinal theories posited that children born into "stable" families, another code word to encourage parents to abide by social norms, possessed more fruitful childhood and adolescent experiences. Wendy Kline, *Building a Better Race: Gender, Sexuality, and Eugenics from the Turn of the Century to the Baby Boom.*

19. Allan Bérubé, *Coming Out Under Fire: The History of Gay Men and Women in World War II*, 6.

20. For more information, see Nan Alamilla Boyd, *Wide-Open Town: A History of Queer San Francisco to 1965*; George Chauncey, *Gay New York: Gender, Urban Culture, and the Making of the Gay Male World, 1890–1940*; Carolyn Herbst Lewis, *Prescription for Heterosexuality: Sexual Citizenship in the Cold War Era*.

21. Joanne Meyerowitz, *Not June Cleaver: Women and Gender in the Postwar American, 1945–1960*.

22. Susan J. Douglas, *Where the Girls Are: Growing Up Female with the Mass Media*; Jessamyn Neuhaus, "The Way to a Man's Heart: Gender Roles, Domestic Ideology, and Cookbooks in the 1950s."

23. Elizabeth A. Wood, *The Baba and the Comrade: Gender and Politics in Revolutionary Russia*, 1–10.

24. Sarah Ashwin, Introduction to *Gender, State, and Society in Soviet and Post-Soviet Russia*, 1.

25. Ibid., 9–12.

26. Igor Kon, *The Sexual Revolution in Russia: From the Age of Czars to Today*, 51–59.

27. Ibid., 59.

28. Dan Healey, "Sexual and Gender Dissent: Homosexuality as Resistance in Stalin's Russia," 150.

29. Dan Healey, "Homosexual Existence and Existing Socialism: New Light on the Repression of Male Homosexuality in Stalin's Russia," 358.

30. Marina Kiblitskaya, "Russia's Female Breadwinners: The Changing Subjective Experience," 58.

31. Olga Issoupova, "From Duty to Pleasure? Motherhood in Soviet and Post-Soviet Russia," 30–38.

32. Kon, *Sexual Revolution*, 152.

33. Healey, "Homosexual Existence," 359–362.

34. Ashwin, *Gender, State, and Society*, 18.

35. Robert L. Griswold, "'Russian Blonde in Space': Soviet Women in the American Imagination, 1950–1965," 881. Griswold also explains that three stereotypes evolved within the US imagination, each stemming from specific cultural needs. Along with the image of the "unsexed" Soviet woman, the United States focused on Nina Khrushchev, wife of the Soviet premiere. This construct granted the Soviets a more humanistic, matronly countenance. Additionally, the "Russian blonde in space," an image that emerged following *Sputnik* and the publicity of female astronaut Valentina Tereshkova, showcased the progress permitted by including women in education and science.

36. Helen Laville, "Gender and Women's Rights in the Cold War," 529.

37. Jeffrey Montez de Oca, "The 'Muscle Gap': Physical Education and U.S. Fears of a Depleted Masculinity, 1954–1963," 129. The "missile gap" was the perceived Soviet dominance in weaponry stemming from exaggerated estimates by the Gaither

Committee and the United States Air Force. Christopher A. Preble, *John F. Kennedy and the Missile Gap.*

38. In a 1960 *Sports Illustrated* article, the president-elect articulated the development of sound bodies as a specifically Cold War Western endeavor. According to Kennedy, "The knowledge that the physical well-being of the citizen is an important foundation for the vigor and vitality of all activities of the nation, is as old as Western civilization itself." John F. Kennedy, "The Soft American," 14–17.

39. Schultz, *Qualifying Times*, 86.

40. Ibid., 84–89.

41. Verbrugge, *Active Bodies*, 206.

42. James Riordan, *Sport under Communism: The U.S.S.R., Czechoslovakia, the G.D.R., China, Cuba*, 20.

43. James Riordan, "The Role of Sport in Soviet Foreign Policy," 585.

44. Despite its popularity domestically, the forum failed to contend with the Olympics as a premiere global event. Rob Beamish, *Steroids: A New Look at Performance-Enhancing Drugs*, 43–46.

45. Ibid., 43.

46. John N. Washburn, "Sport as a Soviet Tool."

47. In 1947 the Soviet Union issued a resolution in which it declared that individuals who broke world records or earned Olympic medals would be financially compensated.

48. Riordan, "Role of Sport."

49. Stephen Wagg and David L. Andrews, *East Plays West: Sport and the Cold War*, 2.

50. Guttmann, *Olympics*, 86–90.

51. In a 1963 bulletin the IOC asked national federations to "disregard questions of national prestige" when discussing human enhancement with athletes. "Doping," 60.

52. Along with illustrating this tendency of the Western media, Wiederkehr shows a similar bias in communist presses. According to the author, both capitalist and communist journalists highlighted their country's conventionally feminine women; however, Eastern bloc accounts ignored all "ugly" sportswomen whereas Western reports emphasized opposing nation's non-feminine athletes. Wiederkehr, "'. . . If Jarmila Kratochvilova Is the Future of Women's Sports, I'm Not Sure I'm Ready for It,'" 320.

53. The 400-meter and 800-meter races were eliminated from the women's track and field program following the women's "collapse" in the 1928 Amsterdam Games. Consequently, for the 1946 and 1950 European Athletics Championships and the 1932–1956 Olympic Games, the 200-meter race was the longest distance permitted for women.

54. "Red Speedster," *Times Herald*, June 15, 1958, C6; Eugene Correia, "He or She?" *Times of India*, August 27, 1972, A18.

55. "Miss Sin Kim Dan in Controversy," *Times* (London), November 14, 1963, 3; "North Korean Girl Betters Sprint Mark," *Chicago Daily Tribune*, July 1, 1962, B5.

56. "Miss Sin Kim Dan Evokes Masculine Blushes," *Times* (London), November 15, 1961, 4.

57. Kidd, "'Another World Is Possible.'"

58. "North Koreans Feted," *Times* (London), October 6, 1964, 4; Edward Seldon Sears, *Running through the Ages*, 260; "North Korea Girl Sets Second Mark," *New York Times*, November 14, 1963, 57.

59. "Intense Human Drama at Tokyo," *Times of India*, October 11, 1964.

60. "Change of Sex," 36.

61. The US women's 4 x 100-relay team, comprised of Mae Faggs, Catherine Hardy, Barbara Jones, and Janet Moreau earned gold, the lone medal awarded to the United States in a women's event outside of swimming and diving.

62. Shirley Povich, "This Morning," *Washington Post*, August 4, 1952, 8.

63. Sarah Jane Eikleberry, "More Than Milk and Cookies: Revisiting the College Play Day."

64. Cahn, *Coming on Strong*, 111–112.

65. Susan K. Cahn, "From the 'Muscle Moll' to the 'Butch' Ballplayer: Mannishness, Lesbianism, and Homophobia in U.S. Women's Sport," 352.

66. Ritchie, "Sex Tested, Gender Verified," 87.

67. According to IAAF Rule 141, all women's entries required a medical certificate, issued by a qualified doctor, except in area games or championships. As denoted in Rule 11, for area games and championships, women competitors had to be inspected by a panel of three female doctors prior to participation. Letter to Johann Westerhoff from Donald T. P. Pain, December 14, 1967, IAAF Correspondence, 1967–1975, OSC Archives.

68. Arne Ljungqvist, *Doping's Nemesis*, 183.

69. Several accounts suggest the IAAF first introduced sex testing in the 1966 European Athletics Championships; however, the British Empire and Commonwealth Games actually occurred two weeks earlier. The success of the exam in Jamaica permitted its continuation in the European Championships. As Porritt explained to Brundage, the application of sex testing in the British Empire and Commonwealth Games "allowed David [Burghley] to carry on during the European Championships." Letter to Avery Brundage from Arthur Porritt, November 10, 1966, Commission Medicale Correspondance, 1960–1967, OSC Archives.

70. Mary Peters, *Mary P: Autobiography*, 56–57.

71. Mary Jollimore, "Gender Bender Hunt Not Necessary in the Olympics," *Globe and Mail*, June 15, 1992, LexisNexis.

72. Ferguson-Smith and Ferris, "Gender Verification," 17.

73. Pirie Enzo, "Mona Sulaiman—First Woman to Win 100/200m Double at Asian Games," *Pinyoathletics*, August 28, 2012, http://www.Pinoyathletics.com/2012/08/28/mona-sulaiman-first-woman-to-win-100200m-double-at-asian-games.

74. Marvin Zim, "Asia: Beneath the Rising Sun," 18.

75. Enzo, "Mona Sulaiman."

76. "Pan Am Doctors Begin Tests to Be Sure Girls Are Girls," *Washington Post*, July 21, 1967, D5.

77. Ibid.

78. Quoted in Heggie, "Testing Sex and Gender," 159.

79. "Tamara Press, Olympic Track Star, Resigns," *Chicago Tribune*, December 5, 1967, C4.

80. Letter to Johann Westerhoff from David Burghley, the Marquees of Exeter, January 10, 1967, Biography and Correspondence of David Burghley, OSC Archives.

81. Trio cited religious beliefs as the reason for her refusal. "2d Woman Athlete Refuses 'Sex Check,'" *New York Times*, September 4, 1966, 147.

82. True, "Red 'Wolves' in Skirts?" 17.

83. Murray L. Barr and Ewart G. Bertram, "A Morphological Distinction between Neurones of the Male and Female, and the Behaviour of the Nucleolar Satellite during Accelerated Nucleoprotein Synthesis," 676–677.

84. "Mosaic in X & Y," 74.

85. Letter to Alexandre de Mérode from Włodzimierz Reczek, October 14, 1967, Commission Medicale Correspondance, 1960–1967, OSC Archives.

86. Letter from Avery Brundage to Arthur Porritt, November 1, 1966, Box 104, IOC Commissions and Committees—Medical Commission, Part III, 1966–1969 Folder, Brundage Collection.

87. Minutes of the Meeting of the Medical Commission, July 14–17, 1968, Box 89, IOC Meetings, 1968, IOC Meetings—67th Session Folder, Brundage Collection.

88. Paul Dimeo, *A History of Drug Use in Sport, 1876–1976*, 55.

89. The IOC defended its inaction by blaming the medical and legal authorities who failed to release the autopsy and cause of death. The report explained, "It is not the responsible directive bodies of sports who are intervening to put down this danger, but the police. Yes . . . the police!" "Waging War against Dope," 46.

90. Dimeo, *History of Drug Use*, 60–61.

91. "Extracts of the Minutes of the 57th Session of the International Olympic Committee."

92. Alison M. Wrynn, "The Human Factor: Science, Medicine and the International Olympic Committee, 1900–70," 214.

93. Thomas M. Hunt, *Drug Games: The International Olympic Committee and the Politics of Doping, 1960–2008.*

94. Wrynn, "Human Factor."

95. Par Gian-Paolo Ormezzano, "Interview du Prince de Mérode 'Grand Chef' de l'Antidopage aux Jeux Olympiques," 1969, Correspondence of Alexandre de Mérode, OSC Archives.

96. Paul Dimeo et al. "Saint or Sinner? A Reconsideration of the Career of Prince Alexandre de Mérode, Chair of the International Olympic Committee's Medical Commission, 1967–2002," 929.

97. Letter to Otto Mayer from Arthur Porritt, October 27, 1962, Commission Medicale Correspondance, 1962–1967, OSC Archives.

98. Letter to Arthur Porritt from Johann Westerhoff, March 13, 1967, Biography and Correspondence of Arthur Porritt, OSC Archives.

99. Letter to Johann Westerhoff from Arthur Porritt, March 13, 1967, Biography and Correspondence of Arthur Porritt, OSC Archives.

100. "Medical Commission," 71–73.

101. Dimeo et al., "Saint or Sinner?" 930.

102. Wrynn, "Human Factor," 214.

Chapter 3. The IOC's Chromosomal Construction of Womanhood

1. "Male Hormones Outlawed: Sex, Doping Tests Set for Olympians," *Washington Post,* May 9, 1967, D2.

2. Daniel F. Hanley, "Medical News, Chromosomes Do Not an Athlete Make," 54–55.

3. Wamsley, "Social Science Literature."

4. Historically, several cultures have embraced "hermaphrodites" and intersex individuals, proving the existence of social arrangements based on a sex/gender continuum. In the premodern era, for example, Aristotle categorized hermaphrodites as a type of twin. Physicians in the Middle Ages similarly posited that differentiation was based on heat: the heat on the right side of the uterus produced males, the coolness on the left created females, and fetuses in the middle became manly women or womanly men. During the Renaissance, various religious institutions intervened in the controlling of hermaphrodites and intersex persons. Jill A. Fisher, *Gender and the Science of Difference: Cultural Politics of Contemporary Science and Medicine.* In the nineteenth century, legal institutions increasingly demanded sexual clarity as the institution of marriage gained authority and required sex segregation. Sharon E. Preves, "Sexing the Intersexed: An Analysis of Sociocultural Reponses to Intersexuality," 537.

5. Fausto-Sterling, *Sexing the Body,* 3.

6. The nineteenth-century postulations guaranteed the longevity of the two-sexed model. Allen Petersen, "Sexing the Body: Representations of Sex Difference in *Gray's Anatomy,* 1858 to the Present."

7. Alice Domurat Dreger, *Hermaphrodites and the Medical Invention of Sex,* 11.

8. Ibid., 145–151.

9. Thomas Laqueur, *Making Sex: Body and Gender from the Greeks to Freud,* 149–150.

10. Ibid., 39.

11. Nelly Oudshoorn, *Beyond the Natural Body: An Archeology of Sex Hormones,* 20–27.

12. Fausto-Sterling, *Sexing the Body,* 163.

13. Ibid., 188.

14. Oudshoorn, *Beyond the Natural Body,* 36.

15. John Money, one of the founders of the Johns Hopkins Gender Identity Clinic, which performed sex-reassignment surgeries in the United States, notably dismissed

psychoanalytical and biological models of gender. Instead he argued that social learning shapes gender roles. Money also believed that infants remain gender-free and, therefore, can be assigned a sex without psychological damage. Meyerowitz, *How Sex Changed*, 114–120.

16. Janice Raymond, *The Transsexual Empire: The Making of a She-Male*, 44.

17. Meyerowitz, *How Sex Changed*, 125.

18. Barr and Bertram, "Morphological Distinction," 676–677.

19. Fiona Alice Miller, "'Your True and Proper Gender': The Barr Body as a *Good Enough* Science of Sex," 461.

20. The Barr body is the inactive X chromosome in a somatic cell. Therefore, women typically have only one sex chromatin per body cell while men typically have zero. Susumu Ohno and T. S. Hauschka, "Allocycly of the X-Chromosome in Tumors and Normal Tissues."

21. Murray L. Barr, "Cytological Tests of Sex," 47.

22. Letter to Roger Jackson from Murray Barr, July 2, 1987, Commission Medicale, Mai-Aout 1987, OSC Archives.

23. Allan J. Ryan, "Letters, Physician Participation in Olympic Game Planning," 960–961; Thomas B. Quigley, "Letters, Physician Participation in Olympic Game Planning," 959–960; British Association of Sport and Medicine, "Doping and the Use of Chemical Agents to Modify the Human Performance in Sport: Policy Statement," 40–42.

24. Raymond G. Bunge, "Sex and the Olympic Games," 196.

25. "Introducing the, Uh, Ladies," 1117.

26. According to the seven members of the *JAMA* editorial board, the possible existence of genetic or biological variety "serves to stress the fact that the ultimate determination of sex should not be based on chromatin patterns alone but on a consideration of the total psycho-physical personality." "Nuclear Sex," 679.

27. "Introducing the, Uh, Ladies," 1118.

28. Raymond G. Bunge, "Narration: Sex and the Olympic Games No. 2," 267.

29. Bernard Lennox, "Some Observations on the Difficulties of Determining Sex," 80.

30. Keith L. Moore, "The Sexual Identity of Athletes," 788.

31. Hanley, "Medical News," 55.

32. Jacques Defrance and Jean-Marc Chamot, "The Voice of Sport: Expressing a Foreign Policy through a Silent Cultural Activity: The Case of Sport in French Foreign Policy after the Second World War."

33. Theirry Terret, "France."

34. Kristin Ross, *Fast Cars, Clean Bodies: Decolonization and the Reordering of French Culture*, 4.

35. Ibid., 77–78.

36. Press Release, September 27, 1967, Box 73, Circular Letters, 1955–1968, Circular Letters—IOC, NOC, and IF Folder, Brundage Collection.

37. Circular Letter to the International Federations, October 3, 1967, Box 73, Cir-

cular Letters, 1955–1968, Circular Letters—IOC, NOC, and IF Folder, Brundage Collection.

38. The International Canoe Federation, International Federation for Equestrian Sports, International Hockey Federation, and International Shooting Sport Federation sought assistance from the IOC. Commission Medicale Correspondance, 1962–1967, OSC Archives.

39. In the 1965 Sports Competition, 205 participants from seventeen countries competed in boxing, cycling, fencing, gymnastics, swimming, and track and field. The next year, 500 athletes from twenty-two nations embraced the opportunity to rehearse for the Olympics. Along with host country Mexico, Canada, Cuba, East Germany, Finland, France, Italy, Japan, Norway, Poland, Rumania, the Soviet Union, Spain, Sweden, Tunisia, West Germany, and the United States participated. "'Little Olympics' Begins Monday," *Washington Post*, October 10, 1965, C8; "Athletes Gather in Mexico City," *New York Times*, October 11, 1965, 58.

40. "Mexico City Will Stage Olympiad Rehearsal," *Washington Post,* September 19, 1965, C7.

41. Wrynn, "Human Factor."

42. Alison M. Wrynn, "'A Debt Paid Off in Tears': Science, IOC Politics, and the Debate about High Altitude in the 1968 Mexico City Olympics."

43. "Mexico City Opens Sports Spree Today," *Washington Post,* October 12, 1966, E1; "Mexico Reveals Possibilities of Human Body," *Times of India*, October 26, 1967, 12.

44. Letter to Donald T. P. Pain from Johann Westerhoff, January 4, 1968, IAAF Correspondence, 1967–1975, OSC Archives.

45. Meeting of the IOC Executive Board at Mon Repos, Lausanne, January 26–27, 1968, Box 86, IOC Meetings—Executive Board, Lausanne, January 26–27, 1968, Folder, Brundage Collection.

46. "Extracts of the Minutes of the 65th Session of the International Olympic Committee," 94.

47. Monique Berlioux, "Femininity," 1.

48. Ibid., 1–2. According to Berlioux, while "one feels sorry for the 'unfortunate' girl who has been disqualified," it is more important to consider the other competitors "who have been ousted from first place simply because they are women and they have taken part honestly."

49. Report on the Medical Organization at the Grenoble Games, July 14–17, 1968, Box 89, IOC Meetings, 1968, IOC Meetings—67th Session, Mexico City, Reports by Commissions, Part II, Folder, Brundage Collection.

50. Ibid.

51. "Medical Commission," 72; "International Federations," 65.

52. Shirley Povich, "This Morning," *Washington Post,* February 5, 1968, D1.

53. The three individuals selected athletes from the following countries: Italy (6), Soviet Union (5), Austria (4), East Germany (4), United States (4), Great Britain (3), Holland (3), Sweden (3), Czechoslovakia (2), Finland (2), France (2), Japan (2), Swit-

zerland (2), West Germany (2), Argentina (1), Canada (1), Czech Socialist Republic (1), Hungary (1), Poland (1), and Norway (1). Rapport de la Commission Medicale pour le Controle du sex, 1968 Grenoble Winter Olympics, Olympic Files, OSC Archives.

54. Povich, "This Morning," D1.

55. "At Grenoble: 1-in-5 Test of Sex said 'Ludicrous,'" *Washington Post*, February 3, 1968, D1.

56. Giuseppe la Cava, "Report on the Activity of the Medical Commission of the CIO at the Winter Games in Grenoble," April 4, 1968, Commission Medicale Correspondance, OSC Archives.

57. The following competitors, considered retrospectively questionable, did not compete: Soviet Claudia Bayarskikh, Austrian Erika Schinegger, and Austrian Krastana Stoesa.

58. Report on the Medical Organization at the Grenoble Games, July 14–17, 1968, Box 89, IOC Meetings, 1968, IOC Meetings—67th Session, Mexico City, Reports by Commissions, Part II, Folder, Brundage Collection.

59. Rick Broadbent, "From Erika to Erik, A Long Journey of Self-Discovery," *Times* (London), October 22, 2009, 92; "Former Women's Ski Champion," *Los Angeles Times*, April 18, 1972, A2; United Press International, "Ski World Loses a Queen as Erika Becomes 'Erik,'" *Los Angeles Times*, June 16, 1968, 17.

60. Julia Sloan, "Carnivalizing the Cold War: Mexico, the Mexican Revolution, and the Events of 1968," 3–5.

61. Ibid., 5.

62. Located to the east of Mexico City, the City of Sport had an eighty-two-hundred-seat stadium, thirty-six football grounds, twenty-six basketball courts, twenty-five baseball grounds, nineteen volleyball nets, two Olympic pools, one diving pool, and one hockey ground. Marte R. Gómez, "Mexico's New City of Sport," 30–31.

63. Estimations on the number of deaths range and remain unclear. Official reports first declared four deaths, followed by the hospitals citing twenty-six. Some more current approximations suggested the death toll was closer to two hundred.

64. Eric Zolov, "'Showcasing the Land of Tomorrow': Mexico and the 1968 Olympics."

65. Circular Letter to IF, NOC, and IOC, August 26, 1968, Box 73, Circular Letters, 1955–1968, Circular Letters—IOC, NOC, and IF Folder, Brundage Collection.

66. Letter to Executive Board from Alexandre de Mérode, September 10, 1968, Box 73, Circular Letters, 1955–1968, Circular Letters—IOC, NOC, and IF Folder, Brundage Collection.

67. Letter to Alexandre de Mérode from Avery Brundage, September 14, 1968, Box 73, Circular Letters, 1955–1968, Circular Letters—IOC, NOC, and IF Folder, Brundage Collection.

68. Marie Hart, "Sport: Women Sit in the Back of the Bus," *Chicago Tribune*, January 2, 1972, E3.

69. Monique Berlioux, "Doping, Drugs, and Sport," 563.

70. Bil Gilbert, "Problems in a Turned-On World," 64–72.

71. Jack Scott, "Drugs in Sport: And May the Man with the Best Pharmacist Win," *Chicago Tribune*, October 24, 1971, A1.

72. Sam Goldberg, "Letters to the Editor," *New York Times*, November 14, 1971, SM6.

73. Scott, "Drugs in Sport," A1.

74. Charles Maher, "Olga Connolly: No Hope for Medal: She'll Compete at Munich for the Fun of It," *Los Angeles Times*, April 12, 1972, G1.

75. Japanese "modernization" was selective in its incorporation of ideals and conventions from elsewhere, which enabled the country to develop as an Asian "Other" (from the Western vantage) and simultaneously as superior to its nearby Asian neighbors. Accordingly, Japan existed as both "ultra-Oriental" and "trans-Oriental." John Horne, "Understanding Sport and Body Culture in Japan," 73–74; S. Collins, "East and West: Confrontational Diplomacy," 1004; William W. Kelly, preface to *The Olympics in East Asia: Nationalism, Regionalism, and Globalism on the Center Stage of World Sports*, 1–3.

76. Sandra Wilson, "Exhibiting a New Japan: The Tokyo Olympics of 1964 and Expo '70 in Osaka," 159.

77. Christian Tagsold, "Modernity, Space, and National Representation at the Tokyo Olympics 1964," 196.

78. Horne, "Understanding Sport," 81–82.

79. Rio Otomo, "Narratives, the Body, and the 1964 Tokyo Olympics," 121.

80. 1972 Medical Commission Pamphlet, Box 105, Commissions, IOC Commissions and Committees—Medical Commission, 1970–1973 Folder, Brundage Collection.

81. For the 1972 Olympics, Alexandre de Mérode remained the president of the IOC Medical Commission, while Arnold Beckett, Albert Dirix, Nina Grashinskaia, Daniel F. Hanley, Eduardo Hay, Yoshio Kuroda, Ludwig Prokop, and Jacques Thiebault served as members. January 29–30, 1972, Minutes of the Meetings of the IOC Medical Commission, Box 105, Commissions, IOC Commissions and Committees—Medical Commission, 1970–1973 Folder, Brundage Collection.

82. 1972 Medical Commission Pamphlet, Box 105, Commissions, IOC Commissions and Committees—Medical Commission, 1970–1973 Folder, Brundage Collection.

83. Sapporo Olympic Organizing Committee, *The XI Olympic Winter Games Sapporo 1972 Official Report*, part 2, 386.

84. Cahn, *Coming on Strong*, 3.

85. Within the three sports, women competed in alpine skiing, cross-country skiing, figure skating, luge, and speed skating. Women were not permitted to participate in the biathlon (until 1992), bobsled (until 2002), ice hockey (until 1998), Nordic combined (still not permitted as of 2015), and ski jumping (until 2014).

86. "A Memorandum on the Use of Sex Chromatin Investigation of Competitions in Women's Division of the Olympic Games," February 3, 1972, Box 105, Commissions, IOC Commissions and Committees—Medical Commission, 1970–1973 Folder, Brundage Collection.

87. Two weeks after the Danish medical doctors sent the report, the Danish NOC president clarified in a letter to Brundage that he had no part in the study. Letter to IOC from Danish NOC President, February 18, 1972, Box 105, Commissions, IOC Commissions and Committees—Medical Commission, 1970–1973 Folder, Brundage Collection.

88. Letter to Alexandre de Mérode from Avery Brundage, April 24, 1972, Box 105, Commissions, IOC Commissions and Committees—Medical Commission, 1970–1973 Folder, Brundage Collection.

89. "Meetings in May," 205.

90. Quoted in Hunt, *Drug Games*, 23.

91. Eduardo Hay, "Sex Determination in Putative Female Athletes," 998.

92. Letter to Malcolm Andrew Ferguson-Smith from Albert de la Chapelle, November 16, 1989, Correspondence Concerning the Buccal Smear Test, Papers of Andrew Ferguson-Smith, University of Glasgow Archives, Scotland (hereafter cited as Ferguson-Smith Papers).

93. Schiller and Young, *1972 Munich Olympics*, 2–4.

94. Ibid., 6.

95. Munich Olympics Organizing Committee, *The Official Report of the Organizing Committee for the Games of the XXth Olympiad Munich 1972*, vol. 1, part 1, 115.

96. Letter to Elizabeth Ferris from Eduardo Hay, February 22, 1981, Correspondence between Ferguson-Smith and Dr. Elizabeth A. Ferris on Proposed Joint Article on Chromosomal Abnormalities and Sex Test of Femininity, Ferguson-Smith Papers.

97. Fox, "Gender Verification," 148–149.

98. Letter to Ferris from Hay, February 22, 1981, Correspondence between Ferguson-Smith and Dr. Elizabeth A. Ferris on Proposed Joint Article on Chromosomal Abnormalities and Sex Test of Femininity, Ferguson-Smith Papers.

99. Letter to Michele Verroken from Martin Bobrow, June 23, 1988, Copies of Correspondence between Professor Albert de la Chapelle and Dr. Martin Bobrow Regarding Challenges to the Buccal Smear Test, Ferguson-Smith Papers.

100. Letter to Alexandre de Mérode from Albert de la Chapelle, July 31, 1987, Copies of Correspondence between Professor Albert de la Chapelle and Dr. Martin Bobrow Regarding Challenges to the Buccal Smear Test, Ferguson-Smith Papers.

101. According to Karsten Schützmann et al., a person's quality of life typically deteriorates after he/she is labeled as having a Disorder of Sex Development (DSD). For individuals with DSD, self-harming behaviors and suicidal tendencies occur at rates comparable to women with histories of physical or sexual abuse. Similarly, as Milton Diamond and Linda Ann Watson explain, people with DSD are treated as medical oddities and usually informed by physicians in a demeaning manner. Schützmann et al., "Psychological Distress, Self-Harming Behavior, and Suicidal Tendencies in Adults with Disorders of Sex Development"; Diamond and Watson, "Androgen Insensitivity Syndrome and Klinefelter's Syndrome: Sex and Gender Considerations."

102. Letter to Martin Bobrow from Albert de la Chapelle, February 25, 1987, Copies of Correspondence between Professor Albert de la Chapelle and Dr. Martin Bobrow Regarding Challenges to the Buccal Smear Test, Ferguson-Smith Papers.

103. Malcolm Andrew Ferguson-Smith, "The Sex Test in International Sport," Ferguson-Smith Papers.

104. Letter to Alexandre de Mérode from Federation Internationale de Volley-Ball, September 7, 1972; Letter to Sung Jip Kim from Alexandre de Mérode, Medical Matters at the 1972 Summer Games in Munich, OSC Archives.

105. "Press Release of the IOC. Games of the XXth Olympiad," 390.

106. Eduardo Hay, "The Stella Walsh Case," 222.

107. She also questioned a "man who has too much grace." Marie-Thérèse Eyquem, "Women Sports and the Olympic Games," 49–50.

Chapter 4. Steroids, Nationalism, and Femininity Testing

1. From the introduction of swimming in 1896 to the 1972 Munich Games, the US men had won 63 of the 124 total gold medals. Similarly, since the inclusion of women's swimming in the 1912 Stockholm Games, the US women, who joined in 1920, had won 47 of the 84 total gold medals.

2. Bill Shirley, "World's First Bionic Swim Team: East Germans Devise a System That Has Enabled Them to Dominate Women's Swimming," *Los Angeles Times*, June 15, 1976, D1; Neil Amdur, "Femininity or Prowess: U.S. Women Must Choose," *Chicago Tribune*, August 2, 1976, E2.

3. Rick Talley, "U.S. Men Win, but Women Whimper," *Chicago Tribune*, July 23, 1976, C1.

4. Steven Ungerleider, *Faust's Gold: Inside the East German Doping Machine.*

5. Lord Killanin, *My Olympic Years*, 87–92.

6. "Lord Killanin at Brighton," 671.

7. The anabolic component builds tissue while androgens promote the development of "male" secondary sex characteristics. Jennifer L. Dotson and Robert T. Brown, "The History of the Development of Anabolic-Androgenic Steroids," 761.

8. John Hoberman, *Testosterone Dreams: Rejuvenation, Aphrodisia, Doping*, 3.

9. Erica Freeman et al., "A Brief History of Testosterone," 371.

10. Dotson and Brown, "History," 762.

11. John M. Hoberman and Charles E. Yesalis, "The History of Synthetic Testosterone," 77.

12. Freeman et al., "Brief History of Testosterone," 371.

13. Hoberman and Yesalis, "History of Synthetic Testosterone," 77.

14. Dotson and Brown, "History," 763–764.

15. As a result of his work on sex hormones, Butenandt was jointly awarded the Nobel Prize in Chemistry in 1939 with Leopold Ruzicka; however, due to Nazi governmental policies he rejected the award. Butenandt eventually accepted in 1949, after World War II.

16. H. M. Behre et al., "Pharmacology of Testosterone Preparations."

17. Hoberman, *Testosterone Dreams*, 55–57.

18. Jan Todd and Terry Todd, "Significant Events in the History of Drug Testing and the Olympic Movement: 1960–1999."

19. Hunt, *Drug Games*, 29.

20. Cedric Shackleton, "Steroid Analysis and Doping Control, 1960–1980: Scientific Developments and Personal Anecdotes."

21. Todd and Todd, "Significant Events," 73.

22. "Denver," 53.

23. "The Inept USOC," *Los Angeles Times*, February 3, 1973, D3; Associated Press, "1976 Winter Olympics Awarded to Innsbruck," *Los Angeles Times*, February 5, 1973, E1.

24. "Innsbruck," 63; "Innsbruck Tightens Belt for '76," *Montreal Gazette*, December 11, 1973, 47.

25. "Bloc Voting," *Los Angeles Times*, February 11, 1976, E1.

26. "E. German Skier Keeps Nordic-Combined Title," *New York Times*, February 10, 1976, 49; "Miss Hamill Wins Gold Skate Medal," *Los Angeles Times*, February 13, 1976, A1.

27. Lisette Hilton, "Relaxed Hamill Gives Gold Medal Performance," *ESPN.Com*, February 13, 1976, http://espn.go.com/classic/s/add_hamill_dorothy.html.

28. "Olympics Coverage," *Chicago Tribune*, February 3, 1976, C1.

29. Peggy Polk, "Hormone Test Required for Women," *Beaver County (PA) Times*, February 2, 1976, B3.

30. "Olympic Sex Tests Designed to Tell Jacques from Jills," *Chicago Tribune*, February 3, 1976, C2.

31. Ibid.

32. Will Grimsley, "Women Ask: How about Sex Tests for Men?" *Los Angeles Times*, February 3, 1976, D1.

33. "Canadian Luge Racer Resents Sex Test," *Toronto Star*, February 3, 1976, C2.

34. Grimsley, "Women Ask," D1.

35. Lake Placid Olympic Organizing Committee, *Official Report of the XIII Olympic Winter Games in Lake Placid in 1980*, 188.

36. Innsbruck Olympic Organizing Committee, *Final Report*, 195.

37. "Olympic Sex Tests," C2.

38. Werner W. Franke and Brigitte Berendonk, "Hormonal Doping and Androgenization of Athletes: A Secret Program of the German Democratic Republic Government," 1264.

39. Bill Shirley, "The Olympic Factory: East Germany Mixes Marx and Marks and Comes Up a Winner in Innsbruck," *Los Angeles Times*, June 11, 1976, G1.

40. Michael Getler, "East Germany's Mighty Sports Machine," *Washington Post*, June 13, 1976, D1.

41. "East Germany Trying to Build 'Super Athletes,'" *Chicago Tribune*, February 12, 1976, C1.

42. For example, in the 1976 US Olympic trials, twenty-three athletes failed the drug controls in track and field events in Eugene, Oregon; none were punished. Franke and Berendonk, "Hormonal Doping," 73.

43. Giselher Spitzer, "Sport and the Systematic Infliction of Pain: A Case Study of State-Sponsored Mandatory Doping in East Germany," 413–425.

44. Matthew Syed, "How Blue Pills Turned Heidi Krieger into a Man," *Times* (London), July 5, 2008, http://transgriot.blogspot.com/2008/07/how-blue-pills-turned-heidi-krieger.html.

45. Guttmann, *Olympics*, 141.

46. Quoted in "'76 Olympics to Montreal," *Chicago Tribune*, May 13, 1970, E2.

47. Joe Alex Morris Jr., "Sacre Bleu! Montreal Pulls an Olympian Upset," *Los Angeles Times*, May 13, 1970, D1.

48. Bruce Kidd claims that the difficulties in organization must be understood within the context of nationalism. During the 1970s the collective identity of Quebeckers opposed the pan-Canadian identity of the federal government. Furthermore, Montreal served as a volatile microcosm of the conflicts, as it was dominated by a small Anglophone elite and home to a large population of French speakers. Kidd, "The Cultural Wars of the Montreal Olympics."

49. Guttmann, *Olympics*, 143.

50. International Olympic Committee, *Olympic Rules and Regulations*.

51. International Olympic Committee, *Olympic Rules, By-Laws, and Instructions*, 17.

52. Rebecca Ann Lock, "The Doping Ban: Compulsory Heterosexuality and Lesbophobia," 405.

53. Amdur, "Femininity of Prowess," E2.

54. Shirley, "World's First Bionic Swim Team," D1.

55. Lock, "Doping Ban," 404.

56. Amdur, "Femininity of Prowess," E2.

57. Scott, "Drugs in Sports," A1.

58. Kathleen Burns, "Interscholastic Sports Set for Girls," *Chicago Tribune*, July 2, 1972, NW9.

59. "Sex Test Disqualifies Athlete," *New York Times*, September 16, 1967, 28.

60. Volga Boatman was a derogatory nickname for Soviets used in the West. The name originally appeared in a Russian folk song, "The Song of the Volga Boatmen." According to folklore, Russian barge haulers sang the tune, about heaving trees, while working on the Volga River.

61. Jim Murray, "Russians Pull a Fast One," *Los Angeles Times*, September 3, 1971, B1.

62. Jim Murray, "100 Years from Now," *Los Angeles Times*, August 8, 1976, C1.

63. Jim Murray, "The New Order Comes to the World of Sports," *Los Angeles Times*, February 8, 1977, D1.

64. "Readers Correspondence," 507–512.

65. Toby Miller, *Sportsex*, 25–26.

66. Jim Murray, "Comaneci Olympics," *Los Angeles Times*, July 21, 1976, F1; Cheryl Bentsen, "It's the End of a Love Affair," *Los Angeles Times*, June 3, 1976, F1.

67. Tony Kornheiser, "Olga Korbut, Still the One They Like to Watch," *New York Times*, December 17, 1976, 71.

68. "Gymnastics Set Flips over the Olga Show," *Los Angeles Times*, September 2, 1972, B1; Neil Allen, "Sweet and Sour Tastes of Sport in 1972," *Times* (London), De-

cember 23, 1972, 10; "84-Pound Powerhouse Thrills Munich Fans," *New York Times*, September 2, 1972, 10.

69. Robert Markus, "Comaneci Is Games' New Golden Girl," *Chicago Tribune*, July 22, 1976, C1.

70. Murray, "Comaneci Olympics," F1.

71. Janice Kaplan, "Views of Sport: Women Athletes Are Women," *New York Times*, March 4, 1979, S2.

72. Bill Shirley, "The Nadia & Olga Show," *Los Angeles Times*, July 20, 1976, E1.

73. Hunt, *Drug Games*, 31–32.

Chapter 5. Gender Testing, Doping Checks, and Olympic Boycotts

1. Joseph M. Turrini, "'It Was Communism Versus the Free World': The USA-USSR Dual Track Meet Series and the Development of Track and Field in the United States, 1958–1985," 427–435.

2. Jill Gerston, "At 86 Pounds, She's Star of 3 Continents," *New York Times*, August 12, 1973, 195; Dave Distel, "The Girl Who Beat the Russians: Little Mary Decker Suddenly Very Big in the World of Track," *Los Angeles Times*, August 21, 1973, B1.

3. "In This Race, Decker Runs around the Bloc," *Los Angeles Times*, August 11, 1983, I1; Pat Butcher, "After the Fall, Mary's Still Quite Contrary," *Times* (London), March 8, 1985, 13.

4. Minutes of the Meeting of the IOC Medical Commission, July 13–14, 1968, Commission Medicale, 1967–1969, OSC Archives.

5. Minutes of the Meeting of the IOC Medical Commission, October 12, 1968, Commission Medicale, 1967–1969, OSC Archives.

6. Minutes of the Meeting of the IOC Medical Commission, August 21, 1972, Commission Medicale, 1972–1979, OSC Archives.

7. Letter to Paul Libaud from Alexandre de Mérode, September 8, 1972, Medical Matters at the 1972 Summer Games in Munich, OSC Archives.

8. Minutes of the Meeting of the IOC Medical Commission, July 10–August 1, 1976, Commission Medicale, 1972–1979, OSC Archives.

9. Minutes of the Meeting of the IOC Medical Commission, July 28, 1976, 1976 Montreal Summer Games, Commission Medicale, OSC Archives.

10. Medical Report of the 1976 Montreal Olympic Games, 1976 Montreal Summer Games, Commission Medicale, OSC Archives.

11. Letter to Alexandre de Mérode from Adrian Paulen, August 12, 1976, Commission Medicale Correspondance, Juillet-Septembre 1976, OSC Archives.

12. Letter to Alexandre de Mérode from Lord Killanin, September 24, 1976, Commission Medicale Correspondance, Juillet-Septembre 1976, OSC Archives.

13. The International Handball Federation and the International Luge Federation tested in international competitions. Under the direction of its secretary-general, FIBA required femininity control for the European Championships for Junior Women

and Girls, European Championships for Women, and the World Championships for Women. FIVB provided femininity certificates during the Senior and Junior World Championships, as well as during the World Cup. Finally, the IAAF oversaw controls in most area and international competitions, including the Asian Games, Commonwealth Games, European Championships, European Cup, and European Indoor Championships. Circular Letter to International Federations Re: Femininity Certificates from Arpad Csanadi, July 7, 1978, Commission Medicale Correspondance, Juin-Aout 1978, OSC Archives.

14. Minutes of the Meeting of the IOC Medical Commission, October 8–12, 1979, Commission Medicale, 1972–1979, OSC Archives.

15. "Lake Placid Has Changed Little, Olympics a Lot," *Los Angeles Times*, November 25, 1979, C1.

16. In particular, the LPOOC required renovations for the Olympic Arena, the ski jump, and the ski lodge, along with refrigerator enhancements on the bobsled run and speed-skating oval. Furthermore, construction of a sport complex—complete with two modern ice skating rinks, eight thousand seats, and locker rooms to accommodate up to ten teams at once—was required, in addition to a new outdoor speed skating track, a press center, and the Olympic Village. Ronald M. MacKenzie, "Lake Placid, 'Olympic City,'" 84–86.

17. "Lake Placid Grows Stormy over Olympics Deficit Issue," *Los Angeles Times*, December 7, 1978, OC-A22; "Innsbruck Held Ready If Lake Placid Falters," *Washington Post*, January 5, 1977, D16.

18. "Lake Placid 1980: The President of the IOC in America," 167–168.

19. Letter to Lord Killanin from J. Bernard Fell, April 27, 1978, Minutes and Correspondence Concerning the Medical Files of the Winter Olympic Games, 1980 Lake Placid Olympic Files, OSC Archives; emphasis in original.

20. Letter to Lord Killanin from Ignaty Novikov, June 5, 1978; Letter to Ignaty Novikov from Lord Killanin, June 13, 1978, Commission Medicale Correspondance, Juin-Aout 1978, OSC Archives.

21. Telex to Willy Grut from Monique Berlioux, January 20, 1979, Minutes and Correspondences Concerning the Medical Files of the Winter Olympic Games, 1980 Lake Placid Olympic Files, OSC Archives.

22. Medical Report of the Services, Equipment, Personnel, Doping, and Femininity Performed by the Medical Department for the Lake Placid Olympic Organizing Committee, Minutes and Medical Reports of the Olympic Winter Games of Lake Placid, 1980 Lake Placid Olympic Files, OSC Archives.

23. Minutes of the Meeting of the IOC Medical Commission, July 19–23, 1980, Commission Medicale, 1980–1992, OSC Archives.

24. "Morning Briefing: Save Time and Money; Ban Olympic Drug and Sex Tests," *Los Angeles Times*, January 3, 1976, C2.

25. Ken Denlinger, "Warfare on Drugs Increases," *Washington Post*, February 12, 1980, D1; Phil Musick, "Sex Test Director Provides Genetic Approval for Olympians," *Pittsburgh Post-Gazette*, February 18, 1980, 16.

26. Nicholas Evan Sarantakes, *Dropping the Torch: Jimmy Carter, the Olympic Boycott, and the Cold War*, 60–94.

27. Stagflation describes a situation where a country's inflation rate is high and economic growth is slow. In times of stagflation, the unemployment rate is typically high.

28. Edward Walsh, "Carter Insists Soviets Quit Afghanistan," *Washington Post*, January 21, 1980, A6; Jimmy Carter, *Keeping Faith: Memoirs of a President*, 481.

29. "Remarks by Mr. Cyrus Vance," 109–110.

30. Killanin, *My Olympic Years*, 183.

31. Sarantakes, *Dropping the Torch*, 1–13.

32. Carter, *Keeping Faith*, 489.

33. Guttmann, *Olympics*, 151; emphasis in original.

34. Neil Amdur, "Los Angeles Preparing Its Bid for '80 Olympics," *New York Times*, October 12, 1973, 53; "Los Angeles Asked to Hold Olympics," *New York Times*, February 23, 1974, 23.

35. Alison Rowley, "Sport in the Service of the State: Images of Physical Culture and Soviet Women, 1917–1941."

36. Kateryna Kobchenko notes that ideology was occasionally different from reality. Although the communist regime proclaimed notions of gender equality, women nevertheless faced opposition from patriarchal organizations that maintained traditional attitudes. Kobchenko, "Emancipation within the Ruling Ideology: Soviet Women in Fizkul'tura and Sport in the 1920s and 1930s," 255–265.

37. Anke Hilbrenner, "Soviet Women in Sports in the Brezhnev Years: The Female Body and Soviet Modernism," 298–299.

38. Jim Riordan, "Revolt against the Fitness Fraud: Sport in the Soviet Union," *Times* (London), April 5, 1989, LexisNexis; Hilbrenner, "Soviet Women in Sports," 299.

39. Wiederkehr found that both trivialized sportswomen, presented female athletes in conventional gender roles, highlighted supposed psychological issues, and sexualized the participants. A slight difference in linguistic tendencies, the West was more likely, at the beginning of the Cold War, to naturalize difference. Wiederkehr, "'If Jarmila Kratochvilova Is the Future.'"

40. Organising Committee of the 1980 Olympic Games in Moscow, *Games of the XXII Olympiad: Official Report*, vol. 2, part 1, 193.

41. "Sex Discrimination of a Different Kind," *Times* (London), August 2, 1980, 6.

42. "Olympic Medical Aides Deny Report of Sex Test Failures," *Washington Post*, August 3, 1980.

43. Letter to Alexandre de Mérode from Ludwig Prokop, December 21, 1980, Commission Medicale Correspondance, Juillet-Decembre 1980, OSC Archives.

44. "Medical Commission Working Group on Gender Verification," January 27, 1987, Copies of Correspondence between Professor Albert de la Chapelle and Dr. Martin Bobrow Regarding Challenges to the Buccal Smear Test, Ferguson-Smith Papers.

45. "Stella Walsh Day," Carl B. Stokes, Monday, April 13, 1970, Folder 1, Stella Walsh Papers, Western Reserve Historical Society Library.

46. "Stella Walsh Defense Fund Established," *Nationality Newspaper & Services*, Folder 7, Stella Walsh Papers, Western Reserve Historical Society Library.

47. Victor Cohn, "Famed Olympic Medalist Stella Walsh Wasn't a 'She,' Autopsy Finds," *Washington Post*, January 24, 1981, A5; W. C. Miller, "Stella Walsh 'Lived and Died' a Female, *Cleveland Plain Dealer*, February 12, 1981, 1.

48. Dan Balz, "Heroine or Hero?" *Washington Post*, December 16, 1980, A1; Cohn, "Famed Olympic Medalist," A5; Noel Jeffries, "Canadian a Winner of Gold?" *Globe and Mail*, February 12, 1981, LexisNexis.

49. "1932 Medalist Wants Her Gold," *Globe and Mail*, August 9, 1984, LexisNexis.

50. Letter to Eduardo Hay from Monique Berlioux, January 30, 1980, Commission Medicale Correspondance, Janvier-Avril 1981, OSC Archives.

51. Hay, "Stella Walsh Case," 221–222.

52. Terry Todd, "Anabolic Steroids: The Gremlins of Sport," 100.

53. Craig Neff, "Caracas: A Scandal and a Warning," 18.

54. David Miller, "Tracking Down the Drug Runners," *Times* (London), March 1, 1984, 14.

55. Todd, "Anabolic Steroids," 100.

56. "The Candidate Cities for 1984," 283–284.

57. Todd, "Anabolic Steroids."

58. Letter to Juan Antonio Samaranch from Alexandre de Mérode, June 1983, Commission Medicale Correspondance, Juin 1983; Juan Antonio Samaranch Meeting with Alexandre de Mérode, April 9, 1987, Commission Medicale Correspondance, Janvier-Avril 1987, OSC Archives.

59. Minutes of the Meeting of the IOC Medical Commission, February 6–7, 1982, Commission Medicale, 1980–1982, OSC Archives.

60. Letter to Alexandre de Mérode from Paul Libaud, June 22, 1983, Commission Medicale Correspondance, Juillet-Aout 1983, OSC Archives.

61. Letter to Alexandre de Mérode from JB Holt, May 27, 1983, Commission Medicale Correspondance, Juin 1983, OSC Archives.

62. "IOC Says Sex Tests Will Be Kept Strictly Secret," *Los Angeles Times*, July 29, 1984, H43.

63. Anthony Daly, "Focus: On Health."

64. Organising Committee for the Olympic Winter Games in Sarajevo in 1984, *Final Report Sarajevo'84*, 146–148.

65. "IOC Says Sex Tests Will Be Kept Strictly Secret," H43.

66. Seymour Martin Lipset and William Schneider, "The Decline of Confidence in American Institutions."

67. Robert M. Collins, *Transforming America: Politics and Culture in the Reagan Years*, 7.

68. "1984 (IOC Official)," 664.

69. Rick Gruneau and Robert Neubauer, "A Gold Medal for the Market: The 1984 Los Angeles Olympics, the Reagan Era, and the Politics of Neoliberalism," 147.

70. Ibid., 134.

71. John Woolley and Gerhard Peters, "Address before a Joint Session of the Con-

gress on the State of the Union," *American Presidency Project,* accessed January 17, 2013, http://www.presidency.ucsb.edu/ws/index.php?pid=38069.

72. Robert H. Johnson argues that the Reagan Doctrine illustrated both continuity and change with regard to presidential doctrines. While the ideology behind the Reagan Doctrine hinged upon notions of American exceptionalism and unilateralism, the policy also moved the country from a defensive orientation to a more preemptive stance. Johnson, "Misguided Morality: Ethics and the Reagan Doctrine."

73. Kenneth Reich, "Soviets Boycott Olympics: Charge U.S. Won't Ensure Safety," *Los Angeles Times,* May 8, 1984, A1.

74. Regarding the change in position, see Kenneth Reich and Douglas Shuit, "Reagan Cools on Olympic Boycott," *Los Angeles Times,* March 28, 1980, A12. Reagan reportedly altered his opinion when he realized that other countries refused to join the United States in the boycott. The timing just happened to coincide with his presidential campaign. For information on Reagan's response to the Soviet's announcement, see Raymond Coffey, "U.S. Charges Foul Play: Soviet Olympic Pullout 'Political' Olympics," *Chicago Tribune,* May 9, 1984, 1.

75. Iran and Libya also did not attend, but not because of Cold War allegiances.

76. Jim Murray, "You'd Never Think She Is One of Them," *Los Angeles Times,* December 29, 1981, D1.

77. Ibid.

78. John Scheibe, "To Run Faster, Decker Tabb Had to Slow Down," *Los Angeles Times,* January 8, 1983, C8.

79. Murray, "You'd Never Think," D1; emphasis in original.

80. Rick Reilly, "Will It Be a Double for Decker?" *New York Times,* April 19, 1984, G1.

81. Decker passed the exam and competed in the 1984 Games. In the 3,000-meter women's final, the much-adored US athlete collided with South African runner Zola Budd. As a result, Decker crashed to the ground and was unable to continue. Although originally empathetic, the US public grew frustrated with her refusal to move beyond the "brutal kilometer." Decker maintained a successful season in 1985, setting a new world record for the women's mile yet failed to medal in 1988 and did not qualify in 1992. For the Atlanta Games Decker resurfaced; however, she became embroiled in a doping controversy, was eliminated in the qualification heats, and fell from the US conscious. The IAAF banned Decker from competition in 1997. For more information, see Tim Layden, "Paralysis by Urinalysis," 108.

82. Letter to Anthony Daly from Monique Berlioux, March 1, 1983, 1984 Los Angeles Summer Olympics Medical Matters: Correspondence, OSC Archives.

83. Minutes of the Meeting of the IOC Medical Commission, July 24, 1984, Commission Medicale 1984, OSC Archives.

84. Los Angeles Olympic Organizing Committee, *Official Report of the Games of the XXIIIrd Olympiad Los Angeles, 1984,* vol. 1, part 2, 358.

85. Linda Kay, "Olympic Women Seek 'XX' Rating," *Chicago Tribune,* July 26, 1984, C1.

86. Ibid.

87. "IOC Medical Commission Working Group on Gender Verification," July 2, 1988, Copies of Correspondence between Professor Albert de la Chapelle and Dr. Martin Bobrow Regarding Challenges to the Buccal Smear Test, Ferguson-Smith Papers.

88. Nancy Hogshead-Makar, phone interview by author, January 19, 2015.

89. Ellie Almond, Julie Cart, and Randy Harvey, "IOC Might Order New Sex Check," *Los Angeles Times*, January 26, 1984, E1.

90. "IOC Says Sex Test Results Will be Kept Strictly Secret," *Los Angeles Times*, July 29, 1984, H43.

91. Almond, Cart, and Harvey, "IOC Might Order New Sex Check."

Chapter 6. The Development of a Protest

1. The organizers tested all female competitors except those who competed in fencing, gymnastics, and tennis. Three competitors produced inconclusive results and two refused further testing. H. Sakamoto, "Femininity Control at the XXth Universiade in Kobe, Japan," 193–195.

2. Kirsten Wengler, phone interview by author, December 30, 2014.

3. Alison Carlson, "Y Doesn't Always Mark the Spot," 43.

4. Kirsten Wengler, phone interview by author, December 30, 2014.

5. Carlson, "Y Doesn't Always Mark the Spot," 43.

6. When discussing Wengler's case, de la Chapelle approximated that the misidentification of a Y chromatin could occur in 6–15 percent of competitors. Letter to Martin Bobrow from Albert de la Chapelle, February 25, 1987, Copies of Correspondence between Prof. Albert de la Chapelle and Dr. Martin Bobrow Regarding Challenges to the Buccal Smear Test, Ferguson-Smith Papers.

7. "A Question of Gender: The Sex Testing of Female Athletes," *ABC Radio*, July 8, 2012, http://www.abc.net.au/radionational/programs/rearvision/a-question-of -gender-the-sex-testing-of-female/4087112#transcript.

8. María José Martínez Patiño, "Personal Account: A Woman Tried and Tested," S38.

9. Alison Carlson, "When Is a Woman Not a Woman?"

10. According to Nicholas Sarantakes, both Killanin and his wife blamed his heart attack on the stress induced by a boycott sparked by New Zealand's allowance in the 1976 Montreal Games, after the country allowed the national rugby team to compete in Apartheid South Africa. Sarantakes, *Dropping the Torch*, 31.

11. "Lord Killanin . . . Five Years of Presidency . . . and China," 538; Killanin, *My Olympic Years*, 220.

12. Juliet Macur, "Samaranch Pushed for Inclusion of Women," *New York Times*, April 21, 2010, http://www.nytimes.com/2010/04/22/sports/olympics/22olympics .html.

13. Joanna Davenport noted that Lord Killanin also attempted to include women. Notably, he extended membership to US Olympian Tenley Albright, who refused his offer. Davenport, "Breaking into the Rings: Women on the IOC," 26–30.

14. During Samaranch's presidency, the IOC added badminton, biathlon, curling, cycling, field hockey, football, ice hockey, judo, pentathlon, sailing, shooting, softball, table tennis, taekwondo, tennis, triathlon, and weight lifting.

15. Letter to James R. Owen from Malcolm Ferguson-Smith, November 6, 1969; Letter to Col. John Fraser from Malcolm Ferguson-Smith, November 21, 1969, Correspondence Regarding the Buccal Smear Examination at the 1970 Edinburgh Commonwealth Games, Ferguson-Smith Papers.

16. J. Francois and Matton-Van Leuven, "Sexual Evaluation of 'Female' Athletes."

17. Malcolm Andrew Ferguson-Smith, "The Sex Test in International Sport," 1976, Ferguson-Smith Papers.

18. Elizabeth Ferris, "Sportswomen and Medicine," 336–338; emphasis in original; Letter to Monique Berlioux from Elizabeth Ferris, December 19, 1979, Commission Medicale Correspondance, Janvier-Juin 1980, OSC Archives.

19. Letter to Elizabeth Ferris from Eduardo Hay, February 22, 1981, Commission Medicale Correspondance, Janvier-Avril 1981, OSC Archives.

20. In an IOC memo, Berlioux explained that "he [de Mérode] does not wish to discuss the femininity controls with them [the IAAF] on this occasion as the Finns are so adamantly against any kind of femininity control." IOC Memo, Notes for Madame Berlioux, April 15, 1983, Medicale Commission Correspondance, Mars 1983, OSC Archives.

21. Letter to de Alexandre de Mérode from Albert de la Chapelle, August 17, 1982, Commission Medicale Correspondance, Avril 1983, OSC Archives.

22. Letter to Albert de la Chapelle from Eduardo Hay, April 25, 1983, Commission Medicale Correspondance, Avril 1983, OSC Archives.

23. Letter to Juan Antonio Samaranch from Albert de la Chapelle, May 7, 1987, Commission Medicale Correspondance, Mai-Aout 1987, OSC Archives.

24. Letter to Albert de la Chapelle from Alexandre de Mérode, July 14, 1987, Medicale Commission Correspondance, Mai-Aout 1987, OSC Archives.

25. IOC President Samaranch suggested de Mérode add Ljungqvist to the IOC's Medical Commission. De Mérode acknowledged that Ljungqvist wanted to be included; however, he was unsure if Ljungqvist's addition would enhance the group's work. Meeting with Alexandre de Mérode and Juan Antonio Samaranch, April 9, 1987, Commission Medicale Correspondance, Janvier-Avril 1987, OSC Archives.

26. Minutes of the Meeting of the IAAF Medical Committee, May 23, 1981, Medicale Commission Correspondance, 1981–1982, OSC Archives.

27. Letter to Martin Bobrow from Albert de la Chapelle, April 14, 1987, Copies of Correspondence between Professor Albert de la Chapelle and Dr. Martin Bobrow Regarding Challenges to Buccal Smear Test, Ferguson-Smith Papers.

28. Patiño, "Personal Account," S38.

29. To ascertain the opinions of the "medical community," this work assessed the following journals: *American Family Physician, British Journal of Sport Medicine, British Medical Journal, British Journal of Medical Practice, British Medical Bulletin, Discover, Genetics, International Journal of Sports Medicine, JAMA: The Journal of the American Medical Association, Journal of the Medical Association of Georgia, Journal*

of the Royal Society of Medicine, Journal of Sports Medicine, Lancet, New Scientist, New Studies in Athletes, Physician and Sports Medicine, and *Science.*

30. De la Chapelle contacted Christos Bartsocas (Athens, Greece), Kare Berg (Oslo, Norway), Herman van den Berghe (Leuven, Belgium), Kirk Bootsma (Rotterdam, Netherlands), Marco Fraccaro (Pavia, Italy), Jean Frezal (Paris, France), Nemat Hashem (Cairo, Egypt), Janusz Limon (Gdansk, Poland), Jan Lindsten (Stockholm, Sweden), John Philip (Copenhagen, Denmark), Elizabeth Robson (London, England), Carlos San Roman (Madrid, Spain), Ivan Subrt (Prague, Czechoslovakia), Ulrich Wolf (Freiburg, Germany), and Liljana Zergollern (Zagreb, Croatia). Letter to Geneticists from Albert de la Chapelle, January 27, 1987, Copies of Correspondence between Professor Albert de la Chapelle and Dr. Martin Bobrow Regarding Challenges to Buccal Smear Test, Ferguson-Smith Papers.

31. Albert de la Chapelle, "The Use and Misuse of Sex Chromatin Screening for 'Gender Identification' of Female Athletes," 1920–1921.

32. Joe Leigh Simpson, "Gender Testing in the Olympics," 1938; Denise Grady, "Sex Test of Champions," 75–78.

33. Ferguson-Smith and Ferris, "Gender Verification in Sport," 18–20.

34. Letter to Myron Genel from John Money, September 29, 1987, Correspondence Regarding the Petition by the "Heinonen Sixteen" on Gender Verification, March-April 1994, Ferguson-Smith Papers.

35. Letter to Martin Bobrow from Albert de la Chapelle, February 25, 1987, Copies of Correspondence between Professor Albert de la Chapelle and Dr. Martin Bobrow Regarding Challenges to the Buccal Smear Test, Ferguson-Smith Papers.

36. Minutes of the Meeting of the IAAF Medical Committee, May 23, 1981, Medicale Commission Correspondance, 1981–1982, OSC Archives.

37. Michael Farber, "Free Condoms Distributed by Organizers Not Yet a Hot Commodity with Athletes," *Montreal Gazette*, February 6, 1992, B2; Randy Havery, "Notebook: Bobsledder in Dispute Is Invited," *Los Angeles Times*, February 11, 1988, D6; Phil Hersch, "Olympics: SEC Commissioner Tops List for Olympic Post," *Chicago Tribune*, October 14, 1987, C3; Frank Orr, "Cardinals Keeping Careful Eye on What Papers Say about Them," *Toronto Star*, October 25, 1987, G3.

38. Letter to Roger Jackson from Murray Barr, June 2, 1987, Commission Medicale Correspondance, Mai-Aout 1987, OSC Archives.

39. Letter to Juan Antonio Samaranch to Albert de la Chapelle, May 7, 1987, Commission Medicale Correspondance, Mai-Aout 1987, OSC Archives.

40. Brian Lowry and D. I. Hoar, "Gender Verification for the 1988 Winter Olympics," 9.

41. Letter to Albert de la Chapelle from E. B. Challis, March 18, 1987; Letter to Martin Bobrow from Joe J. Hoo, August 8, 1988, Copies of Correspondence between Professor Albert de la Chapelle and Dr. Martin Bobrow Regarding Challenges to the Buccal Smear Test, Ferguson-Smith Papers.

42. Letter to Albert de la Chapelle from Joe J. Hoo, January 6, 1987, Correspondence Concerning the Buccal Smear Test, Ferguson-Smith Papers.

43. Letter to Alexandre de Mérode from Albert de la Chapelle, July 31, 1987, Copies

of Correspondence between Professor Albert de la Chapelle and Dr. Martin Bobrow Regarding Challenges to the Buccal Smear Test, Ferguson-Smith Papers.

44. IOC Medical Commission Working Group on Gender Verification, July 2, 1988, Copies of Correspondence between Albert de la Chapelle and Dr. Martin Bobrow Regarding Challenges to the Buccal Smear Test, Ferguson-Smith Papers.

45. Letter to Malcolm Andrew Ferguson-Smith from Albert de la Chapelle, November 16, 1989, Correspondence Concerning the Buccal Smear Test, Ferguson-Smith Papers.

46. Ljungqvist, *Doping's Nemesis*, 186.

47. James F. Larson and Heung S. Park, *Global Television and the Politics of the Seoul Olympics*, 149–170.

48. Sam Jameson, "South Korea Sees '88 Olympics as Key to National Revitalization," *Los Angeles Times*, August 12, 1982, D1.

49. Jarol B. Manheim, "Rites of Passage: The 1988 Seoul Olympics as Public Diplomacy," 282.

50. Roh's election quieted protestors and fostered political stability. Clyde Haberman, "South Korea Walks Fine Line," *New York Times*, September 21, 1987, C1; Peter Maass, "Optimism on Olympics Grow," *Washington Post*, December 27, 1987, B2.

51. "Soviet Claims Seoul Unsafe for Olympics," *Washington Post*, November 20, 1984, E2.

52. Chun cut political ties with the Soviet Union in 1983 after a Korean Air Lines jetliner strayed into Soviet territory and was shot down. All 269 passengers on board were killed. "Seoul Makes a Play for Soviet Bloc," *Chicago Tribune*, October 5, 1984, 5; Philip Taubman, "Soviet Union Will Join Olympics but North Korea May Stay Home," *New York Times*, January 12, 1988, A1.

53. Robert McCartney, "Samaranch: Soviet Bloc Won't Boycott Olympics," *Washington Post*, September 18, 1987, B1; John Burgess, "North and South Korea Meet to Discuss 1988 Olympics," *Washington Post*, October 8, 1985, D3.

54. Seoul Olympic Organizing Committee, *Official Report*, vol. 1, part 3, 182.

55. Ljungqvist, *Doping's Nemesis*, 185.

56. IAF Workshop on Approved Methods of Femininity Verification, October 1990, Papers Relating to the International Athletic Foundation Workshop on Approved Methods of Femininity Verification, Ferguson-Smith Papers.

57. IAF Workshop on Approved Methods of Femininity Verification, List of Participants, November 10–11, 1990, Papers Relating to the International Athletic Foundation Workshop on Approved Methods of Femininity Verification, Ferguson-Smith Papers.

58. C. L. Cole, "Testing for Sex or Drugs," 332.

59. Arne Ljungqvist and Joe Leigh Simpson, "Medical Examination for Health of All Athletes Replacing the Need for Gender Verification in International Sports: The International Amateur Athletic Federation Plan," 851.

60. Letter to Martin Bobrow from Albert de la Chapelle, October 12, 1987, Copies of Correspondence between Professor Albert de la Chapelle and Dr. Martin Bobrow Regarding Challenges to the Buccal Smear Test, Ferguson-Smith Papers.

61. Letter from Joe Leigh Simpson to Arne Ljungqvist, October 8, 1991, Gender Verification Correspondences, September-November, 1991, Ferguson-Smith Papers.

62. M. Hurst, "Athletic Sex Test Snipped," *Herald Sun*, August 23, 1991, LexisNexis.

63. David Powell, "Sex Tests Cause Complaint," *Times* (London), August 21, 1991, LexisNexis.

64. James Christie, "Identity Crisis," *Globe and Mail*, May 6, 1991, LexisNexis.

65. The remaining 204 possessed IAAF femininity certificates from earlier competitions. Letter to Myron Genel from Arne Ljungqvist, October 15, 1991, Gender Verification Correspondence, September-November, 1991, Ferguson-Smith Papers.

66. Ljungqvist and Simpson, "Medical Examination," 851.

67. Letter to All Members of the Gender Verification Workshop from Arne Ljungqvist, March 4, 1991, Papers Relating to the International Athletic Foundation Workshop on Approved Methods of Femininity Verification, Ferguson-Smith Papers.

68. Letter to Arne Ljungqvist from Joe Leigh Simpson, March 18, 1991, Papers Relating to the International Athletic Foundation Workshop on Approved Methods of Femininity Verification, Ferguson-Smith Papers.

69. Letter to Arne Ljungqvist from Myron Genel, April 3, 1991, Papers Relating to the International Athletic Foundation Workshop on Approved Methods of Femininity Verification, Ferguson-Smith Papers.

70. Letter to Arne Ljungqvist from Alison Carlson, March 16, 1991, Papers Relating to the International Athletic Foundation Workshop on Approved Methods of Femininity Verification, Ferguson-Smith Papers; emphasis in original.

71. Thomas Netter, "Barcelona, French City Gets '92 Games," *Chicago Tribune*, October 18, 1986, A1; "Barcelona, French Alpine Town to Host '92 Olympics," *Los Angeles Times*, October 17, 1986, 1; Robert J. McCartney, "Barcelona, Albertville Named 1992 Olympic Sites," *Washington Post*, October 18, 1986, D1.

72. Stuart Wavell and Andrew Alderson, "Row Looms over Olympic Sex Test," *Sunday Times* (London), January 26, 1992, LexisNexis.

73. "Fanfare: Olympics," *Washington Post*, January 29, 1992, C2; "Olympic Chiefs Brush Off Sex Test Storm," Reuters, January 29, 1992, Factiva.

74. Fox, "Gender Verification," 149.

75. P. Vignetti et al. "'Sex Passport' Obligation for Female Athletes: Consideration and Criticisms on 364 Subjects," 220.

76. Louis J. Elsas et al., "Gender Verification at the Centennial Olympic Games," 50.

77. Letter to Elizabeth Ferris from Bernard Dingeon, March 11, 1993, Ferguson-Smith's Correspondence Regarding Test Results from the 1992 Barcelona Olympic Games, Ferguson-Smith Papers.

78. "Olympic Chiefs Brush Off Sex Test Storm."

79. "Olympic Sex Test No Game," *Tulsa World*, February 1, 1992, Factiva.

80. B. Dingeon et al., "Sex Testing at the Olympics," 447.

81. Albertville Olympic Organizing Committee, *Official Report of the Olympic Winter Games of Albertville and Savoie*, 215.

82. "Gender Verification, Report on the XVI Olympic Winter Games in Albert-

ville," Correspondence on the Progress of PCR Testing in Albertville Winter Olympic Games, Ferguson-Smith Papers.

83. Concerned gynecologist James C. Puffer noted that even with 99 percent accuracy, the possibility remained that seven of the approximately seven hundred women in the Winter Olympics and twenty of the approximately two thousand women in the Summer Olympics could be falsely deemed positive. Puffer, "Gender Verification: A Concept Whose Time Has Come and Passed?" 278; "Olympic Games: Sex Test Is Criticised by Doctors," *Independent*, January 29, 1992, 29.

84. According to Vyv Simson and Andrew Jennings, "The Club," one of the most secretive and influential societies in the world, controlled the 1992 bidding process. This unofficial group was comprised of "self-promoting 'Presidents'"—including FIFA president and IOC delegate Dr. João Havelange, Adidas president and creator of International Sport and Leisure Horst Dassler, and IOC president Samaranch—who "between them . . . run world sport" (4). Samaranch sued the two journalists for criminal libel, citing inaccuracies regarding his role in the Spanish Civil War. Simson and Jennings failed to attend the trial and were found guilty in absentia. If the two appeared in Lausanne, Switzerland, they would have to serve five days in jail. Simson and Jennings, *The Lord of the Rings: Power, Money and Drugs in the Modern Olympics*; Alex Duff, "Juan Antonia Samaranch, Olympics Head for 21 Years, Dies at 89 in Spain," *Bloomberg.com*, April 21, 2010, http://www.bloomberg .com/news/2010-04-21/juan-antonio-samaranch-olympics-head-for-21-years-dies -at-89-in-spain.html.

85. This claim is disputable. Tennis and track and field athletes often earned payment for victories; however, they still maintained amateur status. Some might also suggest that the financial support state-sponsored athletes received in various communist countries rendered them more professional than amateur. Nevertheless, as demonstrated in the Barcelona Olympics, the IOC completely abandoned Pierre de Coubertin's amateur ideal in 1992.

86. Michael Janofsky, "Rare Air and New Rules for Olympics," *New York Times*, July 19, 1992, SO1.

87. Christopher Anderson, "Olympic Row over Sex Testing," 784.

88. Only women oversaw the sampling to ensure contamination did not occur. Angels Serrat and Antonio García de Herreros, "Gender Verification in Sports by PCR Amplification of SRY and DYZ1 Chromosome Specific Sequences: Presence of DYZ1 Repeat in Female Athletes," 310–312.

89. After retesting the eleven "irregular" results for SRY, Serrat and de Herreros concluded that six samples amplified ZFY and not SRY, while five samples amplified both ZFY and SRY. SRY is a specific gene located on the Y chromosome; its presence spurred the IOC's decision to mandate physical examinations for the five athletes. Letter to Malcolm Andrew Ferguson-Smith from Antonio García de Herreros, February 24, 1993, Ferguson-Smith's Correspondence Regarding Test Results from the 1992 Barcelona Olympic Games, October 1992–1993, Ferguson-Smith Papers.

90. De la Chapelle guessed the four had androgen insensitivity syndrome. Letter to

Joe Leigh Simpson from Malcolm Andrew Ferguson-Smith, Correspondence Chiefly Concerning Model Resolutions on Gender Verification Testing, For Adoption by Professional Bodies, Ferguson-Smith Papers.

91. Letter to Malcolm Andrew Ferguson-Smith from Myron Genel, February 17, 1993, Ferguson-Smith's Correspondence Regarding Test Results from the 1992 Barcelona Olympic Games, October 1992–1993, Ferguson-Smith Papers.

92. "Insert C," June 14, 1993, Correspondence Chiefly Concerning Model Resolutions on Gender Verification Testing, for Adoption by Professional Bodies, Ferguson-Smith Papers; Elsas et al., "Gender Verification," 50.

Chapter 7. The IAAF's and the IOC's Continued Control

1. Bernard Dingeon, "Gender Verification and the Next Olympic Games," 357.

2. Joe Leigh Simpson et al., "Gender Verification and the Next Olympic Games—Reply," 358; emphasis in original.

3. Letter to Alison Carlson, Anke Ehrhardt, Myron Genel, Malcolm Andrew Ferguson-Smith, Elizabeth Ferris, Arne Ljungqvist, and Joe Leigh Simpson from Albert de la Chapelle, March 23, 1993, Ferguson-Smith's Correspondence Regarding Test Results from the 1992 Barcelona Olympic Games, Ferguson-Smith Papers.

4. Letter to Alison Carlson, Albert de la Chapelle, Anke Ehrhardt, Malcolm Andrew Ferguson-Smith, Elizabeth Ferris, Myron Genel, and Joe Leigh Simpson from Arne Ljungqvist, June 23, 1993, Correspondence Chiefly Concerning Model Resolutions on Gender Verification Testing, for Adoption by Professional Bodies, Ferguson-Smith Papers.

5. In this article Virginia Scahill appeared to alter her position radically. She told Brady that "we are just flat-out not doing the test. . . . It's been done for 25 years now, and it's unfair and unnecessary." Erik Brady, "University Games Drop Gender Test," *USA Today*, July 15, 1992, Factiva.

6. Louis J. Elsas et al., "Gender Verification of Female Athletes," 251.

7. Letter to Alison Carlson, Albert de la Chapelle, Myron Genel, Joe Leigh Simpson, Malcolm Andrew Ferguson-Smith, Anke Ehrhardt, and Elizabeth Ferris from Arne Ljungqvist, April 10, 1995, The Need to Re-Examine Policy, Ferguson-Smith Papers.

8. Katia Mascagni, "World Conference on Women and Sport," 23–27.

9. Letter to Alison Carlson, Albert de la Chapelle, Anke Ehrhardt, Malcolm Andrew Ferguson-Smith, Elizabeth Ferris, Arne Ljungqvist, and Joe Leigh Simpson from Myron Genel, December 20, 1996, Correspondence Regarding the Statement on Gender Verification for Consideration by Women's Sport Foundation, Ferguson-Smith Papers.

10. Alan Riding, "Olympics: One Year to Lillehammer," *New York Times*, February 12, 1993, B11.

11. The IOC voted to alter the format of the Olympics to space the organizational time required between the games. Furthermore, the IOC receives greater income during the years when the Olympics are held.

12. Jon Helge Lesjo, "Lillehammer 1994: Planning, Figurations, and the 'Green' Winter Games."

13. This notably did not extend to married women. Access to craft and commerce occurred in 1839–1865, equal right of inheritance in 1842, and property rights in 1865. Gro Hagemann, "Citizenship and Social Order: Gender Politics in Twentieth-Century Norway and Sweden," 418–419.

14. Ibid., 421.

15. United Nations, "The Universal Declaration of Human Rights," *UN.org*, accessed September 15, 2015, http://www.un.org/en/documents/udhr/index.shtml. For more analysis on Human Rights and Sex Testing, see Stacy Larson, "Intersexuality and Gender Verification Tests: The Need to Assure Human Rights and Privacy," 240–241. Larson also notes that Article 29 provided leeway to national legislation that could maintain that an individuals' rights are outweighed by the necessity of fair play in sport.

16. Convention on the Elimination of All Forms of Discrimination against Women, "Text of the Convention," *UN.org*, accessed September 15, 2015, http://www.un.org /womenwatch/daw/cedaw/cedaw.htm.

17. Hagemann, "Citizenship and Social Order," 421.

18. Gerd von der Lippe, "Medical Tests on Gender, Sexuality, and Sport in Norway, 1890–1950: Changing Metaphors on Femininities and Masculinities."

19. Kari Fasting, "Women and Sport in Norway," 24–25.

20. Jorid Hovden, "Gender and Leadership Selection Processes in Norwegian Sporting Organizations."

21. Arne Ljungqvist et al., "The History and Current Policies on Gender Testing in Elite Athletes," 229.

22. Lillehammer Olympic Organizing Committee, *Official Report of the XVII Olympic Winter Games Lillehammer 1994*, vol. 2, part 1, 89–93.

23. Berit Skirstad found that 66 percent favored gender verification and only 20 percent found the tests humiliating. Skirstad, "Gender Verification in Competitive Sport: Turning from Research to Action," 118.

24. Ibid., 119–122. Skirstad estimated that one out of four female competitors had been unfairly excluded and that the current measures no longer served its original purpose of detecting male masqueraders.

25. Meeting Minutes of the International Olympic Committee Session in Paris, September 4–5, 1994, OSC Archives.

26. Nancy Hogshead-Makar, phone interview by author, January 19, 2015.

27. Fox, "Gender Verification," 148–149.

28. Skirstad, "Gender Verification," 121.

29. Organization for Economic Co-Operation and Development, *Genetic Testing: A Survey of Quality Assurance Proficiency Standards*, 124.

30. Ljungqvist, "Gender Verification," 190–191.

31. Skirstad, "Gender Verification," 119–122.

32. Ljungqvist, "Gender Verification," 190–191.

33. Bruce Lowitt, "IOC Medical Official Predicts Abolishment of Sex Tests," *St. Petersburg Times*, December 7, 1997, 11C.

34. Phil Hersh, "Chinese Runners Suspect," *Chicago Tribune*, September 14, 1993, http://articles.chicagotribune.com/1993–09–14/sports/9309140145_1_wang-junxia -chinese-women-record.

35. Darcy C. Plymire, "Too Much, Too Fast, Too Soon: Chinese Women Runners, Accusations of Steroid Use, and the Politics of American Track and Field."

36. John Goodbody, "Allison Voices Fear of Drug Use by Chinese," *Times* (London), September 14, 1993, LexisNexis.

37. Plymire, "Too Much, Too Fast, Too Soon," 160.

38. Yan Xuetong, "The Rise of China and Its Power Status."

39. "Female Athlete Fails Sex Test," *Courier-Mail*, October 1, 1990, LexisNexis.

40. Sport Around the World, "Women Stopped in Their Tracks by Tests," July 24, 1993, Gender Verification Correspondence, July-December, 1993, Ferguson-Smith Papers.

41. Janet Heinonen, "A Decent Proposal," *Keeping Track*, May 1994, Correspondence Regarding the Petition by the "Heinonen Sixteen" on Gender Verification, Ferguson-Smith Papers.

42. Throughout her career, Heinonen maintained such postulations. When South African runner Caster Semenya faced international criticism in 2009, Heinonen argued that the situation was not novel in the world of sport. She not only suggested that Semenya be prohibited from competition but also referenced Chinese athletes who similarly depended upon "gender miscues" for success. Larry Eder, "Caster Semenya Saga Moves On: What Is Gender?" *RunBlogRun*, September 9, 2009, http:// www.runblogrun.com/2009/09/caster-semenya-saga-moves-on-what-is-gender -commentary-by-larry-eder.html.

43. Letter to Arne Ljungqvist, Malcolm Ferguson-Smith, Liz Ferris, and Myron Genel from Alison Carlson, April 19, 1994, Correspondence Regarding the Petition by the "Heinonen Sixteen" on Gender Verification, Ferguson-Smith Papers.

44. The sixteen athletes who signed the petition all maintained US citizenship: Darcy Arreola, Cathie Twomey Bellamy, Kelly Blair, Melody Fairchild, Eryn Forbes, Kathy Hayes Herrmann, Lynn Jennings, Kristy Johnston, Anne Marie Letko, Lisa Ondicki, Annette Peters, PattiSue Plumer, Colleen de Reuck, Mary Slaney, Shelly Steele, and Elizabeth Wilson. Letter to Arne Ljungqvist from Olympic and International World Class Athletes, February 24, 1994, Correspondence Regarding the Petition by the "Heinonen Sixteen" on Gender Verification, Ferguson-Smith Papers.

45. Letter to Albert de la Chapelle, Anke Ehrhardt, Malcolm Andrew Ferguson-Smith, Elizabeth Ferris, Myron Genel, Arne Ljungqvist, and Joe Leigh Simpson from Alison Carlson, April 19, 1994, Correspondence Regarding the Petition by the "Heinonen Sixteen" on Gender Verification, Ferguson-Smith Papers.

46. Letter to Arne Ljungqvist from Olympic and International World Class Athletes, February 24, 1994, Correspondence Regarding the Petition by the "Heinonen Sixteen" on Gender Verification, Ferguson-Smith Papers.

47. Phyllis Fang, "Games—Sports Still Perplexed by Man-Woman Question," Reuters News, October 12, 1994, Factiva.

48. Letter to Arne Ljungqvist from Malcolm Ferguson-Smith, March 16, 1994; Letter to Arne Ljungqvist, Malcolm Ferguson-Smith, Liz Ferris, and Myron Genel from Alison Carlson, April 19, 1994, Correspondence Regarding the Petition by the "Heinonen Sixteen" on Gender Verification, Ferguson-Smith Papers.

49. Fang, "Games—Sports Still Perplexed."

50. Of the women's airtime, 61 percent showed swimming, diving, and gymnastics while power sports, such as discus and shot put, received hardly any mention. Susan Tyler Eastman and Andrew C. Billings, "Gender Parity in the Olympics: Hyping Women Athletes, Favoring Men Athletes."

51. C. A. Tuggle and Ann Owen, "A Descriptive Analysis of NBC's Coverage of the Centennial Olympics."

52. Joan Stephenson, "Female Olympians' Sex Tests Outmoded," 177.

53. Elsas et al., "Gender Verification," 50.

54. Letter to Alison Carlson, Albert de la Chapelle, Anke Ehrhardt, Malcolm Andrew Ferguson-Smith, Elizabeth Ferris, Arne Ljungqvist, and Joe Leigh Simpson from Myron Genel, June 15, 1993, Correspondence Chiefly Concerning Model Resolutions on Gender Verification Testing, for Adoption by Professional Bodies, Ferguson-Smith Papers.

55. Atlanta Committee for the Olympic Games, *Official Report of the Centennial Olympic Games*, vol. 1, 292.

56. Correspondences between Myron Genel and Skip Elsas, September 22, 1995, The Need to Re-Examine Policy, Ferguson-Smith Papers.

57. Elsas et al., "Gender Verification," 50–51. Of the female participants, 379 women did not need verification, because they competed in open events, and 296 had previously been granted a certificate.

58. S. Boyd Eaton et al., "The Polyclinic at the 1996 Atlanta Olympic Village," 599–602.

59. Elsas, "Gender Verification," 53.

60. Herb Weinberg, "Robert Helmick: The Salt Lake City Candidacy," 6.

61. "Nagano: In the Japanese Heartland," 21–24.

62. Organising Committee for the Olympic Winter Games in Nagano, *The XVIII Olympic Winter Games: Official Report Nagano 1998*, 288–295.

63. Bill Mallon, Jeroen Heijmans, *Historical Dictionary of the Olympic Movement*, 34.

64. "Athletes Elect Athletes," 19–20.

65. "Athletes' Commission Election," 48.

66. Janet Rae Brooks, "Gender Testing at Olympics Abolished at Last," *Globe and Mail*, April 7, 2000, S13.

67. Myron Genel, "Gender Verification No More?" 7218.

68. Ibid.

69. Meeting Minutes of the 109th IOC Session, July17–20, 1999, Seoul, OSC Archives.

70. Myron Genel and Arne Ljungqvist, "Essay: Gender Verification of Female Athletes," 541.

71. Puffer, "Gender Verification," 278; Barry D. Dickinson et al., "Gender Verification of Female Olympic Athletes," 1542.

72. Haley K. Olsen-Acre, "The Use of Drug Testing to Police Sex and Gender in the Olympics."

73. Joe Leigh Simpson et al., "Gender Verification in the Olympics," 1568–1569; Jill Pilgrim et al., "Far from the Finish Line: Transsexualism and Athletic Competition."

74. A British heptathlon athlete, Brazilian judoka Edinanci Silva, and Brazilian volleyball player Érika Coimbra underwent testing. Silva and Coimbra reportedly were born with both male and female genitalia. Surgery allowed the two to compete as women. Despite passing all required tests, Silva experienced cruel media attacks. Colin Adamson, "The Girls from Brazil Who Share a Sydney Secret," *Evening Standard* (London), September 27, 2000, 22.

75. The Stockholm Consensus divided transgender athletes into two groups. One set of stipulations referred to individuals who had undergone sex-reassignment surgery before reaching puberty; for these individuals the Stockholm Consensus allowed them to compete in the resultant gender division without restriction. For the other group the IOC established the narrow set of regulations.

76. International Olympic Committee Medical Commission, "Statement of the Stockholm Consensus on Sex Reassignment in Sports," *Olympic.org,* December 11, 2003, http://multimedia.olympic.org/pdf/en_report_905.pdf.

77. For several transgender athletes who so desire, surgery remains an impossibility. Sex-reassignment is expensive, thereby making it affordable for only wealthy individuals. In addition, several countries do not have the necessary medical background or scientific technology to perform the operations, and sex reassignment for female-to-male transgender individuals has yet to be perfected. Legal recognition by "appropriate official authorities" is also problematic. Transgender people outside of North America and Europe have difficulty changing legal status.

78. Ljungqvist, *Doping's Nemesis*, 183.

Epilogue

1. Letter to Alison Carlson, Albert de la Chapelle, Anke Ehrhardt, Malcolm Andrew Ferguson-Smith, Elizabeth Ferris, Myron Genel, and Joe Leigh Simpson from Arne Ljungqvist, June 23, 1999, Correspondence Concerning the News that Genetic Based Screening for Female Gender Was to Be Abandoned by the IOC and Reaction, Ferguson-Smith Papers.

2. Nilanjania Bhowmick and Jyoti Thottam, "Gender and Athletics: India's Own Caster Semenya," *Time,* September 1, 2009, http://www.time.com/time/world/article/0,8599,1919562,00.html.

3. Samantha Shapiro, "Caught in the Middle: A Failed Gender Test Crushed Santhi Soundarajan's Olympic Dreams."

4. "Sex Test Failure Attempts Suicide," *Fox Sports,* September 6, 2007, http://www

.foxsports.com.au/breaking-news/sex-test-failure-attempts-suicide/story-e6frf33c
-1111114358075?nk=8a38a3db3f1187a0f340434cc13804ac.

5. Anna Kessel, "Caster Semenya Wins 800m Gold but Cannot Escape Gender Controversy," *Guardian*, August 19, 2009, http://www.guardian.co.uk/sport/2009 /aug/19/caster-semenya-800m-world-athletics-championships-gender.

6. Christopher Clarey and Gina Kolata, "Gold Is Awarded, but Dispute over Runner's Sex Intensifies," *New York Times*, August 21, 2009, B9.

7. Christopher Clarey, "Gender Test after a Gold-Medal Finish," *New York Times*, August 20, 2009, B13.

8. In 2008 Semenya participated in the World Junior Championships, where she won the gold medal in the 800-meter race with a time of 2:04.23. "Young SA Team Strikes Gold," *Independent Online*, October 16, 2008, http://www.iol.co.za/sport /young-sa-team-strikes-gold-1.594712#.VhgUxi5VhBd.

9. Shapiro, "Caught in the Middle."

10. Jaime Schultz, "New Standards, Same Refrain: The IAAF's Regulations on Hyperandrogenism," 32–33.

11. Carina Ray, "Caster Semenya: Twenty-First Century 'Hottentot Venus'?"

12. Ljungqvist claimed that Soundarajan and Semenya did not cause the reintroduction of gender verification. Accordingly, Olympic officials and medical practitioners already had been debating the issue when the two athletes surfaced. However, others point to the two athletes as the primary motivation for new regulations. Stephen Wilson, "IOC to Adopt Rules in Gender Cases," *USA Today*, April 5, 2011, usatoday30. usatoday.com/sports/olympics/2011-04-05-3875669216_x.htm.

13. The timeline of meetings was as follows: December 2009, IAAF Expert Working Group, Monaco; January 2010, IOC/IAF DSD Meeting, Miami; May 2010, IAAF Expert Working Group, Monaco; September 2010, IOC/IAAF Working Session, Stockholm; October 2010, IOC Expert Hyperandrogenism Working Group, Lausanne; and February 2011, IOC/IAAF Working Session, Monaco.

14. Quoted in Cassandra Wells, "Diagnosing Sex-Gender Verification and the IOC," 301.

15. International Olympic Committee Medical and Scientific Department, "IOC Regulations on Female Hyperandrogenism."

16. Richard Budgett, interview by author, Lausanne, Switzerland, June 28, 2013.

17. International Olympic Committee Medical and Scientific Department, "IOC Regulations."

18. Stephanie Findlay, "Olympics Struggle with Policing Femininity," *Star* (London), June 8, 2012, http://www.thestar.com/sports/olympics/2012/06/08/olympics_struggle _with_policing_femininity.html.

19. International Association of Athletics Federation, "IAAF Regulations Governing Eligibility of Females with Hyperandrogenism to Compete in Women's Competition."

20. International Association of Athletics Federation, "Hyperandrogenism Regulations: Explanatory Notes."

21. Schultz, "New Standards, Same Refrain," 32–33.

22. International Association of Athletics Federation, "IAAF Regulations."

23. Some examples of possible treatments include the use of antiandrogens, estrogen replacement therapy, and gonadectomies. Antiandrogens are drugs that block androgen receptors and prevent the expression of biological effects. A gonadectomy, in this instance, refers to the surgical removal of testes.

24. Bill Littlefield, "Dutee Chand: A Woman Banned from Women's Sports," October 11, 2014, National Public Radio, http://onlyagame.wbur.org/2014/10/11/dutee-chand-banned-iaaf.

25. Patrick Fénichel et al., "Molecular Diagnosis of 5α-Reductase Deficiency in 4 Elite Young Female Athletes through Hormonal Screening for Hyperandrogenism," 1056.

26. Ibid., 1057.

27. Juliet Macur, "Fighting for the Body She Was Born With," *New York Times*, October 6, 2014, 11.

28. "Sprinter Battles Gender-Based Ban, Rather than Track Rivals," *Straits Times*, October 15, 2014, Factiva.

29. Dutee Chand v. Athletics Federation of India and the International Association of Athletics Federation, Interim Arbitral Award (CAS 2014/A/3759), http://www.tas-cas.org/fileadmin/user_upload/award_internet.pdf; emphasis in original.

30. Nathan Q. Ha et al., "Hurdling over Sex? Sport, Science, and Equity," 1040.

31. Sullivan, "Gender Verification," 414.

32. Marc Naimark, "A New Study Supports Female Athletes Unfairly Excluded from Sport," *Slate*, September 12, 2014, http://www.slate.com/blogs/outward/2014/09/12/sex_verification_in_sports_a_new_study_supports_unfairly_excluded_female.html.

33. Canadian Centre for Ethics in Sport, *Sport in Transition: Making Sport in Canada More Responsible for Gender Inclusivity*, 8–9.

34. Schweinbenz and Cronk, "Femininity Control."

35. Quoted in Findlay, "Olympics Struggle."

36. Canadian Centre for Ethics in Sport, *Sport in Transition*, 8.

Bibliography

Archival Collections

Avery Brundage Collection. University of Illinois Archives, United States.
Malcolm Andrew Ferguson-Smith Papers. University of Glasgow, Scotland.
Olympic Studies Centre. Lausanne, Switzerland.
Stella Walsh Papers. Western Reserve Historical Society Library, United States.

Other Sources

"1984 (IOC Official)." *Olympic Review* 120 (1977): 664.

Albertville Olympic Organizing Committee. *Official Report of the Olympic Winter Games of Albertville and Savoie.* Albertville: Comité d'organisation des Jeux Olympiques d'hiver de 1992, 1992.

Anderson, Christopher. "Olympic Row over Sex Testing." *Nature* 353, no. 6347 (1991): 784.

"Are Girl Athletes Really Girls?" *Life*, October 7, 1966, 63–72.

Ashwin, Sarah. Introduction to *Gender, State and Society in Soviet and Post-Soviet Russia.* Edited by Sarah Ashwin. London: Routledge, 2000.

"Athletes' Commission Election." *Olympic Review* 20 (April-May 1998): 48.

"Athletes Elect Athletes." *Olympic Review* 10 (August-September 1996): 19–20.

Atlanta Committee for the Olympic Game. *Official Report of the Centennial Olympic Games.* Atlanta: Atlanta Committee for the Olympic Games, 1996.

Ballantyne, Kaye N., Manfred Kayser, and J. Anton Groogtegoed. "Sex and Gender Issues in Competitive Sports: Investigation of a Historical Case Leads to a New Viewpoint." *British Journal of Sports Medicine* 46 (2012): 614–617.

Barr, Murray L. "Cytological Tests of Sex." Letter to the editor. *Lancet* 267, no. 6906 (1956): 47.

Barr, Murray L., and Ewart G. Bertram. "A Morphological Distinction between Neurones of the Male and Female, and the Behaviour of the Nucleolar Satellite during Accelerated Nucleoprotein Synthesis." *Nature* 163, no. 4148 (1949): 676–677.

Beamish, Rob. *Steroids: A New Look at Performance-Enhancing Drugs*. Santa Barbara, CA: Praeger, 2011.

Beamish, Rob, and Ian Ritchie. *Fastest, Highest, Strongest: A Critique of High-Performance Sport*. New York: Routledge, 2006.

Behre, H. M., C. Wang, D. J. Handelsman, and E. Nieschlag. "Pharmacology of Testosterone Preparations." In *Testosterone: Action, Deficiency, Substitution*, edited by E. Nieschlag, 405–444. Cambridge: Cambridge University Press, 2004.

Berg, Stefan. "1936 Berlin Olympics: How Dora the Man Competed in the Woman's High Jump." *Spiegel Online International*, September 15, 2009. http://www.spiegel .de/international/germany/1936-berlin-olympics-how-dora-the-man-competed -in-the-woman-s-high-jump-a-649104.html.

Berlioux, Monique. "Doping, Drugs, and Sport." *Olympic Review* 25 (1969): 561–564.

———. "Femininity." *Olympic Review* 3 (December 1967): 1–2.

Bérubé, Allan. *Coming Out Under Fire: The History of Gay Men and Women in World War II*. Chapel Hill: University of North Carolina Press, 1990.

Birrell, Susan. "Discourses on the Gender/Sport Relationship: From Women in Sport to Gender Relations." *Exercise and Sport Sciences Reviews* 16 (1988): 459–502.

Bostwick, J. Michael, and Michael J. Joyner. "The Limits of Acceptable Biological Variation in Elite Athletes: Should Sex Ambiguity Be Treated Differently from Other Advantageous Genetic Traits?" *Mayo Clinic Proceedings* 87, no. 6 (2012): 508–513.

Boyd, Nan Alamilla. *Wide-Open Town: A History of Queer San Francisco to 1965*. Berkeley: University of California Press, 2005.

British Association of Sport and Medicine. "Doping and the Use of Chemical Agents to Modify the Human Performance in Sport: Policy Statement." *British Journal of Sports Medicine* 1, no. 2 (1964): 40–42.

Bunge, Raymond G. "Narration: Sex and the Olympic Games No. 2." *JAMA: The Journal of the American Medical Association* 200, no. 10 (1967): 267.

———. "Sex and the Olympic Games." *JAMA: The Journal of the American Medical Association* 173 (July 23, 1960): 196.

Cahn, Susan K. *Coming on Strong: Gender and Sexuality in Twentieth-Century Women's Sport*. Cambridge: Harvard University Press, 1994.

———. "From the 'Muscle Moll' to the 'Butch' Ballplayer: Mannishness, Lesbianism, and Homophobia in U.S. Women's Sport." *Feminist Studies* 19 (Summer 1993): 343–368.

———. "Testing Sex, Attributing Gender: What Caster Semenya Means to Women's Sports." *Journal of Intercollegiate Sport* 4, no. 1 (2011): 38–48.

Camporesi, Silvia, and Paolo Maugeri. "Caster Semenya: Sport, Categories and the Creative Role of Ethics." *Journal of Medical Ethics* 36 (2010): 378–379.

Canadian Centre for Ethics in Sport. "Sport in Transition: Making Sport in Canada More Responsible for Gender Inclusivity." July 2012. http://www.cces.ca/files/pdfs /CCES-PAPER-SportInTransition-E.pdf.

"The Candidate Cities for 1984." *Olympic Review* 126 (May 1978): 283–284.

Carlson, Alison. "When Is a Woman Not a Woman?" *Women's Sport and Fitness* 13, no. 2 (1991): 24–29.

———. "Y Doesn't Always Mark the Spot." *Ms.*, 1988, 43.

Carpentier, Florence, and Jean-Pierre Lefévre. "The Modern Olympic Movement, Women's Sport, and the Social Order during the Inter-War Period." *International Journal of the History of Sport* 23, no. 7 (2006): 1112–1127.

Carter, Jimmy. *Keeping Faith: Memoirs of a President*. New York: Bantam Books, 1982.

Cayleff, Susan E. *Babe: The Life and Legend of Babe Didrikson Zaharias*. Urbana: University of Illinois Press, 1995.

"Change of Sex." *Time*, August 24, 1936, 39–40.

Chapelle, Albert de la. "The Use and Misuse of Sex Chromatin Screening for 'Gender Identification' of Female Athletes." *Journal of the American Medical Association* 256, no. 14 (1986): 1920–1923.

Chatziefstathiou, Dikaia. "Reading Baron Pierre de Coubertin: Issues of Race and Gender." *Aethlon* 25, no. 2 (2008): 95–116.

Chauncey, George. *Gay New York: Gender, Urban Culture, and the Making of the Gay Male World, 1890–1940*. New York: Basic Books, 1995.

Cole, C. L. "Testing for Sex or Drugs." *Journal of Sport and Social Issues* 24, no. 4 (2000): 331–333.

Collins, Patricia Hill. *Black Sexual Politics: African Americans, Gender, and the New Racism*. New York: Routledge, 2004.

Collins, Robert M. *Transforming America: Politics and Culture in the Reagan Years*. New York: Columbia University Press, 2006.

Collins, S. "East and West: Confrontational Diplomacy." *International Journal of the History of Sport* 24, no. 8 (2007): 1003–1041.

Cott, Nancy. *No Small Courage: A History of Women in the United States*. New York: Oxford University Press, 2000.

Coubertin, Pierre de. "The Women at the Olympic Games." In *Pierre de Coubertin, 1863–1937—Olympism: Selected Writings*. Lausanne: International Olympic Committee, 2000.

Daly, Anthony. "Focus: On Health." *Olympic Review* 201 (July-August 1984): 510–512.

Davenport, Joanna. "Breaking into the Rings: Women on the IOC." *Journal of Physical Education, Recreation & Dance* 67, no. 5 (1996): 26–30.

Defrance, Jacques, and Jean-Marc Chamot. "The Voice of Sport: Expressing a Foreign Policy through a Silent Cultural Activity: The Case of Sport in French Foreign Policy after the Second World War." *Sport in Society: Cultures, Commerce, Media, Politics* 11, no. 4 (2008): 395–413.

Demak, Richard. "Marfan Syndrome: A Silent Killer." *Sports Illustrated*, February 17, 1986, 30.

"Denver." *Olympic Review* 60–61 (November-December): 53.

Diamond, Milton, and Linda Ann Watson. "Androgen Insensitivity Syndrome and Klinefelter's Syndrome: Sex and Gender Considerations." *Child and Adolescent Psychiatric Clinics of North America* 13, no. 3 (2007): 623–640.

Dickinson, Barry D., Myron Genel, Carolyn B. Robinowitz, Patricia L. Turner, and Gary L. Woods. "Gender Verification of Female Olympic Athletes." *Medicine & Science in Sports & Exercise*, 34 no. 10 (2002): 1539–1542.

Dimeo, Paul. *A History of Drug Use in Sport, 1876–1976*. New York: Routledge, 2007.

Dimeo, Paul, Thomas M. Hunt, and Matthew T. Bowers. "Saint or Sinner? A Reconsideration of the Career of Prince Alexandre de Mérode, Chair of the International Olympic Committee's Medical Commission, 1967–2002." *International Journal of the History of Sport* 28, no. 6 (2011): 925–940.

Dingeon, Bernard. "Gender Verification and the Next Olympic Games." *JAMA: The Journal of the American Medical Association* 269, no. 3 (1993): 357.

Dingeon, Bernard, P. Hamon, M. Robert, P. Schamasch, and M. Pugeat. "Sex Testing at the Olympics." *Nature* 358 (August 6, 1992): 447.

"Doping." *Olympic Review* 84 (November 1963): 60.

Dotson, Jennifer L., and Robert T. Brown. "The History of the Development of Anabolic-Androgenic Steroids." *Pediatric Clinic of North America* 54, no. 4 (2007): 761–769.

Douglas, Susan J. *Where the Girls Are: Growing up Female with the Mass Media*. New York: Three Rivers Press, 1995.

Dreger, Alice Domurat. *Hermaphrodites and the Medical Invention of Sex*. Cambridge: Harvard University Press, 1998.

Dyreson, Mark. *Making the American Team: Sport, Culture, and the Olympic Experience*. Urbana: University of Illinois Press, 1998.

Eastman, Susan Tyler, and Andrew C. Billings. "Gender Parity in the Olympics: Hyping Women Athletes, Favoring Men Athletes." *Journal of Sport and Social Issues* 23, no. 2 (1999), 140–170.

Eaton, S. Boyd, Blane A. Woodfin, James L. Askew, Blaise M. Morrisey, Louis J. Elsas, Jay L. Shoop, Elizabeth A. Martin, and John D. Cantwell. "The Polyclinic at the 1996 Atlanta Olympic Village." *Olympic Medicine: The Medical Journal of Australia* 167, no. 11–12 (1997): 599–602.

Eikleberry, Sarah Jane. "More Than Milk and Cookies: Revisiting the College Play Day." *Journal of Sport History* 42 (2014): 467–486.

Eisen, George. "The Voices of Sanity: American Diplomatic Reports from the 1936 Berlin Olympiad." *Journal of Sport History* 11, no. 3 (1984): 56–78.

Elsas, Louis J., Risa P. Hayes, and Kasinathan Muralidharan. "Gender Verification at the Centennial Olympic Games." *Journal of the Medical Association of Georgia* 86, no. 1 (1997): 50–54.

Elsas, Louis J., Arne Ljungqvist, Malcolm A. Ferguson-Smith, Joe Leigh Simpson, Myron Genel, Alison S. Carlson, Elizabeth Ferris, Albert de la Chapelle, and Anke A. Ehrhardt. "Gender Verification of Female Athletes." *Genetics in Medicine* 2 (2000): 249–254.

Epstein, David. *The Sports Gene: Inside the Science of Extraordinary Athletic Performance*. New York: Penguin, 2014.

"Extracts of the Minutes of the 57th Session of the International Olympic Committee." *Olympic Review* 72 (1960): 61–69.

"Extracts of the Minutes of the 65th Session of the International Olympic Committee." *Olympic Review* 98–99 (May-August 1967): 89–95.

Eyquem, Marie-Thérèse. "Women Sports and the Olympic Games." *Olympic Review* 73 (February 1961): 48–50.

Fakiolas, Efstathios T. "Kennan's Long Telegram and NSC-68: A Comparative Theoretical Analysis." *East European Quarterly* 31, no. 4 (1998): 415–433.

Fasting, Kari. "Women and Sport in Norway." In *Sport and Women: Social Issues in International Perspective,* edited by Ilse Hartmann-Tews and Gertrud Pfister, 15–34. New York: Routledge, 2003.

Fausto-Sterling, Anne. "Gender, Race, and Nation: The Comparative Anatomy of 'Hottentot' Women in Europe, 1815–1817." In *Deviant Bodies: Critical Perspectives on Difference in Science and Popular Culture,* edited by Jennifer Terry and Jacqueline Urla, 19–46. Bloomington: Indiana University Press, 1995.

———. *Sexing the Body: Gender Politics and the Construction of Sexuality.* New York: Basic Books, 2000.

Fénichel, Patrick, Françoise Paris, Pascal Philibert, Sylvie Hiéronimus, Laura Gaspari, Jean-Yves Kurzenne, Patrick Chevallier, Stéphane Bermon, Nicolas Chevalier, and Charles Sultan. "Molecular Diagnosis of 5α-Reductase Deficiency in 4 Elite Young Female Athletes through Hormonal Screening for Hyperandrogenism." *Journal of Clinical Endocrinology & Metabolism* 98, no. 6 (2013): 1055–1059.

Ferez, Sylvain. "From Women's Exclusion to Gender Institution: A Brief History of the Sexual Categorisation Process within Sport." *International Journal of the History of Sport* 29, no. 2 (2012): 272–285.

Ferguson-Smith, M. A., and Elizabeth A. Ferris. "Gender Verification in Sport: The Need for Change?" *British Journal of Sports Medicine* 25, no. 1 (1991): 17–20.

Ferris, Elizabeth. "Sportswomen and Medicine." *Olympic Review* 140 (June 1979): 336–338.

Fisher, Jill A. *Gender and the Science of Difference: Cultural Politics of Contemporary Science and Medicine.* New Brunswick, NJ: Rutgers University Press, 2011.

Fox, John S. "Gender Verification: What Purpose? What Price?" *British Journal of Sports Medicine* 27, no. 3 (1993): 148–149.

Francois, J., and M. Th. Matton-Van Leuven. "Sexual Evaluation of 'Female' Athletes." *Journal of Sports Medicine* 1, no. 3 (1973): 5–11.

Franke, Werner W., and Brigitte Berendonk. "Hormonal Doping and Androgenization of Athletes: A Secret Program of the German Democratic Republic Government." *Clinical Chemistry* 43, no. 7 (1997): 1262–1279.

Freeman, Erica, David A. Bloom, and Edward J. McGuire. "A Brief History of Testosterone." *Journal of Urology* 165, no. 2 (2001): 371–373.

Frost, Dennis. *Seeing Stars: Sports Celebrity, Identity, and Body Culture in Modern Japan.* Cambridge: Harvard University Press, 2010.

Gaddis, John Lewis. *The Cold War: A New History.* New York: Penguin, 2005.

Gallico, Paul. *Farewell to Sport.* Lincoln: University of Nebraska Press, 1937.

———. "The Little Babe from Texas Turned Out to Be One of the World's Greatest Athletes." *Esquire,* March 1955, 48–49.

Genel, Myron. "Gender Verification No More?" *Medscape Women's Health* 5, no. 3 (2000): 7218.

Genel, Myron, and Arne Ljungqvist. "Essay: Gender Verification of Female Athletes." *Lancet* 366 (2005): 541.

Gerber, Ellen W., Jan Felshin, Pearl Berlin, and Waneen Wyrick. *The American Woman in Sport.* Reading, MA: Addison-Wesley, 1974.

Gilbert, Bil. "Problems in a Turned-on World." *Sports Illustrated,* June 23, 1969, 64–72.

"Girl Changes into Man." *Your Body* (June 1936). In *American Sexual Histories,* edited by Elizabeth Reis, 309–311. Oxford: Blackwell.

Gómez, Marte R. "Mexico's New City of Sport." *Olympic Review* 71 (1960): 30–31.

Grady, Denise. "Sex Test of Champions." *Discover* 13, no. 6 (1992): 75–78.

Griswold, Robert L. "'Russian Blonde in Space': Soviet Women in the American Imagination, 1950–1965." *Journal of Social History* 45, no. 4 (2012): 881–907.

Gruneau, Rick, and Robert Neubauer. "A Gold Medal for the Market: The 1984 Los Angeles Olympics, the Reagan Era, and the Politics of Neoliberalism." In *The Palgrave Handbook of Olympic Studies,* edited by Helen Jefferson Lenskyj and Stephen Wagg, 134–162.

Guttmann, Allen. *The Olympics: A History of the Modern Games.* Urbana: University of Illinois Press, 2002.

———. *Women's Sports: A History.* New York: Columbia University Press, 1991.

Ha, Nathan Q., Shari L. Dworkin, María José Martínez Patiño, Alan D. Rogol, Vernon Rosario, Francisco J. Sanchez, Alison Wrynn, and Eric Vilain. "Hurdling over Sex? Sport, Science, and Equity." *Archives of Sexual Behavior* 43, no. 6 (2014): 1035–1042.

Hagemann, Gro. "Citizenship and Social Order: Gender Politics in Twentieth-Century Norway and Sweden." *Women's History Review* 11, no. 3 (2002): 417–429.

Hall, M. Ann. "Alexandrine Gibb: In 'No Man's Land of Sport.'" *International Journal of the History of Sport* 18, no. 1 (2001): 149–172.

Hanley, Daniel F. "Medical News, Chromosomes Do Not an Athlete Make." *JAMA: The Journal of the American Medical Association* 202, no. 11 (1967): 54–55.

Hanson, Sharon Kinney. *The Life of Helen Stephens: The Fulton Flash.* Carbondale: Southern Illinois University Press, 2004.

Hargreaves, Jennifer. "Olympic Women: A Struggle for Recognition." In *Women and Sports in the United States: A Documentary Reader,* edited by Jean O'Reilly and Susan K. Cahn, 3–14. Lebanon, NH: Northeastern University Press, 2007.

———. *Sporting Females: Critical Issues in the History and Sociology of Women's Sports.* New York: Routledge, 1994.

Hay, Eduardo. "Femininity Tests at the Olympic Games." *Olympic Review* 76–77 (March-April 1974): 119–124.

———. "Sex Determination in Putative Female Athletes." *JAMA: The Journal of the American Medical Association* 221, no. 9 (1972): 988–999.

———. "The Stella Walsh Case." *Olympic Review* 162 (April 1981): 221–222.

Healey, Dan. "Homosexual Existence and Existing Socialism: New Light on the Repression of Male Homosexuality in Stalin's Russia." *GLQ: A Journal of Gay and Lesbian Studies* 8, no. 3 (2002): 349–378.

———. "Sexual and Gender Dissent: Homosexuality as Resistance in Stalin's Russia." In *Contending with Stalinism: Soviet Power and Popular Resistance in the 1930s*, edited by Lynne Viola, 139–169. Ithaca, NY: Cornell University Press, 2002.

Heggie, Vanessa. "Testing Sex and Gender in Sports; Reinventing, Reimagining and Reconstructing Histories." *Endeavour* 34, no. 4 (2010): 157–163.

Hilbrenner, Anke. "Soviet Women in Sports in the Brezhnev Years: The Female Body and Soviet Modernism." In *Euphoria and Exhaustion: Modern Sport in Soviet Culture and Society*, edited by Nikolaus Katzer, Sandra Budy, Alexandra Köhring, and Manfred Zeller, 295–315. Frankfurt: Campus Verlag, 2010.

Hoberman, John. *The Olympic Crisis: Sport, Politics, and the Moral Order*. New Rochelle, NY: Caratzas, 1986.

———. *Testosterone Dreams: Rejuvenation, Aphrodisia, Doping*. Berkeley: University of California Press, 2005.

Hoberman, John M., and Charles E. Yesalis. "The History of Synthetic Testosterone." *Scientific American* 27, no. 2 (1995): 27–33.

Horne, John. "Understanding Sport and Body Culture in Japan." *Body & Society* 6, no. 2 (2000): 73–86.

Hovden, Jorid. "Gender and Leadership Selection Processes in Norwegian Sporting Organizations." *International Review for the Sociology of Sport* 35, no. 1 (2000): 75–82.

Hunt, Thomas M. *Drug Games: The International Olympic Committee and the Politics of Doping, 1960–2008*. Austin: University of Texas Press, 2011.

"Innsbruck." *Olympic Review* 74–75 (1974): 63–66.

Innsbruck Olympic Organizing Committee. *Final Report*. Innsbruck: Organisationskomitee der XII. Olympischen Winterspiele, cop., 1976.

International Association of Athletics Federation. *Competition Rules, 2014–2015*. Monaco: International Association of Athletics Federation, 2013.

———. "Hyperandrogenism Regulations: Explanatory Notes." *International Association of Athletics Federation*, May 1, 2011. http://www.iaaf.org/about-iaaf/documents /medical.

———. "IAAF Regulations Governing Eligibility with Hyperandrogenism to Compete in Women's Competition." *International Association of Athletics Federation*, May 1, 2011. http://www.iaaf.org/about-iaaf/documents/medical.

"International Federations." *Olympic Review* 5 (February 1968): 62–65.

International Olympic Committee. *Olympic Rules, Bye-Laws, and Instructions*. Lausanne: International Olympic Committee, 1975. http://www.olympic .org/Documents/Olympic%20Charter/Olympic_Charter_through_time/1975 -Olympic_Charter-Olympic_Rules.pdf.

———. *Olympic Rules and Regulations*. Lausanne: International Olympic Committee, 1974. http://www.olympic.org/olympic-charter/documents-reports-studies -publications.

International Olympic Committee Medical and Scientific Department. "IOC Regulations on Female Hyperandrogenism." *International Olympic Committee*, June 22, 2012. http://www.olympic.org/Documents/Commissions_PDFfiles/Medical

_commission/2012-06-22-IOC-Regulations-on-Female-Hyperandrogenism-eng
.pdf.

"Introducing the, Uh, Ladies." *JAMA: The Journal of the American Medical Association* 198, no. 10 (1966): 1117–1118.

Issoupova, Olga. "From Duty to Pleasure? Motherhood in Soviet and Post-Soviet Russia." In *Gender, State, and Society in Soviet and Post-Soviet Russia,* edited by Sarah Ashwin, 30–55. London: Routledge, 2000.

Johnson, Robert H. "Misguided Morality: Ethics and the Reagan Doctrine." *Political Science Quarterly* 103, no. 3 (1988): 509–529.

Jutel, Annemarie. "Sociology of Diagnosis: A Preliminary Review." *Sociology of Health & Illness* 31, no. 2 (2009): 278–299.

Kelly, William W. Preface to *The Olympics in East Asia: Nationalism, Regionalism, and Globalism on the Center Stage of World Sports,* edited by Susan Brownell and William K. Kelly, 1–4. New Haven, CT: Yale University Press, 2011.

Kennedy, John F. "The Soft American." *Sports Illustrated,* December 1960, 14–17.

Kiblitskaya, Marina. "Russia's Female Breadwinners: The Changing Subjective Experience." In *Gender, State, and Society in Soviet and Post-Soviet Russia,* edited by Sarah Ashwin, 55–70. London: Routledge, 2000.

Kidd, Bruce. "'Another World Is Possible': Recapturing Alternative Olympic Histories, Imagining Different Games." In *Global Olympics: Historical and Sociological Studies of the Modern Games,* edited by Kevin Young and Kevin B. Wamsley, 145–160. San Diego: Elsevier, 2005.

———. "The Cultural Wars of the Montreal Olympics." *International Review for the Sociology of Sport* 27, no. 2 (1992): 151–164.

Kietlinski, Robin. *Japanese Women and Sport: Beyond Baseball and Sumo.* London: Bloomsbury, 2011.

Killanin, Lord [Michael Morris]. *My Olympic Years.* New York: William Morrow, 1983.

Kline, Wendy. *Building a Better Race: Gender, Sexuality, and Eugenics from the Turn of the Century to the Baby Boom.* Berkeley: University of California Press, 2001.

Kobchenko, Kateryna. "Emancipation within the Ruling Ideology: Soviet Women in Fizkul'tura and Sport in the 1920s and 1930s." In *Euphoria and Exhaustion: Modern Sport in Soviet Culture and Society,* edited by Nikolaus Katzer, Sandra Budy, Alexandra Köhring, and Manfred Zeller, 255–267. Frankfurt: Campus Verlag, 2010.

Kon, Igor. *The Sexual Revolution in Russia: From the Age of Czars to Today.* New York: Free Press, 1995.

Krüger, Arnd, and William Murray. *The Nazi Olympics: Sport, Politics, and Appeasement in the 1930s.* Urbana: University of Illinois Press, 2003.

Kyle, Donald G. *Sport and Spectacle in the Ancient World.* Oxford: Blackwell, 2007.

"Lake Placid 1980: The President of the IOC in America." *Olympic Review* 125–126 (March-April 1978): 167–168.

Lake Placid Olympic Organizing Committee. *Official Report of the XIII Olympic Winter Games in Lake Placid in 1980.* Lake Placid, NY: Lake Placid Olympic Organizing Committee, 1980.

Lansbury, Jennifer H. *A Spectacular Leap: Black Women Athletes in Twentieth-Century America*. Fayetteville: University of Arkansas Press, 2014.

Laqueur, Thomas. *Making Sex: Body and Gender from the Greeks to Freud*. Boston: Harvard University Press, 1990.

Larson, James F., and Heung S. Park. *Global Television and the Politics of the Seoul Olympics*. Oxford: Westview Press, 1993.

Larson, Stacy. "Intersexuality and Gender Verification Tests: The Need to Assure Human Rights and Privacy." *Pace International Law Review* 23, no. 1 (2011): 240–241.

Laville, Helen. "Gender and Women's Rights in the Cold War." In *The Oxford Handbook of the Cold War*, edited by Richard H. Immerman and Petra Goedde, 523–539. Oxford: Oxford University Press, 2013.

Layden, Tim. "Paralysis by Urinalysis." *Sports Illustrated*, May 1997, 108.

Leigh, Mary H. "The Enigma of Avery Brundage." *Arena Review* 4, no. 2 (1980): 11–21.

Lennartz, Karl. "Biographies of IOC-Members." *Journal of Olympic History* 11, no. 1 (2003): 56–58.

Lennox, Bernard. "Some Observations on the Difficulties of Determining Sex." *Bulletin of the British Association of Sport Medicine* 3, no. 2 (1968): 80–85.

Lesjo, Jon Helge. "Lillehammer 1994: Planning, Figurations, and the 'Green' Winter Games." *International Review for the Sociology of Sport* 35, no. 3 (2000): 282–293.

Lewis, Carolyn Herbst. *Prescription for Heterosexuality: Sexual Citizenship in the Cold War Era*. Chapel Hill: University of North Carolina Press, 2010.

Lillehammer Olympic Organizing Committee. *Official Report of the XVII Olympic Winter Games Lillehammer 1994*. Lillehammer: Organising Committee for the Olympic Winter Games in Lillehammer, 1994.

Lippe, Gerd von der. "Medical Tests on Gender, Sexuality, and Sport in Norway, 1890–1950: Changing Metaphors on Femininities and Masculinities." *Journal of Sport History* 27, no. 3 (2000): 481–495.

Lipset, Seymour Martin, and William Schneider. "The Decline of Confidence in American Institutions." *Political Science Quarterly* 98, no. 3 (1983): 379–402.

Ljungqvist, Arne. *Doping's Nemesis*. Cheltenham, UK: SportsBooks Limited, 2011.

———. "Gender Verification." In *The Encyclopedia of Sports Medicine: An IOC Medical Commission Publication*, edited by Barbara L. Drinkwater, 183–193. Paris: Blackwell Science, 2000.

Ljungqvist, Arne, and Joe Leigh Simpson. "Medical Examination for Health of All Athletes Replacing the Need for Gender Verification in International Sports: The International Amateur Athletic Federation Plan." *JAMA: The Journal of the American Medical Association* 267, no. 6 (1992): 850–852.

Ljungqvist, Arne, and María José Martínez-Patiño, A. Martinez-Vidal, Luisa Zagalaz, Pino Díaz, and Covadonga Mateos. "The History and Current Policies on Gender Testing in Elite Athletes." *International SportMed Journal* 7, no. 3 (2006): 225–230.

Lock, Rebecca Ann. "The Doping Ban: Compulsory Heterosexuality and Lesbophobia." *International Review for the Sociology of Sport* 38, no. 4 (2003): 397–411.

Los Angeles Olympic Organizing Committee. *Official Report of the Games of the*

XXIIIrd Olympiad Los Angeles, 1984. Los Angeles: Los Angeles Olympic Organizing Committee, 1984.

"Lord Killanin at Brighton." *Olympic Review* 134 (1978): 670–677.

"Lord Killanin . . . Five Years of Presidency . . . and China." *Olympic Review* 119 (September 1977): 536–539.

Lowry, Brian, and D. I. Hoar. "Gender Verification for the 1988 Winter Olympics." *Bulletin of the Hereditary Diseases Program of Alberta* 5, no. 3 (1986): 9.

Loy, John W., Fiona McLachlan, and Douglas Booth. "Connotations of Female Movement and Meaning." *Olympika: The International Journal of Sports Studies* 18 (2009): 1–24.

MacKenzie, Ronald M. "Lake Placid, 'Olympic City,'" *Olympic Review* 112 (February 1977): 84–86.

Magubane, Zine. "Spectacles and Scholarship: Caster Semenya, Intersex Studies, and the Problem of Race in Feminist Theory." *Signs: Journal of Women in Culture and Society* 39, no. 3 (2014): 761–785.

Mallon, Bill, and Jeroen Heijmans, *Historical Dictionary of the Olympic Movement.* Lanham, MD: Scarecrow Press, 2011.

Mandell, Richard. *The Nazi Olympics.* Urbana: University of Illinois Press, 1987.

Manheim, Jarol B. "Rites of Passage: The 1988 Seoul Olympics as Public Diplomacy." *Western Political Quarterly* 43, no. 2 (1990): 279–295.

Mascagni, Katia. "World Conference on Women and Sport." *Olympic Review* 26, no. 12 (1996): 22–31.

May, Elaine Tyler. *Homeward Bound: American Families in the Cold War.* New York: Basic Books, 1988.

McBride, Rachel, and Jehannine Austin. "Sex Testing or Gender Verification: Is There a Difference and Does it Matter?" *Journal of Genetic Counseling* 20, no. 1 (2011): 113–114.

"Medical Commission." *Olympic Review* 5 (February 1968): 71–73.

"Meetings in May." *Olympic Review* 56–57 (May-June 1972): 203–210.

Meyerowitz, Joanne. *How Sex Changed: A History of Transsexuality in the United States.* Cambridge: Harvard University Press, 2002.

———. *Not June Cleaver: Women and Gender in the Postwar American, 1945–1960.* Philadelphia: Temple University Press, 1994.

Miller, Fiona Alice. "'Your True and Proper Gender': The Barr Body as a *Good Enough* Science of Sex." *Studies in History and Philosophy of Biological and Biomedical Sciences* 37 (2006): 459–483.

Miller, Toby. *Sportsex.* Philadelphia: Temple University Press, 2001.

Mitchell, Sheila. "Women's Participation in the Olympic Games, 1900–1926." *Journal of Sport History* 4, no. 2 (1977): 208–228.

Moore, Keith L. "The Sexual Identity of Athletes." *JAMA: The Journal of the American Medical Association* 205, no. 11 (1968): 787–788.

"Mosaic in X & Y." *Time*, September 29, 1967, 70.

Mouratidis, John. "Heracles at Olympia and the Exclusion of Women from the Ancient Olympic Games." *Journal of Sport History* 11, no. 3 (1984): 41–55.

Munich Olympics Organizing Committee. *The Official Report of the Organizing Committee for the Games of the XXth Olympiad Munich 1972*. Munich: Munich Olympics Organizing Committee, 1972.

Munthe, Christian. "Selected Champions: Making Winners in the Age of Genetic Technology." In *Sport Ethics*, edited by William Morgan, 273–284. Champaign, IL: Human Kinetics, 2007.

"Nagano: In the Japanese Heartland." *Olympic Review* 19 (February-March 1998): 21–24.

Neff, Craig. "Caracas: A Scandal and a Warning." *Sports Illustrated*, September 5, 1983, 18–23.

Neuhaus, Jessamyn. "The Way to a Man's Heart: Gender Roles, Domestic Ideology, and Cookbooks in the 1950s." *Journal of Social History* 32, no. 3 (1999): 529–555.

"Nuclear Sex." *JAMA: The Journal of the American Medical Association* 179, no. 6 (1959): 679.

Nyong'o, Tavia. "The Unforgiveable Transgression of Being Caster Semenya." *Women & Performance: A Journal of Feminist Theory* 20, no. 1 (2010): 95–100.

Oca, Jeffrey Montez de. "The 'Muscle Gap': Physical Education and U.S. Fears of a Depleted Masculinity, 1954–1963." In *East Plays West: Sport and the Cold War*, edited by Stephen Wagg and David L. Andrews, 123–148. New York: Routledge, 2007.

Ohno, Susumu, and T. S. Haushka. "Allocycly of the X-Chromosome in Tumors and Normal Tissues." *Cancer Research* 20, no. 4 (1960): 541–545.

Olsen-Acre, Haley K. "The Use of Drug Testing to Police Sex and Gender in the Olympics." *Michigan Journal of Gender and Law* 13, no. 2 (2007): 207–236.

Organising Committee for the Olympic Winter Games in Nagano. *The XVIII Olympic Winter Games: Official Report Nagano 1998*. Nagano: Organising Committee for the Olympic Winter Games in Nagano in 1998, 1998.

Organising Committee for the Olympic Winter Games in Sarajevo in 1984. *Final Report Sarajevo '84*. Sarajevo: Organising Committee for the Olympic Winter Games in Sarajevo in 1984, 1984.

Organising Committee of the 1980 Olympic Games in Moscow. *Games of the XXII Olympiad: Official Report*. Moscow: Organising Committee of the 1980 Olympic Games in Moscow, 1980.

Organization for Economic Co-Operation and Development. *Genetic Testing: A Survey of Quality Assurance and Proficiency Standards*, 2007. http://www.oecd.org/sti/biotech/39534160.pdf.

Otomo, Rio. "Narratives, the Body, and the 1964 Tokyo Olympics." *Asian Studies Review* 31, (June 2007): 117–132.

Oudshoorn, Nelly. *Beyond the Natural Body: An Archeology of Sex Hormones*. New York: Routledge, 1994.

Patiño, María José Martínez. "Personal Account: A Woman Tried and Tested." *Lancet* 366 (December 2005): S38.

Pearson, Helen. "Physiology: Freaks of Nature?" *Nature* 444 (December 2006): 1000–1001.

Peters, Mary. *Mary P: Autobiography*. London: Stanley Paul, 1974.

Petersen, Allen. "Sexing the Body: Representations of Sex Difference in *Gray's Anatomy*, 1858 to the Present." *Body & Society* 4, no. 1 (1998): 1–15.

Pilgrim, Jill, David Martin, and Will Binder. "Far from the Finish Line: Transsexualism and Athletic Competition." *Fordham Intellectual Property, Media and Entertainment Law Journal* 13, no. 2 (2003): 496–549.

Plymire, Darcy C. "Too Much, Too Fast, Too Soon: Chinese Women Runners, Accusations of Steroid Use, and the Politics of American Track and Field." *Sociology of Sport Journal* 16 (June 1999): 155–173.

Preble, Christopher A. *John F. Kennedy and the Missile Gap*. DeKalb: Northern Illinois University Press, 2004.

"Press Release of the IOC. Games of the XXth Olympiad." *Olympic Review* 59 (October 1972): 390.

Preves, Sharon E. "Sexing the Intersexed: An Analysis of Sociocultural Reponses to Intersexuality." *Signs: Journal of Women in Culture & Society*, 27 no. 2 (2002): 523–556.

Puffer, James C. "Gender Verification: A Concept Whose Time Has Come and Passed?" *British Journal of Sports Medicine* 30, no. 4 (1996): 278.

Quigley, Thomas. "Letters, Physician Participation in Olympic Game Planning." *JAMA: The Journal of the American Medical Association* 189, no. 12 (1964): 959–960.

Ray, Carina. "Caster Semenya: Twenty-First Century 'Hottentot Venus'?" *New African* (November 2009): 18–19. http://www.africanexecutive.com/modules/magazine/articles.php?article=4857.

Raymond, Janice. *The Transsexual Empire: The Making of a She-Male*. Boston: Beacon Press, 1979.

"Readers Correspondence." *Olympic Review* 107–108 (September-October 1976): 507–512.

Reeser, J. C. "Gender Identity and Sport: Is the Playing Field Level?" *British Journal of Sports Medicine* 39, no. 10 (2005): 695–699.

Reis, Elizabeth. *Bodies in Doubt: An American History of Intersex*. Baltimore: John Hopkins University Press, 2009.

"Remarks by Mr. Cyrus Vance." *Olympic Review* 149 (March 1980): 109–110.

Riordan, James. "The Role of Sport in Soviet Foreign Policy." *International Journal* 43, no. 4 (1988): 569–595.

———. *Sport under Communism: The U.S.S.R., Czechoslovakia, the G.D.R., China, Cuba*. London: C. Hurst, 1981.

Ritchie, Ian. "Sex Tested, Gender Verified: Controlling Female Sexuality in the Age of Containment." *Sport History Review* 34, no. 1 (2003): 80–98.

Rosenberg, Emily S. "Consuming Women: Images of Americanization in the American Century." *Diplomatic History* 23, no. 3 (1999): 479–497.

Ross, Kristin. *Fast Cars, Clean Bodies: Decolonization and the Reordering of French Culture*. Cambridge: MIT University Press, 1995.

Rowley, Alison. "Sport in the Service of the State: Images of Physical Culture and Soviet Women, 1917–1941." *International Journal of the History of Sport* 23, no. 8 (2006): 1314–1340.

Ryan, Allan J. "Letters, Physician Participation in Olympic Game Planning." *JAMA: The Journal of the American Medical Association* 189, no. 12 (1964): 960–961.

Sakamoto, H. "Femininity Control at the XXth Universiade in Kobe, Japan." *International Journal of Sports Medicine* 9 (1988): 193–195.

Sapporo Olympic Organizing Committee. *The XI Olympic Winter Games Sapporo 1972 Official Report*. Sapporo: Le Comité d'organisation des Elèmes Jeux Olympiques d'hiver, 1973.

Sarantakes, Nicholas Evan. *Dropping the Torch: Jimmy Carter, the Olympic Boycott, and the Cold War*. Cambridge: Cambridge University Press, 2011.

Scanlon, Thomas F. *Eros & Greek Athletics*. Oxford: Oxford University Press, 2002.

Schiller, Kay, and Christopher Young. *The 1972 Munich Olympics and the Making of Modern Germany*. Berkeley: University of California Press, 2010.

Schultz, Jaime. "Caster Semenya and the 'Question of Too': Sex Testing in Elite Women's Sport and the Issue of Advantage." *Quest* 63, no. 2 (2011): 228–243.

———. "New Standards, Same Refrain: The IAAF's Regulations on Hyperandrogenism." *American Journal of American Bioethics* 12 (July 2012): 32–33.

———. *Qualifying Times: Points of Change in U.S. Women's Sport*. Urbana: University of Illinois Press, 2014.

Schützmann, Karsten, Lisa Brinkmann, Melanie Schacht, and Hertha Richter-Appelt. "Psychological Distress, Self-Harming Behavior, and Suicidal Tendencies in Adults with Disorders of Sex Development." *Archives of Sexual Behavior* 38 (2009): 16–33.

Schweinbenz, Amanda Nicole, and Alexandria Cronk. "Femininity Control at the Olympic Games." *Third Space: A Journal of Feminist Theory & Culture* 9, no. 2 (2010). http://journals.sfu.ca/thirdspace/index.php/journal/article/viewArticle /schweinbenzcronk/329.

Sears, Edward Seldon. *Running through the Ages*. Jefferson, NC: McFarland, 2001.

Serrat, Angels, and Antonio García de Herreros. "Gender Verification in Sports by PCR Amplification of SRY and DYZ1 Chromosome Specific Sequences: Presence of DYZI Repeat in Female Athletes." *British Journal of Sports Medicine* 30, no. 4 (1996): 310–312.

Seoul Olympic Organizing Committee. *Official Report*. Seoul: Korean Textbook Publishing, 1988.

Shackleton, Cedric. "Steroid Analysis and Doping Control, 1960–1980: Scientific Developments and Personal Anecdotes." *Elsevier* 74, no. 3 (2009): 288–295.

Shapiro, Samantha. "Caught in the Middle: A Failed Gender Test Crushed Santhi Soundarajan's Olympic Dreams." *ESPN The Magazine*, August 1, 2012. http://espn .go.com/olympics/story/_/id/8192977/failed-gender-test-forces-olympian-redefine -athletic-career-espn-magazine.

Simpson, Joe Leigh. "Gender Testing in the Olympics." *JAMA: The Journal of the American Medical Association* 256, no. 14 (1986): 1938.

Simpson, Joe Leigh, Arne Ljungqvist, Albert de la Chapelle, Malcolm Ferguson-Smith, Elizabeth Ferris, Myron Genel, Anke Ehrhardt, and Alison Carlson. "Gender Verification and the Next Olympic Games—Reply." *JAMA: The Journal of the American Medical Association* 269, no. 3 (1993): 358.

Simpson, Joe Leigh, Arne Ljungqvist, Malcolm A. Ferguson-Smith, Albert de la Chapelle, Louis J. Elsas, A. Ehrhardt, Myron Genel, Elizabeth Ferris, and Alison Carlson. "Gender Verification in the Olympics." *JAMA: The Journal of the American Medical Association* 284, no. 12 (2000): 1568–1569.

Simson, Vyv, and Andrew Jennings. *The Lord of the Rings: Power, Money, and Drugs in the Modern Olympics.* New York: Simon & Schuster, 1991.

Skirstad, Berit. "Gender Verification in Competitive Sport: Turning from Research to Action." In *Values in Sport: Elitism, Nationalism, Gender Equality and the Scientific Manufacture of Winners,* edited by Torbjörn Tannsjo and Claudiö Tamburrini, 116–122. London: Kluwer Academic Publishers, 2000.

Sloan, Julia. "Carnivalizing the Cold War: Mexico, the Mexican Revolution, and the Events of 1968." *European Journal of American Studies* 1 (2009): Document 1.

Spitzer, Giselher. "Sport and the Systematic Infliction of Pain: A Case Study of State-Sponsored Mandatory Doping in East Germany." In *The Ethics of Sport: A Reader,* edited by Mike McNamee, 413–425. New York: Routledge, 2010.

Stephenson, Joan. "Female Olympians' Sex Tests Outmoded." *JAMA: The Journal of the American Medical Association* 276, no. 3 (1996): 177–178.

Sullivan, Claire. "Gender Verification and Gender Policies in Elite Sport: Eligibility and 'Fair Play.'" *Journal of Sport & Social Issues* 35, no. 4 (2011): 400–419.

Suny, Ronald Grigor. *The Revenge of the Past: Nationalism, Revolution, and the Collapse of the Soviet Union.* Redwood City, CA: Stanford University Press, 1993.

Sykes, Heather. "Transsexual and Transgender Policies in Sport." *Women in Sport and Physical Activities Journal* 15, no. 1 (2006): 3–13.

Tagsold, Christian. "Modernity, Space, and National Representation at the Tokyo Olympics 1964." *Urban History* 37, no. 2 (2010): 289–300.

Terret, Theirry. "France." In *European Cultures in Sport: Examining the Nations and Regions,* edited by James Riordan and Arnd Krüger, 103–122. Bristol, UK: Intellect Books, 2003.

Todd, Jan, and Terry Todd. "Significant Events in the History of Drug Testing and the Olympic Movement: 1960–1999." In *Doping in Elite Sport: The Politics of Drugs in the Olympic Movement,* edited by Wayne Wilson and Ed Derse, 65–128. Champaign, IL: Human Kinetics, 2001.

Todd, Terry. "Anabolic Steroids: The Gremlins of Sport." *Journal of Sport History* 14, no. 1 (1987): 87–107.

Tomlinson, Alan. "Carrying the Torch for Whom?" In *The Olympics at the Millennium: Power, Politics, and the Games,* edited by Kay Schaffer and Sidonie Smith, 167–181. New Brunswick, NJ: Rutgers University Press, 2000.

Tuggle, C. A., and Ann Owen. "A Descriptive Analysis of NBC's Coverage of the Centennial Olympics." *Journal of Sport and Social Issues* 23, no. 2 (1999): 171–182.

Turrini, Joseph M. "'It Was Communism Versus the Free World': The USA-USSR Dual Track Meet Series and the Development of Track and Field in the United States, 1958–1985." *Journal of Sport History* (Fall 2001): 427–471.

Ungerleider, Steven. *Faust's Gold: Inside the East German Doping Machine.* New York: St. Martin's, 2001.

Vannini, April, and Barbara Fornssler. "Girl, Interrupted: Interpreting Semenya's Body, Gender Verification Testing, and Public Discourse." *Cultural Studies ←→ Critical Methodologies* 11, no. 243 (2011): 243–257.

Verbrugge, Martha H. *Active Bodies: A History of Women's Physical Education in Twentieth-Century America.* Oxford: Oxford University Press, 2012.

Vignetti, P., A. Rizzuti, L. Bruni, M. C. Tozzi, P. Marcozzi, and L. Tarani. "'Sex Passport' Obligation for Female Athletes: Consideration and Criticisms on 364 Subjects." *International Journal of Sports Medicine* 17, no. 3 (1996): 239–240.

Wackwitz, Laura A. "Verifying the Myth: Olympic Sex Testing and the Category of 'Woman.'" *Women's Studies International Forum* 26, no. 6 (2003): 553–560.

Wagg, Stephen, and David L. Andrews. *East Plays West: Sport and the Cold War.* New York: Routledge, 2007.

"Waging War against Dope." *Olympic Review* 77 (February 1962): 46.

Wamsley, Kevin B. "Social Science Literature on Sport and Transitioning/Transitioned Athletes." *Prepared for the Promising Practices: Working with Transitioning/Transitioned Athletes in Sport Project.* http://www.caaws.ca/e/resources/pdfs/Wamsley_lit_review%282%29.pdf.

Washburn, John N. "Sport as a Soviet Tool." *Foreign Affairs* 34, no. 3 (1956): 490–499.

Weinberg, Herb. "Robert Helmick: The Salt Lake City Candidacy." *Journal of Olympic History* 11, no. 2 (2003): 6–10.

Wells, Cassandra. "Diagnosing Sex-Gender Verification and the IOC." In *Rethinking Matters Olympic: Investigations into the Socio-Cultural Study of the Modern Olympic Movement*, edited by Robert K. Barney, Janice E. Forsyth, and Michael K. Heine, 301–311. London: University of Western Ontario, 2011.

Wickets, Donald Furthman. "Can Sex in Humans Be Changed?" *Physical Culture* 77 (January 1937): 16–17.

Wiederkehr, Stefan. "' . . . If Jarmila Kratochvilova Is the Future of Women's Sports, I'm Not Sure I'm Ready for It.' Media, Gender, and the Cold War." In *Euphoria and Exhaustion: Modern Sport in Soviet Culture and Society*, edited by Nikolaus Katzer, Sandra Budy, Alexandra Köhring, and Manfred Zeller, 315–335. Frankfurt: Campus Verlag, 2010.

———. "'We Shall Never Know the Exact Number of Men Who Have Competed in the Olympics Posing as Women': Sport, Gender Verification, and the Cold War." *International Journal of the History of Sport* 23, no. 7 (2006): 1152–1172.

Wilson, Sandra. "Exhibiting a New Japan: The Tokyo Olympics of 1964 and Expo '70 in Osaka." *Historical Research* 85, no. 227 (2012): 159–178.

Wood, Elizabeth A. *The Baba and the Comrade: Gender and Politics in Revolutionary Russia.* Bloomington: Indiana University Press, 1997.

Wrynn, Alison. M. "'A Debt Paid Off in Tears': Science, IOC Politics and the Debate about High Altitude in the 1968 Mexico City Olympics." *International Journal of the History of Sport* 23, no. 7 (2006): 1152–1172.

———. "The Human Factor: Science, Medicine and the International Olympic Committee, 1900–70." *Sport in Society* 7, no. 2 (2004): 211–231.

X (George Kennan). "The Sources of Soviet Conduct." *Foreign Affairs* 65, no. 4 (1987): 852–868.

Xavier, Neena A., and Janet B. McGill. "Hyperandrogenism and Intersex Controversies in Women's Olympics." *Journal of Clinical Endocrinology & Metabolism* 97, no. 11 (2012): 3902–3907.

Xuetong, Yan. "The Rise of China and Its Power Status." *Chinese Journal of International Politics* 1, no. 1 (2006): 5–33.

Zim, Marvin. "Asia: Beneath the Rising Sun." *Sports Illustrated* 26, January 1967, 18.

Zolov, Eric. "'Showcasing the Land of Tomorrow': Mexico and the 1968 Olympics." *Americas* 61, no. 2 (2004): 159–188.

Index

LINDSAY PARKS PIEPER is an assistant professor of sport management at Lynchburg College.

SPORT AND SOCIETY

The University of Illinois Press
is a founding member of the
Association of American University Presses.

Composed in 10.5/13 Minion Pro
with Univers display
by Jim Proefrock
at the University of Illinois Press
Manufactured by Cushing-Malloy, Inc.

University of Illinois Press
1325 South Oak Street
Champaign, IL 61820-6903
www.press.uillinois.edu